# EVENING CHATS IN BEIJING

# Also by Perry Link

北京

Perry Link

# EVENING CHATS IN BEIJING

### Probing China's Predicament

W · W · Norton & Company

New York    London

First Edition

The text of this book is composed
in 11/13 Goudy Old Style
with the display set in Koch Antiqua
Manufacturing by The Maple-Vail Book Manufacturing Group.
Book design by Margaret M. Wagner.
Calligraphy by Fang Lizhi.

Library of Congress Cataloging-in-Publication Data
Link, E. Perry (Eugene Perry), 1944–
Evening chats in Beijing : probing China's predicament / Perry
Link.
p.   cm.
Includes index.
1.  China—Intellectual life—1976–     2.  China—Politics and
government—1976–     I.  Title.
DS779.23.L57   1992
951.05—dc20                                      91–29724

ISBN 0-393-03052-0

W.W. Norton & Company, Inc.
500 Fifth Avenue, New York, N.Y. 10110
W.W. Norton & Company Ltd.
10 Coptic Street, London WC1A 1PU

1 2 3 4 5 6 7 8 9 0

*To*
*Beulah and Eugene,*
*who showed me how much*
*parents can give to children,*

*and to*
*Monica and Nathan,*
*who taught me that*
*children give parents even more*

# CONTENTS

# FOREWORD

I wonder if any country in the world publishes more books about China than does the United States. At its peak, I am told, the American output of China books reached an average of one per day, whereas recently the rate has dropped off to about two hundred annually. But of all such books that have come to my attention, *Evening Chats in Beijing* stands out as considerably different in both content and style. What amazes me is that a book so compact in size can encompass so much. It not only addresses most of the major problems that face China today but also searches in considerable depth for the origins of those problems in the particularities of Chinese history and society.

Perry Link looks at China primarily through the perceptions and experiences of Chinese intellectuals. To an American reader, it might seem questionable that the thoughts and feelings of a relatively small social group can adequately reflect the whole of Chinese experience. Such a reader needs to understand that, over the past hundred years, Chinese intellectuals have stood at the vortex of the swirling currents of their national history. They have taken on the heavy burden of responsibility for their nation's destiny and, for every step of progress their country has made, have paid prices and accepted sacrifices far in excess of what is normal for intellectuals in most other countries.

Their dedication has been especially evident during the forty-two years of Communist rule of the People's Republic. It should be remembered that during this period Chinese peasants and workers, although deprived of freedom just as much as intellectuals, have still been able to perform their normal life functions. Even without freedom, peasants can till the earth and workers can go to factories. But intellectuals have lost the fundamental conditions for carrying out their work: professors cannot present the ideas and theories they see fit to present; writers and reporters cannot write the truth about life as they find it. They are sometimes forced to pronounce lies and sophistries that they personally find disgusting. Not even natural scientists have been exempt from this kind of political oppression. And beyond that there are the one hundred thousand or more intellectuals who for periods as long as one or two decades have had to abandon their work entirely and live as pariahs performing hard and heavy physical labor. As is well illustrated in the pages of this book, the long tradition of Chinese intellectuals to "be the first in the world to assume its worries and the last to enjoy its pleasures" has persisted in recent generations. This tradition has led intellectuals in the People's Republic—even when (or precisely because?) they have lived in complete deprivation of political rights and in total isolation from normal social life—to perceive reality with more sensitivity than the average person and to ponder the fate of the nation more deeply.

I hope that the present book will not be regarded only as a work of scholarship in the China field. It can and should be appreciated by any reader who has a normal interest in what is happening to a quarter of the world's population. And it is wise for those in the West to show such interest, because it is not only the fate of the Chinese people that depends on what the next ten years bring to China; all of humankind inevitably will feel the effects. China continues to present the world with "riddles": Why, among the great nations of today's world, does this country, with the longest continuous history and richest cultural tradition, turn out to be the poorest and most backward?

Why, when nearly all the countries of "the socialist camp" have undergone radical change, does China stay in its old rut? Interest in such questions should by no means be limited to scholarly and intellectual circles.

This book does not give answers to the major problems facing contemporary China. What it does offer is the opportunity to understand the considerable anxiety and struggle that go on in China, amid pain and perplexity, in the search for a Chinese "way" in the modern world—a way that for the last hundred years has remained frustratingly elusive. By now it seems that the end of this long search may finally be coming into sight. If the present book could somehow be translated and introduced into mainland China (at least, I think, a translation could be published in Hong Kong and brought into China from there), then the book itself could contribute directly to advancing this historical process.

In such an event, readers in China will feel surprise. A book like this should have been written by a Chinese! How come a foreigner wrote it? The reason, of course, is not hard to find. In China this book would not only be refused publication; simply to have written it would constitute an offense.

But this is not to say that just any foreigner who understands Chinese could have written this book. Chinese who know Perry Link will be quick to say that the book must owe its success to his astoundingly good Chinese, which he speaks even better than a lot of Chinese people. In my view, however, the author's nature and temperament may be equally important factors. Somehow, Chinese who come into contact with Link do not feel they are dealing with a foreigner; he has a way of inspiring people's confidence and trust. The modest and conscientious attitude he brings to his scholarship is reflected in the pages of this book, which, although entitled "Evening Chats," is by no means just the record of some conversations. It is clearly the result of a slow culling of materials that were originally several times—or several dozen times—more extensive than the book itself, combined with analyses that come from many years of observation of Chinese society. I feel sure that all readers, even including the Chinese intellectuals with whom Perry Link had his evening chats, will come away from this book feeling—as I did—that they have learned something.

*Liu Binyan*
*December 1990*

# EVENING CHATS IN BEIJING

# INTRODUCTION

> The Chinese Association for Science and Technology, called
> CAST, was founded in 1958. It is a mass organization for Chinese
> scientists, engineers, and technologists and consists of 146 national
> professional societies with a total membership of over 1,710,000,
> plus 46,560 science popularization associations, with 4,160,000
> members, and 80,000 rural research societies of specialized tech-
> nology, with 4,160,000 members. . . . From 1966 to 1976 our work
> was devastated by the machinations of the Gang of Four. . . . Last
> year CAST and its affiliated societies held 1,854 scientific seminars
> and symposia, at which 115,070 academic themes and papers were
> presented. This year . . .

It was a sweltering afternoon in August 1988. I had just arrived
in Beijing, and the combination of the heat, the jet lag, and
the tedium of the message I was hearing made it hard to take
careful notes. I was beginning a one-year term as director of the
Beijing office of the Committee on Scholarly Communication
with the People's Republic of China (CSCPRC), a subcommit-
tee of the National Academy of Sciences that runs the national-
level scholarly exchange program between the United States
and China. I was to work on arrangements for lectures, seminars, and field research across the full range of academic disciplines; but my first task was to pay a series of courtesy calls at

the various Chinese bureaucratic offices charged with management of scholarly affairs.

The scene that day at CAST was fairly representative of these meetings. I was seated at the center of a row of overstuffed sofas crammed between a wall and a line of tea tables. The six CAST officials were seated with me and a CSCPRC colleague in the same row, all of us facing forward, which meant that anyone who wished to look at a speaker had to lean forward and crane the neck in one direction or the other. The CAST officials, suffering the heat in awkwardly fitting coats and ties, had come more for ceremony than for discussion, and clearly expected the same from me. Only the occasional nervous cough or wry smile that accompanied a phrase like "the Gang of Four" signaled the presence of deeper layers of meaning.

After the meeting I returned to the Friendship Hotel, a large compound in northwestern Beijing near the city's major universities, where my family and I had been assigned a small apartment with a bathroom and a hot plate. My wife, Jean, in the midst of a Ph.D dissertation, worried about finding a voltage transformer so that she could plug in her computer. Our daughter, Monica, aged seven, was having fun learning Chinese and looking forward to attending second grade in a Chinese school. Our little boy, Nathan, aged three, wondered confjstantly why we weren't still in California. Our apartment was in one of the older, seedier buildings of the large Friendship compound, which was built in the 1950s to house Soviet advisers. The hotel's service personnel, of whom there were far too many for the modest tasks they performed, had long ago made their peace with the fact that many things just didn't fit or work.

I spent the rest of my afternoon in a tangle of electrical adapters and extension cords, trying to work out how I could plug in my electric shaver without either unplugging the mini-refrigerator or moving my bed. After two hours of fruitless effort, I consulted one of the service workers stationed at the door. "It doesn't matter," he said, as if definitively. Then, after drawing long and deep on a cigarette, he counseled me, "Be patient. Westerners need to shave more often than Chinese, I know. It's no big problem. By the way, why don't you use a razor? No problem!"

That evening we were visited by a young Chinese scholar whom I had known in 1980, when I spent a year in China doing research on modern Chinese literature. The friend could barely contain his excitement at seeing Jean and me, and we, too, were delighted to reconnect. But we were startled at the contrast he presented with the cheerful, optimistic youngster in our memories. "China's hopeless!" he sputtered. "The old men in charge are thoroughly corrupt, and the whole society has gone bad with them. Their 'socialism' is a lie! It doesn't work. They know it. Everybody knows it. Everyone is cynical, selfish, disgusted . . ." I interrupted to recommend that he lower his voice. "I'm sure all the rooms in this hotel are bugged," he said. "But I don't care! I've had it with them! I've seen through them! They can know what I think—I don't care."

The young man's language was vastly different in style and content from what I had heard at CAST in the afternoon. In the months that followed, this divide between "official" and "unofficial" modes of discourse continued to present itself to me on a daily basis. The "unofficial" sphere grew ever larger as the intellectuals I encountered got to know me better. It struck me that Chinese scholars in virtually all fields—from seismology to aesthetics, engineering to sociology—seemed to spend their private time in discussion of only one topic: China. What is the terrible mess we are in? How did it happen? What can we do about it? They seemed to accept it as their duty as intellectuals, in the manner of the Confucian literati of Chinese tradition, to *youguo youmin*, "worry about the country and the people." It was obvious that their informal talk also had a cathartic function; it was a way for them to release frustrations.

Although I had come to China expecting to hear some pessimistic views, I was unprepared for such a dour consensus about China's major problems: entrenched, pandemic corruption; a state led by doddering men still trapped in the ways of the 1930s–1950s, their formative period, and opposed to basic freedoms and any shifts toward democracy; an economy stalled halfway through a critical reform program; an educational system crippled by a serious lack of funds and flawed even in its basic conception, producing a populace that was ever more mercenary, illiterate, and uncivil; and a social structure ossified by a rigid hierarchy of "work units" too often run by cynical bullies—people whose moral or political ideals had succumbed to the system and who now simply manipulated their positions and connections to their private advantage. If these problems seemed born of moribund leadership, there were others that even a vigorous government would find daunting: overpopulation, looming grain shortages, and mounting inflation and foreign debt. The distraught intellectuals could, moreover, see no clear hope—no inspiring ideology, no prospect of improvement in the political leadership, no sign of any movement from below.

As I listened, and inevitably began to sympathize, I found it necessary to remind myself that the Chinese people, including intellectuals, certainly enjoyed more wealth and freedom in late 1988 than they had fifteen years earlier, when Maoist policies were still firmly in place. But during the 1980s the growth of popular expectations had far exceeded improvements in daily life. The comparison to the outside world (especially to other Chinese societies such as those of Taiwan, Hong Kong, and Singapore) only exacerbated the despairing sense that China was falling ever further behind and was doomed to continue to do so by the stubbornness of a wrongheaded government. Chinese intellectuals in their fifties, who could remember the pain and strife of World War II, the civil war, the disastrous Antirightist Campaign and Great Leap Forward of the 1950s, and the debacle of the Cultural Revolution, often observed that they had never felt as depressed as they did right then, in the late 1980s.

My routine work in Beijing presented a daily contrast between the "official" and the "unofficial" modes of expression in China. One I heard in my office, at meetings, and on the telephone in any business concerning formal arrangements for scholarly exchange; the other I heard after hours, in the homes of Chinese friends, and in other informal situations. The very language of communication—content, style, vocabulary, and even grammar—was different in these respective worlds. As I struggled to learn how to switch off between two versions of the Chinese language, I also began to reflect on what this bifurcation implied about Chinese society and daily life.[1] These reflections became key to my understanding of China's contemporary crisis.

It is perhaps the natural response of an outsider, in discovering dissidence under the rug in an authoritarian society, and especially when finding so much of it, to assume that the unofficial mode represents what people "really" think and that the formulaic official language is merely a cover. On the whole, this assumption is fairly accurate—at least far more accurate than its reverse would be—for China as I found it in 1988. But the relations between official and unofficial language uses are more complicated than that. Both kinds of language are fully "real" and are equally essential to getting along in Chinese life.

First, I had to interpret the puzzle that some intellectuals, and some bureaucrats as well, could move quite comfortably between the official and unofficial modes of speaking, almost as if donning and doffing a cap. The striking differences between the two kinds of language raised questions about this ability to shift easily. Could it be that moving back and forth amounted to donning and doffing integrity as well as idiom? Sometimes, rather clearly, it did. But then consider this case. At a large meeting about six weeks after I arrived in Beijing, I listened to a bureaucrat from the Chinese Academy of Sciences deliver a fairly stuffy account of his organization's current work and plans. I was then surprised at lunch, where by chance he and I were sitting alone at a table, to hear him gradually tell me how

1. The distinction has close, but not precise, parallels in the Marxist-Leninist experience of the Soviet Union and Eastern Europe. See Vladimir Shlapentokh, *Soviet Intellectuals and Political Power: The Post-Stalin Era* (Princeton: Princeton University Press, 1990), pp. 80–84 and passim, where essentially the same distinction is discussed as "public" versus "private"; Václav Havel, "The Power of the Powerless," trans. P. Wilson, in *Václav Havel; or, Living in Truth,* ed. Jan Vladislav (London: Faber and Faber, 1987), where Havel's brilliant discussion of the interface of "ideology" and ordinary life has deep resonance with the Chinese case (see especially pp. 41–50); and Czeslaw Milosz, *The Captive Mind,* trans. Jane Zielonko (New York: Octagon Books, 1981), especially the discussion of Ketman (pp. 54–55ff.) and the examples of Beta, Gamma, and Delta (pp. 134, 141, and 188).

"hopeless" it all was and how awkward he felt about his own role. As I got to know him better during the year, I came to understand that his inner feelings corresponded much more closely to his expression of hopelessness than to his official account. His confession on the day we met had not been calculated to impress me or to gain sympathy and personal help from a foreigner. (Many times during my year in China I did encounter such attempts.) He felt genuinely ambivalent about the official language that he was obliged to use; yet he accepted the necessity of using it, and, on the whole, struggled to do some good with it wherever and however he could. It would be inaccurate to consider his official expression insincere or merely superficial; instead, he was following the rules of a game. His official use of words, at its cleverest, resembled a go player's placing of stones: perhaps initially of opaque intent, yet well considered, sometimes sophisticated, and always with a final goal in mind.

Second, there was the problem that both the official and the unofficial languages, distinct though they were on the surface, were grounded in common assumptions that lie fairly deep in Chinese culture. Broadly speaking, these common assumptions include the notions that to speak is above all to act and that speech acts are to be evaluated by how "well" or "properly" they are performed. "Proper" has often meant "morally proper"; for centuries in China the assumption that the proper use of language could cultivate moral character was implicit in the practice of requiring children to memorize classical texts. But "proper" can also mean "prudentially proper" when the task is to reach one's goal most efficiently. For example, one day the son of a Chinese friend came to the CSCPRC office to ask me how to fill out an application for an American graduate school. I assumed that he wanted help in understanding the questions on the form, but what he really wanted, and asked for without guile, was advice about what answers to give in order to maximize his chances for admission. He seemed bewildered when I suggested that he just write down the true answers. His naive bewilderment revealed that he had not exactly begun with an intent to "lie," as a Westerner might think of it. He had come to learn how to perform verbally in the requisite way. To him, the right answers to this impressive-looking official form were obviously the ones that the form called for, not information he might dig out of his ordinary life in China.

The assumption in Chinese culture that speech is to be evaluated as action or performance also entails—more, at least, than in the modern West—that the *manner* of expression is important. Beyond a "fitting" thing to say, there is often a "set'" way to say it. These conventions, sometimes called *tifa*, or "ways of mentioning," although common in official and unofficial language alike, are most easily illustrated in highly politicized usage. During the Cultural Revolution (1966–76), Mao Zedong was known as "the great [*weida*] Chairman Mao" and Zhou Enlai as "the beloved [*jing'ai*] Premier Zhou." After Mao's death, Hua Guofeng was added as "the wise [*yingming*] Chairman Hua." To mismatch modifier and name in these cases would have seemed at best a stupid mistake and at worst sarcasm that smacked of sedition.[2] Not only word selection but also word order must be fitting. The "great glorious, correct Communist party" cannot be the "correct, glorious, great" party or the "glorious, great, correct" party without deflating the impression of greatness, glory, and correctness.

Such ludicrous extremes are, of course, partly the Orwellian products of modern totalitarian government. But the assumptions that speech is action, that style and content are inseparable, and that there are "correct" ways of expressing style/content run much deeper in Chinese culture than does Marxism-Leninism. In the Chinese of daily life, a phrase as common as *ni shuo de hen hao* can equally well mean "what you said was good" and "you said it well." (Chinese people have no trouble distinguishing these two ideas when they want to, but in common use the phrase means both, without the question of a distinction arising.) Similarly a false statement can be rebutted by

---

2. Actually, Mao Zedong qualified for all three modifiers—"great," "beloved," and "wise"—provided they were embedded properly in larger set patterns. But to call Zhou or Hua "great" in the official language would be a serious mistake.

*bushi neme shuo de,* "that's not the way you say it." Peculiar or undesirable behavior can be described as *buxiangyang,* "not resembling the pattern," or equally well as *buxianghua,* "not resembling words." The Chinese word *xue,* "study," originally means "imitate," although without the negative connotation that the behavior is derivative; "emulate" might be closer.

The habits of observing *tifa,* or "ways of expressing," are evident even in people who are trying to free themselves from old patterns. The leaders of China's overseas "democracy movement," while seeking to escape the moral and political hegemony of their country's official language, still draw on its grammar and lexicon. One manifesto written in 1990 calls for "men of strong will" to "offer themselves to the great mission" and "resolutely struggle for Chinese democracy."[3] In opposing the Communist party, as in obeying it, there is a place for set phrases and standardized ideas. To a Westerner, these formulations may seem to be clichés—indicative of unoriginality and even hypocrisy in those who repeat them. But in China, people often repeat the standard phrases with sincerity, to signal true feelings and moral commitment. I began to notice a pronounced similarity in the observations of Chinese intellectuals on some subjects. These patterns result in part from the commonalities of their experience, but also in part from the assumptions intellectuals share about "the way things are to be said." Because their concerns are so strongly tied to the very language that they use, I have included discussions of language use at several places in this book.

I also frequently discuss the cultural roles of Chinese intellectuals, for these are as deeply embedded in Chinese culture and society as assumptions about proper language use. But there is a tension at the heart of the Chinese intellectual's cultural identity that has from time to time over the centuries been the source of much personal ambivalence, pain, and sacrifice: it lies in the intellectual's paradoxical relation to the state. Chinese intellectuals have long been considered pillars of the state, and

3. " 'Dangdai Zhongguo yanjiu zhongxin' zujian jihua" (Organizational plan for a "Center for the Research of Contemporary China").

yet it is their duty as well to criticize and even oppose China's rulers when these rulers compromise their moral authority. The intellectuals I met complained caustically about Deng Xiaoping's China yet were reluctant to break with the state. Just as their willingness to "go along" seems to call into doubt the significance of their criticism, so the extreme bitterness of their complaining seems to raise moral questions about their willingness to go along.[4] How should we understand their alienation cum compliance?

Most of this book can be viewed as an exploration of the causes of this ambivalence. Since any understanding of the problem must be grounded in China's history, we must begin by looking, however briefly, at who "the intellectuals" were, both during the imperial history of recent centuries and during the Communist history of recent decades.

For more than thirteen centuries of imperial Chinese history, until the early twentieth century, "literati" competed for appointment to offices of the Chinese state by taking civil service examinations that tested their literary ability and mastery of classic texts. Despite occasional breaks and irregularities in its history, the examination system was based throughout on a theory of benign human nature, perfectible through education, that had its origins in the teachings of Confucius (ca. 551–479 B.C.), Mencius (ca. 372–289 B.C.), and others in China's ancient past. The examination system rested on assumptions that scholars who mastered classical texts would absorb from them the knowledge of morality and proper behavior that would guide their actions and equip them to rule society wisely as officials of the state. In the logical continuity of these assumptions, we can appreciate how formal language, literary education, moral cultivation, and service to society via the state were understood not just as closely related but as aspects of a seamless whole. (The marked contrast on these points with the modern West is too obvious to need explanation.) During the last two centuries the modern world has provoked great social and political storms

---

4. I am indebted to Andrew J. Nathan for this formulation of the problem.

that have changed the face of China and, in particular, led to several revolutions in Chinese education—in matters of examinations, curricula, administration, and so on. But the underlying cultural assumptions in China about the role of intellectuals, and about the fundamental identity of learning, proper behavior, and service to society via the state, have been much slower to change. Chinese intellectuals today still enjoy quoting maxims that capture the ideals of their literati predecessors: that the educated man should "take responsibility for all under heaven" and "be the first in the world to assume its worries, the last to enjoy its pleasures."[5] And they continue to assume that the route through which to tender their assistance to society is—where else?—the state authority. If the state authority accepts their aid, fine; if not, one withdraws to await a more propitious time.

Chinese tradition offers many stories of courageous literati who opposed state policy by remonstrating with the emperor, knowing well that their actions would lead to beating, banishment, or even death. For centuries the poet Qu Yuan (343–289 B.C.) has been an inspirational example of responsible action. In a period of fragmented rule, Qu Yuan advised the king of the southern state of Chu to ally with other states and to resist the stronger state of Qin. But when rival courtiers intrigued against him, Qu Yuan lost the trust of the king, who banished him to wander the countryside south of the Yangzi River. In exile, Qu Yuan wrote allegorical poetry about his frustrated patriotism and unjust treatment and eventually drowned himself in despair.[6] The dissent of Qu Yuan, and of other literati like him, was almost always that of a loyal adviser. Although critical of a ruler's policies, literati did not appeal beyond the emperor to

5. Both these sayings are attributed to the scholar Fan Zhongyan (989–1052), although the textual source for the first is not known. The second appears in Fan's "Yueyanglou ji" (Recorded at the Yueyang pavilion). See *Guwen guanzhi* (Essence of the classics), vol. 9 (Hong Kong: Xuelin Bookstore, n.d.), p. 138.

6. On the many and shifting mythological conceptions that have surrounded Qu Yuan for more than two thousand years, see Laurence A. Schneider, *A Madman of Ch'u: The Chinese Myth of Loyalty and Dissent* (Berkeley and Los Angeles: University of California Press, 1980).

an "opposition"—which, in any case, did not exist except when the state was threatened by major rebellion or invasion.

China's imperial history helps explain the ambiguous position of Chinese intellectuals in relation to the state. But the pattern of alienation cum compliance that we observe today has also resulted importantly from the recent experience of Communist rule. Drawn to the patriotic and egalitarian ideals of the revolution in the late 1940s and early 1950s, most Chinese intellectuals willingly, even enthusiastically, offered their idealism to the new regime. Then a series of anti-intellectual campaigns conducted by the Communists in the 1950s and 1960s drove home the unwelcome and unexpected message that the party leadership aimed to reject, humiliate, and even destroy the intellectual "class." China's intellectuals were not prepared for the stark alternatives that these campaigns set before them. In imperial China one could "retreat to perfect oneself"; but the zealous Communist regime allowed little opportunity for such retreat, either social or psychological. Its campaigns permeated society, and it demanded "reform from the bone marrow outward." Short of suicide or extremely strict self-censorship, one's only alternative was to embrace the state even while suffering its denunciation.

In the 1980s, the party's pressure on intellectuals abated enough to allow another problem to emerge. What did it now mean to "cultivate oneself"? Cultivate in what? Premodern Confucianism? (It hardly seemed practical to turn the clock back so radically.) Marxism or Maoism? (These were too repulsive by now and, moreover, had clearly failed.) Democracy? (This was not well known, and public advocacy carried risks.) Something else? But despite the prevailing confusion about what one's ideological core should be, the assumptions that a scholar's worth is measured by his contributions in the public arena, that these contributions are properly made through state channels, and that the state's official recognition brings personal and family glory remained strong even among intellectuals who in other ways were utterly disgusted with the state, or at least with the people currently running it.

The question of how to define "intellectual" in today's China is complicated and sometimes controversial. The term *zhishifenzi* ("intellectuals") is usually understood to refer to people with some kind of postsecondary education. Some limit this to university graduates; others include graduates of specialized and two-year colleges and trade schools. A high school degree alone is sufficient to qualify for the term "educated youth" (*zhishi qingnian*). The term "higher intellectual" (*gaoji zhishifenzi*) applies to professionals in universities, research institutes, hospitals, museums, publishing houses, and so on, as well as to scientists, engineers, and doctors wherever they may be based, and to distinguished writers and artists even if they lack college degrees. Controversies arise over narrower, more evaluative definitions—for example, when it is proposed to distinguish true "intellectuals" from technocratic Soviet-style "intelligentsia." In ordinary Chinese life, most people use the term *zhishifenzi* without any precise definition in mind. Depending on where one draws the line, the total number of such *zhishifenzi* would fall somewhere in the low tens of millions, or about I to 5 percent of the Chinese population. In this book I will be referring mostly to the "higher intellectuals," but I omit the word "higher" not only because of its elitist connotations but because the problems that emerge extend well beyond the "higher" circles.

I was forcefully struck in fall 1988 not only by how freely Chinese intellectuals were then speaking their minds but by how radical their questioning seemed to be. The contrast with 1979–80, when I last lived in China, was startling. That earlier year had seen the high tide of post-Mao "scar literature," when China's writers filled literary magazines with stories about the violence and inhumanity of the Cultural Revolution, as well as about current social problems such as bureaucratism and bribery. These literary magazines circulated in the hundreds of thousands and stimulated discussion that was fully as lively as that which would pervade China in the late 1980s. But there was one outstanding difference. The questions raised in scar literature nearly all had answers—indeed, most of the answers were well known to readers in advance. Was the Cultural Revolution horribly violent? *Of course* it was! Is our country afflicted with bureaucratism? And how! The authors of scar literature were not informing their readers of much, nor were they posing large questions for readers to ponder. What they were doing—and it was a valuable service at the time—was giving public expression to thoughts and complaints that most people had long harbored but had not dared, save in the strictest of confidence, to utter. The release that came from seeing the truth aired in public, arrayed with the prestige of official publication, was powerfully elating. In 1988, by contrast, the important questions intellectuals were raising did not have ready answers—or any answers at all. They were large, probing, frightening questions that took in most of modern Chinese history.

For example: How can we understand, or understand anew, the entire Chinese revolution, starting from the 1930s? Why were we intellectuals so docile in the 1950s when Mao "criticized" us and began to set up his tyranny? What do we make of the "peasant consciousness" that we admired then but that oppresses us now? How can we feel certain that we have really understood the Cultural Revolution? Given the absurdity of blaming the Cultural Revolution on just a "gang" of only four people, what is it in *all of us* that allowed such violence to happen? (If we can't find that characteristic, how do we know it will not rise up to bite us again some day?)

And more broadly: What is happening to the socialist movement worldwide? Have most socialist countries, beginning with Poland and Hungary, and now including even China and the Soviet Union, awakened to the realization that the socialist ideal has been a mirage all along? (Does the world owe China its thanks for having run the experiment full tilt and shown it to be a failure?) Will state socialism go down in history as an aberration, a "peculiar contagious disease" of the twentieth century? If so, where will that leave China? What should we do now? Does China, long accustomed to having a state ideology, need one? Can democracy be implemented in China? Is traditional Chinese culture "flawed" in some way that makes us misfits in the modern world?

And more personally: What should we intellectuals do now?

Should we try to maintain our tradition of "taking responsibility" for the general welfare, and to "worry first" about our country? If so, what exactly do we mean by our country, given the long-standing forcible insistence by our rulers that there must be no distinctions among party, state, nation, and people in these matters? Or, has "patriotic responsibility" been so abused in the past that we are better off refusing it entirely for now and concentrating on our professional work and our families?

The idea that I might write about Chinese intellectuals' struggles with all these questions originated with China's widely admired dissident journalist Liu Binyan, who also gave crucial advice about how to go about this task. I saw Liu frequently in the spring of 1988, when he and I were both teaching at UCLA. A year before the June 1989 upheaval at Tiananmen Square, Liu was already disturbed to find that Western intellectuals could condemn repression in places like the Soviet Union and South Africa but were somehow reluctant to condemn the same in China. I told Liu that I, too, felt frustrated by this double standard, and went on to offer several explanations for it: that many American intellectuals have long opposed the ideological anti-communism that reached its worst extremes in the McCarthy period, remain attached to some of the ideals of socialism, harbor warm feelings for the Chinese people, do not sense in China the nuclear threat posed by the Soviet Union or the ugly and familiar race issue apparent in South Africa, and consider China an alluring, mysterious place, whose culture is different in a way that may make our own political and social standards inapplicable to it. Liu responded immediately—and correctly—that none of these explanations was based on *facts* about China. Hearing this, I urged Liu to write a book or article that would present those facts to the American reading public. The problem, I argued, lay not with the values of American intellectuals (ironically, a "liberal" in the United States resembles what the Chinese Communist government has always called a "rightist"—for example, Liu Binyan himself) but with their ignorance of facts. You, I told Liu, who knew China so extraordinarily well and who can write and speak directly to American audiences, can perform an invaluable service.

I may have badgered Liu too much on this point. One day he suddenly turned to me and said, "Why don't *you* think of playing this role as well? You will be in Beijing next year, working with a broad range of Chinese intellectuals. You know something about Chinese history and literature, but also, because you're American, you know what Americans are interested in and how to write it down in English." Noticing, perhaps, that he had startled me into momentary speechlessness, Liu went on to give me advice that proved uncannily accurate. "Next year, when you are in China, interesting things are bound to happen. Dissatisfaction among intellectuals and urban workers cannot grow much stronger before it bursts to the surface. The seventieth anniversary of the May Fourth movement and the fortieth of the founding of the People's Republic may each provide the spark. There may even be violence. Keep a journal while you are there. *Listen* to the intellectuals. Just listen, and take notes. They dare to talk these days. What they say orally goes far beyond what they can put into print. You should read things, too, of course. But first just listen, until you understand what things are important to read, and why."

Liu Binyan's predictions of upheaval took a year to mature. But his description of the intellectuals' willingness to talk was immediately apparent when I arrived in Beijing in August 1988. One of China's most eminent social scientists told me, "We essentially *have* freedom of speech now. Informally we can say just about anything, and do. What we don't have is freedom of the press." Within a month I had been invited to four or five dinner parties at which the only topic was China; the only attitude, bitter cynicism; and the only two kinds of villain, the top leaders and those who cooperate with them. But there was also a seemingly endless supply of spirited opinions and lurid anecdotes, which generated in the groups a kind of levity and momentum that drove the dinner parties late into the night. I was primarily a silent auditor at such gatherings, since my participation would have slowed things down—as everyone knew. I'm sure my presence was forgotten most of the time.

Some of the tidbits that the intellectuals enjoyed trading orally were the *minyao,* or "popular ditties," that captured publicly unspeakable truths in clever rhymes and rhythms. One, for example, was attributed to Inner Mongolian herdsmen who were obliged to receive a group of party officials sent out to "help them understand politics":

> They came out a bunch of sleepy clunks
> And went home a bunch of sotten drunks.

As a comment on the refuge that people took in informal talk, in stories and anecdotes that spread thickly through a nationwide grapevine, there was this:

> One billion people, nine hundred million tongues churning,
> The other hundred million are in the process of learning.

In the Beijing dialect, the term *kan* had suddenly arisen for this major sociopolitical pastime of "chatting." *Kan,* with an original meaning of "fluent," was also a pun on "to chop down." Someone who really talked up a storm was said to come in "chopping with two axes"; to let out all the stops was to "chop the great mountain" *(kan dashan).*

I began compiling notes on what I heard in both public and private discussions—without, naturally, attaching names, since I had to assume that my office and apartment in the Friendship Hotel were subject to surveillance. I focused on intellectuals' concerns about their own lives and responsibilities, because these issues lay at the heart of their worries. I began organizing my notes under five categories: (1) situation, meaning the intellectuals' worries about official corruption, political repression, the spiraling cynicism and rudeness in public behavior, and other issues in their contemporary environment; (2) livelihood, meaning problems with finances, housing, and other aspects of their personal daily lives; (3) history, meaning their reevaluations of the Communist movement and more generally of twentieth-century China; (4) identity, meaning the complex problems of identifying with the state and its ideology, as well as with China as a nation, and with such smaller groups as the work unit and the family; and (5) responsibility, meaning their views on what actions they should take as individuals and as intellectuals. These five categories have evolved into chapters of the present book, with "identity" having become two.

In January 1989, I drew up a list of people to interview in depth and formulated a series of relatively large, open-ended questions. I chose people who I knew would speak frankly given my promise of anonymity. In the end I conducted about two dozen interviews, divided almost equally among natural scientists, social scientists, and humanists, and including a few investigative journalists as well. About one-third were women. They included a range of the young, middle-aged, and elderly. Most were based in Beijing but some lived in Tianjin, Shanghai, and Guangzhou.[7] Although most were people whom I met for the first time in the fall of 1988 and who opened up to me increasingly during the year I was in Beijing, a few were old friends who were frank at the outset and remained so throughout.

In the wake of the government's harsh crackdown on Chinese intellectuals after June 4, 1989, the problem of preserving the anonymity of friends and interviewees has become much greater than I, or they, originally anticipated. Some of those I spoke with are still living at home and going to their workplaces inside China. Some have fled to other locations in China, and some have left the country. At least two were sent to prison. At the time of our talks, some of my interviewees declined my offer of anonymity, saying that the general situation was relaxed enough that anonymity wasn't so important or that, in any case, their disgust with the leadership was so thorough that they were ready to let the chips fall where they might. I responded in these instances that anonymity was a fixed condition of the inter-

7. Also known as Canton.

view, whether they declined it or not. I have used names for
only a few of those I spoke with—such as Liu Binyan, Fang
Lizhi, Dai Qing, Wang Meng, Li Tuo, and Liu Zaifu. Their
views and standpoints are so well known and well published
that anonymity would serve little purpose. For others, anonymity is imperative. One of my interviewees, who had spoken quite
freely in the relaxed atmosphere of January 1989, became
extremely concerned after the massacre about my notes on what
he had said. When we met in the United States in late 1989,
he went over my transcript line by line, deleting items—
amounting to about two-thirds of the whole—that he wished I
would not mention *even if* anonymously. He was afraid for his
family in China and warned me that the Chinese police would
scrutinize whatever I wrote for the slightest clues to identifying
people. "You Americans are always too naive about these things,"
he said.

In his case and in that of most others, I have thus been
careful to omit not only names but also dates, places, and tell-
tale marks such as institutions, special fields, and family situations. Sometimes I have deliberately altered these details,
without, I hope, obscuring the overall point. I do allow myself
to refer specifically to published sources, but in some cases I
have had to disguise even these as interview material—because
Chinese officials can use a foreigner's approval as "proof" that
a writer's ideas are subversive.

The Chinese government's repressive techniques exert a
pressure on this sort of project that is regrettable both for the
danger it poses to friends and informants and for the need for
editorial gymnastics it imposes on the writer. This pressure also
hurts you, the reader, who deserves full flesh-and-blood descriptions of the wise, funny, and courageous people whose thoughts
you will encounter. I would love to describe eyebrows and dim-
ples, family members and life histories, and the interior details
of living quarters. The people I have written about helped
maintain my own morale as it sometimes flagged under the
chronic frustrations of living and working in the People's
Republic. At times my spirits soared after a chance simply to

sit and talk with them for a few hours. Despite the persecution and humiliation they have had to contend with, and while enduring cramped, even squalid living conditions that made my own look almost attractive, they managed to remain idealistic, generous, witty, and, most poignant of all, patriotic.

How representative of the tens of millions of others called intellectuals were my informants? My conscious aim in including several generations, both sexes, a spectrum of fields, and various locales was to exploit the advantages of "representative sampling." And the fact that certain concerns recurred wherever I happened to look strengthened my sense that they were indeed pervasive. But I have not attempted a survey of the opinions of all "intellectuals" in a properly social scientific way. A sociologist in search of a rigorous and systematic survey would likely find two biases in my data base.

First, there is a certain quality bias in my sample. I have given more attention to the views of people I found broad-minded, selfless, and sincere, and less to those I found petty-minded, selfish, and devious. I have also avoided the standardized expressions of frightened apparatchiks, even though I make no moral judgment about their timidity. I have made these selections with the reader's interest in mind. The higher-quality views not only make for better sustained reading but ultimately allow a fuller grasp of the basic issues that face China. Yet, at the same time, I hope not to leave the impression that all Chinese intellectuals are saints, which certainly they are not. They include as great a proportion of scoundrels as one would find in any large group. The vice of hypocrisy is perhaps especially salient among them, largely because of their wish to maintain the traditional elevated image of the scholar even as their cruel environment drives them ever further toward hard-bitten pursuit of self-interest.

Second, there is in some ways an elite bias in my sample. About half my interviewees were nationally famous intellectual leaders, and while the issues on which they commented were widely discussed by others, their particular opinions, in some cases, would have to be called avant-garde. Again, I believe that you, the reader, are well served to see not only typical views but path-breaking ones as well. Most occur, and will be duly noted, on the topics of "identity" and "responsibility" (chapters 4–6).

Of the various divides within Chinese intellectual opinion, the ones that Chinese intellectuals themselves most often note are groupings by age. The common distinctions—which seem to me basically accurate—are among three generations, each marked by the experience of its formative years: the "old," educated before the revolution of 1949; the "middle-aged," educated under the Soviet system of the 1950s and early 1960s; and the "young," whose education was disrupted during the turmoil of the Cultural Revolution. Some now add a fourth generation, the "very young," educated during the open and somewhat mercenary 1980s. Besides occasionally noting generational differences in the pages that follow, I discuss them explicitly in chapter 5.

But even while noting divisions within Chinese intellectual opinion, I found the opposite phenomenon—of broad agreement, and even the presence of "set views"—more remarkable as I listened to people talk. For example, in the late 1980s seemingly everyone agreed that the families of top officials constantly embezzled public funds and bought luxury items like Mercedes automobiles; that the underfunding of education was a terrible mistake, and maybe even a deliberate policy to keep intellectuals weak and the populace ignorant; and that the leadership's proposal to build a dam across the Yangzi Gorges was stupid and wasteful and served only the egoistic pride of top leaders.

I call these not just common views but set ones, in part because they were expressed in identical or very similar terms all across China. Catchphrases such as "The scalpel of the brain surgeon earns you less than the razor of the barber" (to complain about low pay for intellectuals) were repeated, in fall 1988, by elderly engineers in Beijing as well as by young painters in Guangzhou. Such set views sometimes came and went abruptly, almost faddishly, causing me to wonder how, without a free press or a very good telephone system, word can spread so effectively. One explanation, certainly, is that the very lack of a free press in China forces public opinion into the underground grapevine known as "alleyway news" (*xiaodao xiaoxi*), where it has a breadth and vitality that we are unaccustomed to in the West. Another explanation lies in the surprising number of interconnections among the Chinese intellectual elite. The physicists know who the poets are, and even read them. Families are linked by marriage. There are strong lifetime bonds among classmates and people from the same native locale. "Pick eight Chinese intellectuals, at random," a Beijing editor told me, "put them at the same table, with some food and drink, and before they are done they will have discovered at least eight personal connections of some kind."

As we noted above, the tendency toward set views is caused in part by conventions of language use in Chinese culture. But a more powerful cause for the appearance of consensus among intellectuals in China is the enduring sense of an oppressive governing authority. "They"—the corrupt, dictatorial, misguided leaders—are like a dark cloud that looms so pervasively and incessantly that it creates consensus that otherwise would not exist among those crouching beneath it. The importance of this dark cloud is most easily seen when it goes away, as when Chinese intellectuals move overseas. In a place like New York, the cloud is still visible, but only as a white puff in the distance, and as its menace diminishes, so does the solidarity of Chinese intellectuals living under it. Differing views overlooked in China now come to the fore. Personal rivalries, although visible in the Chinese context, now become dominant issues. The Chinese Communist party's great but unintended contribution to unity among intellectuals is substantially lost.

I must stress that the resentment and despair present in my descriptions of Chinese intellectual opinion "under the cloud" are not my own creation. The sad and undeniable fact is that Chinese intellectuals have been heartsick for several years, beginning well before the shock of June 4, 1989, and certainly continuing in its aftermath. When an outspoken "dissident" like Fang Lizhi suddenly springs from among them, his can seem to an outsider like a minority view. But placed along a spectrum of opinion in its own context, most of Fang Lizhi's views are neither extreme nor very unusual. I heard many views in Beijing, especially from younger intellectuals, that were far more radical than his.[8] Fang stands out in part for the clarity and cogency of his analyses; but the characteristic that catapulted him to fame in the late 1980s was his willingness, as someone who had already achieved considerable status in Chinese society, to erase the line that conventionally separates public from private expression. Fang himself has written, "My airing of [dissident] thoughts has much less to do with any unique insights of mine than with the need to express publicly what many people are thinking privately." He has also observed that some day, when the repression finally ends in China, "these overscrutinized words of [his] will return to their rightful state of obscurity."[9]

Indeed, one of the challenges for me in writing this book has been to resist the tendency to tone down what I heard in order that the result seem more moderate and "professional." Like other American scholars of China, I have found myself subject to subtle but strong pressures against public embarrassment of "China"—meaning really the top leadership of the Chinese Communist party. Occasionally I have needed to remind myself that telling the truth must be a higher priority than preserving face for those who might find the truth an embarrassment.

My decision to write a book brought a generally enthusiastic response from my intellectual friends in Beijing. "You can write down things that we can't," one said. "It's good that someone does it." Some were eager to convey their views to the outside world. "I feel disappointed, even disgusted," said one young man, "when I see Americans come and look at the Great Wall, live in the tourist hotels, and think this is 'China.' They don't know anything about our problems and our actual lives." Some

8. For some examples, see below, p. 120.

9. Fang Lizhi, *Bringing Down the Great Wall: Writings on Science, Culture, and Democracy in China* (New York: Alfred A. Knopf, 1991), pp. xlv, xlvii.

made me feel uneasy by boldly predicting that my perspective as a foreign scholar would be especially "objective." (A latent reason for this enthusiasm, I believe, was the hope to gain a foreigner's imprimatur for their own complaints. It is a sad paradox of Chinese political life that leaders who routinely ignore or repress the voices of their own citizens will sit up and take notice when a foreigner comments.) But the notion of my "objectivity," at least sometimes, had a deeper intellectual interest to some, who hoped that the lens of an outsider might bring fresh insights. After one lengthy interview, fraught with worry over seemingly insoluble dilemmas, a professor of American studies said, "I look forward to reading what you say about our problems. It may be hard for you. We ourselves don't know what to say."

Beyond the questions of how well my sample represents Chinese intellectuals generally and of what the "consensus" within that community is lies the question of the place of intellectual opinions within China's society as a whole. To what extent are the worries of intellectuals shared by the rest of the population?

Some of the issues treated in this book have to do specifically with the roles and responsibilities of intellectuals themselves. Although members of other social groups may have opinions on these topics, they understandably do not worry about them as intellectuals do. But on the broader problems facing China—corruption, repression, stalled reforms, future directions for the country, and so on—there seems to be considerable commonality of interest across the social spectrum, at least in the cities. During my first few months in Beijing, my impressions of popular opinion were limited to chance encounters such as talking with taxi drivers and shop clerks, reading graffiti in parks, and listening in movie theaters to loudly voiced commentary on the heroes and villains in films. (Such commentary is a delightful Chinese custom, amusing in its own right and wonderful for the scholar interested in popular thought.) In these encounters I often heard bitter complaints that resonated with those of the intellectuals. But my sources were so few and so determined by

chance that I could not feel confident about what they represented.

Then, a few months later, evidence of popular discontent
unfolded before me in a way that went far beyond anything the
cleverest research method could have revealed. The evidence
lay in the streets of Beijing, in the responses of the city's people
to the student protests of spring 1989. These responses seemed
to come in roughly four stages, each indicating stronger support
for the students' complaints. During the marches after Hu Yaobang's death on April 15, the Beijing populace tended to watch
guardedly from a distance, with a sense of "Will they get away
with it?" By late April, during the marches that defied the *People's Daily* editorial branding the protests as "turmoil," many
ordinary citizens had moved toward active support of the students. They flashed the V sign, supplied food and water, and
assisted in traffic control. By mid-May, in the demonstrations
that brought around a million people to Tiananmen Square,
there were innumerable banners proclaiming, "Support the
Students!" I saw a worker stand above the crowd and shout,
"Long live the students!" and then listen as the crowd echoed
him in unison. In a public opinion poll taken in the city in
May 1989, 96 percent of those surveyed "thought the democracy movement's demands were reasonable," less than 1 percent
thought them "unreasonable," and the others gave no response.[10]
After the declaration of martial law on May 19 and the approach
of troops on the outskirts of town, the consensus in support of
the students took on an antigovernment siege mentality. One
banner urged, "Protect Our City." A small poster in a tiny back
alley threatened resistance to the military threat in its own way:
"One Billion People, One Billion Vegetable Cleavers."

The events of spring 1989 not only showed how widely some
of the concerns of the intellectuals were shared by the Beijing
populace as a whole; they also revealed a popular acceptance of
students as leaders in bringing grievances before the state. I

10. The survey was done by the psychology department of Beijing Normal University. See Nicholas D. Kristof, "Revel Planned Where Goddess of Democracy Fell," *New
York Times*, September 22, 1989, p. A4.

could not help noting the sharp contrast on this score with American student antiwar demonstrations in the 1960s, when protesters like myself were greeted with catcalls from hard hats, and would have frankly doubted the authenticity of any worker who stood up to shout, "Long live the students!" In the Chinese case, it seemed, the intellectuals' deep-seated notions that they should "take responsibility for the world" and "speak for the people" were not just self-wrought conceits but cultural assumptions shared, at least in the cities, by nonintellectuals as well. I remember overhearing an old man who was watching one of the student marches. Speaking in the heavy Beijing brogue, he referred to the students as "learning sprouts." "They're the best ones our country's got!" he said. "They come from all over the country." In a culture that respects age as much as China's does, for an old man to speak respectfully of "sprouts" only under-scores the power of an equally traditional respect for learning.

The question of what is on the minds of rural people in China is harder to answer, primarily because the population is so vast and varied. My own impressions, except for three stays in a small Cantonese village totaling two weeks, have been gained indirectly from Chinese intellectuals, including writers who describe the countryside in fiction, as well as from Western social scientists. All sources tend to agree that Chinese peasants are most concerned with their immediate environment. Will their families grow and prosper? Will they be better off in the coming year? Will luck be good, the gods kind, the spirits of the ances-tors comfortable? Contemporary intellectuals and their bundle of worries are generally remote from the peasants, despite the latent respect for "learning" in the traditional sense. This dis-tance is often increased by peasant resentment of the intellec-tuals' sometimes arrogant castigation of rural "superstition" and "backwardness."

But it by no means follows, as the Communist party leader-ship sometimes claims, that the distance between peasants and intellectuals implies peasant support for the state. Chinese jour-nalists and Western anthropologists in recent years have described a Chinese peasantry living in chronic resentment of the state, both for the taxes and regulations it imposes on their economic activity and for its denigration of their "feudal" social and spiritual life. Strong evidence that Chinese peasants wish to be free from the state can be seen in the famous reforms of the early and mid-1980s, the most hopeful years in China since the early 1950s. By far the most successful of these reforms was the agricultural policy of shifting control over land and responsibility for harvests out of state hands and into the peasants' own. These changes resulted in a nationwide surge in food production for which state leaders were eager to take credit, seldom acknowledging that it was usually the peasants themselves who pushed for this reform, sometimes even carrying it out before officials had time to declare it as policy. In 1956, peasants in Zhejiang province, defying Mao Zedong's orders to form agricultural collectives, assigned land to individual households. In 1962, peasants in Anhui province seized land from the state when driven to extremes by a terrible three-year famine. In both cases the peasants were eventually forced to hand control of the land back to state institutions. But when the process began again in poor areas of Anhui in 1978, the provincial governor, Wan Li, defended the peasants' actions, thereby earning himself popular acclaim in the ditty "If you want rice, Wan Li is nice," and also creating a prototype for agricultural reform that was followed elsewhere, with the peasants again pushing hardest.[11]

In short, the rift between Chinese intellectuals and the Communist leadership, about which much will be said in this book, seems to be matched by roughly comparable rifts between intellectuals and peasantry, and between peasantry and Communist leadership, discussion of which must be left for other books.

Yet I would stress that, because of assumptions about the connection between learning and governance that lie deep within Chinese tradition, the role of intellectuals in state and society

---

11. I am indebted to Liu Binyan and Fang Lizhi for this information. For more detail see Chen Yizi, *Zhongguo: Shinian gaige yu ba-jiu minyun* (China: Ten years of reform and the 1989 democracy movement) (Taipei: Lianjing Publishing Enterprises, 1990), pp. 17–32. The popular ditty in Chinese is *"Yao chi mi, zhao Wan Li."*

is more important than a Westerner might suspect. The behavior of the Communist leadership itself suggests the implicit power of intellectuals. The party's long series of campaigns against intellectuals—which has extended from the early 1940s into the 1990s and continued even with intellectuals battered into utter docility—offers the best evidence of the party's fear of the moral authority, and thus the power, of intellectuals. In March 1989, when thirty-three leading Chinese intellectuals signed a petition asking the party leadership to declare an amnesty for political prisoners, this simple act shook the Chinese polity at its highest levels. Top leaders consulted in haste; the State Council's official spokesman issued a carefully worded rebuke; within days, news of the petition had spread orally throughout Beijing and then to other cities. It was a catalyst in the chain of events that led to the tremendous uprising later that spring. What Western intellectual can imagine organizing thirty-two colleagues to sign a petition that would have such effects?

The dramatic events of spring 1989 slowed the progress of this book. I had just finished transcribing my interviews when the marches began. As the Chinese intellectual community grew steadily more tense and excited, the mood of reflection and inward probing that pervaded the fall and winter began to give way to a preoccupation with daily events. The dull gloom began to dissipate amid bursts of hope and shouts of defiance. I actually learned considerably less during the political thunderstorm than during the muggy calm that preceded it; hence this is not a "Tiananmen book," although it may be viewed as an exploration of the causes of the protests.

Occasionally the spring events cast a startling new light on aspects of life in China. For me the most spectacular example came when I was forcibly turned away, together with my wife and Professors Fang Lizhi and Li Shuxian, China's famous human rights advocates, from attending President George Bush's farewell banquet in Beijing on February 26, 1989. What I learned from this unusual experience, and from its consequences in the days that followed, had to do both with the nature of repression in China and with how an image generated by exposure to the news media can diverge from actual life.

It was quite by chance that I shared a car with Fang Lizhi and his wife, Li Shuxian, that evening. We agreed to do this on the afternoon of the previous day, at a planning meeting for a conference that was to occur two months later. (The planning meeting was held, ironically, inside the Great Wall Hotel, the very place we would be barred from reaching twenty-four hours later.) In small talk after the meeting, the topic of the Bush banquet came up, and it turned out that Fang, Li, and I had invitations. I suggested that we share a ride. For me it was standard practice to make this kind of invitation to Chinese friends, because I, as a privileged foreigner, had much easier access to cars than they had. Of course, I was aware that Fang Lizhi was out of favor with the Chinese government, but for that very reason felt that to shun him in circumstances where I would not shun other Chinese would be to observe a stigma unworthy of respect. I knew that the foreign press would be eagerly watching for Fang's attendance, and in my mind's eye I pictured Fang having to face a crush of Western reporters at the hotel door. I knew nothing of the backstage standoff that had developed between Chinese and American diplomats over the invitation and did not remotely imagine that the Chinese leadership would choose to settle the matter by ordering the police to bar Fang physically. I assumed that because Fang and Li had already received formal invitations from the White House, any problems between the American and Chinese governments must have been worked out.

En route the next day, Fang, Li, my wife, Jean, and I speculated about what might happen at the banquet. Fang felt that any mention of human rights would be brief at best, and probably only symbolic. He doubted he would have any direct contact with Bush and had no intention of seeking any. Suddenly, about five blocks from the hotel, our car was waved to the side of the road and surrounded by about eight policemen wearing crisp new uniforms and revolvers at their hips. Our driver was summoned and told he had been speeding. After sitting in bewilderment for about five minutes, we got out of the car and prepared to walk the remaining five blocks to the banquet. Immediately about twenty plainclothes police swarmed around us, pulled and pushed us apart, and held us inside two tight circles—one around Fang Lizhi and Li Shuxian, the other around Jean and me—separated by about fifty feet. The police told Fang and Li that their invitations were invalid and that they could not continue toward the hotel. Several minutes later the band of plainclothes police disappeared as abruptly as it had descended, and the four of us were allowed to come together again. Fang suggested that we go to the U.S. embassy to verify the validity of the invitations. Fortunately the embassy was in the opposite direction from the hotel, which clearly was the direction the Chinese police wished us to move in.

But our car had disappeared. We found and boarded a taxi, but it, too, was stopped after six blocks for a "defective tail-light." (Fully seven armed police busily investigated that tail-light.) We tried to board public buses, but they were flagged down before reaching their stops and then drove by without stopping. This happened several times. People waiting at the stops, unaware of the reason for this strange pattern, had comments for the bus drivers that are not repeatable but can easily be imagined. Fang, despite everything else on his mind, felt that we had become an unfair burden to Beijing commuters and suggested that we give up the bus idea and simply walk the three or four miles to the embassy. Li Shuxian and Jean, who had not dressed for the streets of Beijing in February, exercised as they went in order to try to stay warm.

We had company. There were police all along the way—in uniforms, in plainclothes, on foot, on bicycles, on motorcycles, in police vans, in unmarked cars. Some tagged faithfully behind us; others came and went. Having no map, we found it difficult to make our way in an unfamiliar part of the city at night. After getting bad directions once or twice, we knew we had to make judgments about which pedestrians might *not* be plainclothes police, and turned this into a sort of game. We saw a man walking hand in hand with a small child. "Eighty percent safe," Fang noted. When we asked directions and got an especially animated, warm, and lengthy answer, Fang said, "Safe for sure." When we finally arrived at the American ambassador's residence, at 17 Guanghua Road, a cluster of about a dozen police barred the gate and told us no one was inside.

By chance a Canadian diplomat named David Horley and his wife, who were out for an evening stroll, encountered us on the sidewalk and brought us to their nearby apartment. When police tried to block us from entering the building, Horley politely but firmly reminded them of the rights of diplomats to entertain personal guests. From the Horley apartment Li Shuxian called home to inform her son Fang Zhe of what had happened and to assure him that his parents were safe. Within a few minutes this simple act had elicited a barrage of phone calls to the Horley residence. Members of the Western press, having noticed Fang's absence at the banquet, immediately began calling his home to find out the reason for it and now were having all their calls referred by the Fangs' son to the Horley number. Fang and I handled the incoming calls—he taking the Chinese and I the English—until we recognized the futility of repeating the same story over and over. We decided to head for the Shangri-la Hotel, where the press corps was based, and go through the events once for all to hear. David Horley kindly agreed to drive us there in his car. We were again tailed by police, but not stopped. It may have been Horley's diplomatic license plates that kept us from developing a defective taillight. More likely, we were left alone because the banquet was just ending at the time, and the Shangri-la was far from the Great Wall Hotel.

ABC's Todd Carrel, who was waiting for us at the Shangri-la door, whisked us upstairs to ABC headquarters, locked the door behind us, did an interview, and wanted to hurry us out a back door and send us home so that ABC would have a scoop. This quixotic effort was doomed from the start, however, by the mob of reporters already milling at the end of ABC's hallway. Fang decided to withhold further comment until he could get to a large room downstairs and hold an open press conference. After that he wanted to "go home." But ever soft-hearted, he later agreed to return upstairs for an interview with NBC's Tom Brokaw, an "old friend" who had interviewed him the night before. Next a CBS representative, who knew that both ABC and NBC had taped one-on-one interviews, came protesting volubly that CBS was being unfairly left out. Fang agreed to see Bill Plante. Afterwards Todd Carrel took us all home in an ABC van. Again we were tailed, but this time by determined remnants of the Western press corps.

It was about two-thirty in the morning when my wife and I arrived back at our small apartment. The sudden tranquillity accentuated the sense of buzzing absurdity in all that had just happened. We realized we had not had dinner. We sat on folding chairs in our tiny kitchen, snacking on peanut butter sandwiches and straight Scotch. I set the alarm for six, wanting to write down an account of what had happened in order to satisfy further requests for the story without having either to abbreviate it or to exhaust myself in its repetition. I rose at six and by nine-thirty had completed an account—only the facts, in chronological order. At ten I was called to the U.S. embassy, where officials wanted exactly this kind of factual account. A press officer asked if he could share it with reporters, and I said yes.

In the days that followed, I found the consequences of this peculiar experience to be as compelling as the event itself. The first of the aftershocks was a sense of fear—not strong fear, but a kind not quite like any I had experienced before. I do not remember feeling any fear during the banquet incident itself, perhaps because I was so preoccupied by problems at hand. But in the ensuing days I occasionally felt brief and inexplicable surges of apprehension in situations that were wholly ordinary. Was this group of bicyclists suddenly going to veer and crash into me? Was someone going to leap out of a stairwell and cause an "accidental" fall?

One of the more unsettling of these episodes occurred two days after the banquet, the next time I went to see Fang Lizhi and Li Shuxian. They lived on the eleventh floor of a large slab-shaped apartment building served by two elevators, one at either end. One elevator ran on Mondays, Wednesdays, and Fridays and the other on Tuesdays, Thursdays, and Saturdays. (I cannot remember what happened on Sundays.) It was a Tuesday, and I would have to use the elevator at the opposite end from the Fangs' apartment. Then I would have to walk about fifty feet along an exterior walkway eleven stories above the ground. An adequate railing guarded the edge of the walkway. I had taken this route several times in the past without a second thought. But that day, after leaving the elevator at the eleventh floor, I was suddenly visited by the notion that if I were to go out onto the walkway someone might appear to push me over the railing. I told myself that this fear was groundless. Next I told myself it was more than groundless; it was irrational. But I did not step onto the walkway. I resolved the momentary dilemma by telling myself that, in any case, it would not take much more time if I went back down in the elevator, walked to the other end of the building, and climbed the stairs adjacent to the nonworking elevator, thus avoiding the ledge. And that is what I did.

During the same period of days, I also became aware of unusually strong impulses to blame myself when problems arose. For example, when the hotel service workers assigned to care for the CSCPRC office went in after hours and used the photocopier for private purposes, it would properly be my duty to say something about this petty abuse. But when an especially blatant instance occurred in the days after the banquet incident, I could not bring myself to protest. I forced myself to go find a supervisor, but ended up mumbling apologies for bringing the complaint. "I know it's not terribly important, and they're good people, I know, and I don't mean to be unpleasant . . ." I may actually have given him the impression that further minor offenses would be just fine.

I shared these psychological aftereffects with one of my closer Chinese friends—a sensitive, introspective writer who generally stayed away from politics. "Now you know what it really feels like to be Chinese," he said. This comment struck me with considerable force. I had edited three books of China's post-

Mao "scar literature," including first-person accounts of horrible suffering. Beyond these I had heard many oral accounts that were too shocking to be published. I thought I knew about such things. But firsthand experience, even as temporary and comparatively gentle as mine had been, brought insights that no amount of empathy with the stories of others had yielded.

The next surprise for me in the aftermath of the banquet incident was to discover that I had become a kind of underground hero. The banquet story had been broadcast to the world and then back to China via the British Broadcasting Company and the Voice of America. "We support you," whispered a senior historian in the middle of an official meeting two days later. "The Communist party hates him," said a beaming youngster who introduced me to his friends inside his apartment. I received congratulatory letters, some obviously written under pseudonyms, from across China. A young man in Hunan province wrote in English praising "the integrity of the Western intellectual as exemplified by you." An official from People's University in Beijing sent word through a friend, "Because of what's happened, we must cancel your lecture next month. But I hope you will invite our students to your own office to talk with them." A scholar at Beijing University to whom I had offered a ride to a conference, and who had not shown up to accept it, went out of her way to pass me a message that she had missed the ride by accident and not because she was avoiding association with me. An eminent literary scholar sent an oral message through a friend: "In the eyes of Premier Li Peng and President Yang Shangkun, you must be the least welcome foreigner in all of China; in my eyes, you are the most welcome."

What surprised me most about this "image" of mine was neither that it had spread so quickly—the combination of foreign broadcasting and the Chinese grapevine can be very efficient— nor that it attracted sympathy so easily, because I knew that the sympathy had nothing to do with me, and little even with Fang Lizhi, but everything with pent-up resentment of the Chinese authorities. What did surprise me was the discovery that I had been credited with a purposeful act. It is pleasant, of course, to listen to congratulations, but underneath I kept wondering, "What would they say if they knew it was an accident? What if they knew that the bizarre rush of events that night left hardly any room for considered choice?" In retrospect, the only point during the evening at which Jean and I could have chosen a significantly different course came when the plainclothes police released the Fangs and us from our separate confinements. Once the Fangs had been told that they could not attend the banquet, Jean and I could have shaken hands with the Fangs and walked toward the hotel by ourselves. But this did not occur to us. I doubt that it occurred to the Fangs. Nor, I will wager, would it have occurred to you. I suspect that nearly any four human beings—even ones who did not like one another—would feel a strong impulse to band together if suddenly thrust into circumstances as peculiar and intimidating as those. Such impulses issue from a deeper, more instinctive level in human nature than what we normally refer to as either integrity or courage.

I also received—and this is only fair, I suppose—several kinds of criticism to balance the unwarranted praise. The Chinese authorities, embarrassed by publicity of the incident, directed blame at me for making the difference between what had happened and whatever it was that they had planned for the Fangs that evening. (Their assumption that a "smooth" diversion of the Fangs would have kept their empty seats at the banquet out of the world's headlines reveals a serious misunderstanding of the operations of a free press; but that is another issue.) For the next few weeks plainclothes agents watched Jean and me, and even our small children, in ways sufficiently obtrusive to cause us to conclude that the purpose was mild intimidation as much as surveillance. A few months later, when our family's personal effects were shipped from China, the police gave us a simple receipt, but no explanation for "seventy-six items of books, letters, papers, and clothing" that they had confiscated. I believe their treatment of us would have been harsher than this had it not been for their mistaken assumption—which was clear in some of their press accounts—that I was a U.S. government employee. Their strident protests to the American government over the incident appeared, in my view, to have followed partly from the incorrect assumption that the U.S. embassy had deputed me to accompany Fang.

I was also the target of blame from some Americans, who criticized me for flamboyance, for leaping into politics in search of personal fame. That misunderstandings as basic as this could arise from a news story—even a fairly well-reported one—gave me new insight into the workings of public "images." For the first time in my life, I was tempted to sympathize with politicians who hire "image handlers." Other Americans saw me as an accomplice in the delivery of a gratuitous insult to "China." These were people who accepted the Chinese government's claim that the invitation to Fang Lizhi was "an affront to the host country," and who blamed the American ambassador Winston Lord for bad judgment in proposing it. At a distance these people apparently had no way of knowing that the citizens of that "host country" who knew about the Fang invitation generally were, in marked contrast to their rulers, enthusiastic about it and thankful to the Americans for the implicit statement it made. Nor could most of these same critics have known that the decision to invite Fang was personally discussed and approved by President Bush in advance. Later efforts by White House officials to shift responsibility for the "mistake" onto Winston Lord were disingenuous and cowardly.

Another kind of criticism, one that issued primarily from American academic circles, raises important issues that call for reflection. Some said I "drew too close" to Chinese intellectuals, "abused my role" an as official at CSCPRC, made life more difficult for my successors in that role, and needlessly complicated management of future U.S.-China scholarly relations. These criticisms speak to genuine, long-term structural problems in the scholarly relations of any foreign country with the People's Republic of China. They are worth considering in some detail not just for the sake of dialogue with my critics but because they bear on the issues I discuss in this book.

We must begin by removing the question of my allegiances

from the narrow context of the banquet incident, which, although it prompted discussion of the issue, is not a good illustration of it. It is a bad illustration because—and this I must point out to my critics as much as to my would-be admirers—the question of what *causes* an event has to precede the question of praise or blame for it. The four of us who groped our way through the cold streets of Beijing that night, and then spent several hours at bay before the Western press, were by no stretch of the imagination the initiators of these events. The causes of the incident in its broad outlines were fairly simple. The onslaught of the press was caused by Fang Lizhi's empty seat at the banquet; and the cause for that empty seat was the order given to the Chinese police to block Fang Lizhi from the hotel. This order was later reported to have originated with Yang Shangkun or Li Peng, who thus should be primary candidates for whatever praise or blame people wish to assign. (If it seems strange to "credit" Yang and Li with the enhancement of Fang Lizhi's reputation, it should be noted that there are many precedents in the People's Republic—including Bai Hua, Liu Binyan, and Wang Ruowang in the 1980s—for the leadership's making heroes out of the people it attacks.) Once Mr. Yang and Mr. Li made their decision, there was very little possibility of averting the appearance of Fang Lizhi on the cover of *Time* magazine.

The issue of "drawing too close" to Chinese intellectuals should be addressed as part of the broader problem of the intricate balancing that is a daily necessity for any manager of academic exchanges with China. The crux of the problem is that one must maintain good relations with two opposing groups—officials of the state, who mediate the power that can make or break any activity, and intellectuals, who although generally remote from power are the ultimate partners in any successful intellectual exchange. The antagonism of these two groups has a long and bitter history. The problem of bridging the two is complicated by the tendency of most people, including officials and intellectuals, to behave differently in public and in private, in official and unofficial contexts. Intellectuals adopt official language as situations require; some cross the line (or at least want to) and become officials. Some officials, on the other hand, speak and behave differently in public and in private. Yet the overall distinction between "official" and "unofficial" is pervasive and crucial. With few exceptions, the people one deals with as a manager of exchange present themselves fairly consistently in one or the other of the two modes. Thus the sense that one is dealing with two different groups is rather constant.

The two groups have notably different sets of interests. The top priority of the officials is to avoid political mistakes that can leave them vulnerable to criticism by their superiors, who answer to higher superiors and so on right to the top. These political interests can be so sensitive as scarcely to be raised directly in official meetings with a foreigner. But they loom in the background as unquestionable givens and are communicated only by the subtlest of signs—or later, sometimes, in private. The next priority for the officials, at least during my term of service, was money, about which there was much discussion, often very awkward. The officials I encountered began and ended with the unshakable faith that American funds were limitless and that it was their duty to extract the maximum in any way they could. (Although I did my best to dispel this faith, in fairness I should note that, from a Chinese point of view, the size of American wealth can seem so huge that a small subtraction from it still might leave it the same size.) Politics and money were the twin pillars in the negotiating position of Chinese officials. They dwarfed any consideration of intellectual substance and merit. It may be unkind, but not unfair, to say that many of the officials did not even understand what is meant by scholarly merit. Those who did have some understanding of it always put political and financial considerations first.

The Chinese scholarly community was also quite aware of the ways in which politics and money influenced programs of intellectual exchange, and they did their best to handle both to their advantage even while resenting the official's domination in these areas. The scholars and officials divided most clearly over intellectual matters: Not only did the scholars have a much better understanding of intellectual merit, but at least some of them were devoted to giving questions of quality top priority. Some were able to suggest ways in which CSCPRC could lower costs and improve scholarly payoff at the same time—for example, by going through university professors to hire Chinese graduate students as research assistants, instead of using less competent but more expensive state-assigned functionaries. They also knew how to make progress in building politically sensitive fields, such as sociology, without turning them into political minefields. I also discovered that, in a wide variety of disciplines, these serious scholars (who included Fang Lizhi, by the way) were the same ones who were building the strongest professional ties with their American counterparts. For all these reasons I felt a strong affinity with them and did indeed "draw close" to them. I also admit, without apology, that it was sympathy as well as judgment that drew me toward them.

But my critics are correct in saying that the manager of a scholarly exchange program with China has to maintain effective ties with both scholars and officials. There is no alternative. One group is your partner, and the other calls the square dance. Even if you think of the officials (to borrow the image of one especially bitter Chinese intellectual) as rapacious bullies who stand in the roadway between Chinese and Western intellectuals, frightening passersby and demanding tolls, there still is no escape from the fact that they are there. Managers of scholarly exchange can choose, as some have done, basically to ignore the intellectuals and deal only with the officials. This choice makes management easy but carries considerable cost to the quality of exchange as well as to the perception in the Chinese intellectual community that Western colleagues offer independent judgment and integrity. On the other hand, if one sides too closely with the intellectuals, the officials will delay or withhold approvals—and the machinery of exchange will slow down or even stop.

The best route, like it or not, is the awkward middle. The first step down this path is to develop one's own official and unofficial personae for use in these two different spheres. You must learn to handle the two substantially different styles of language. At first the exercise can make you feel two-faced, but the feeling subsides as you gradually understand that the Chinese populace as a whole has come to accept the double language as a necessity of life. Skill in using both levels of language is seldom viewed with moral disapproval, and in most cases the practice is neither intended nor interpreted as deceptive. Some persons even regarded it as a perfectible art.

But to learn to distinguish contexts, audiences, and languages, and to match them appropriately, only equips you for the really difficult choices. Your life is fairly easy as long as its "spheres" remain separate, which they do as long as you are making small talk or speaking abstractly. But in day-to-day work the separation becomes problematic. For example, what do you do when attending a meeting between Chinese officials and a high-level group of American academics who have recently gotten off an airplane from the United States and are about to get back on one, in which the Chinese officials are presenting an ideal official-language version of matters that departs far from reality, and the Americans are busily taking notes? Do you "break the rules of the game" by injecting some questions that are out of bounds in official discourse? Is the benefit of giving the Americans a fuller picture worth the embarrassment of shattering decorum? Although you know that the Chinese officials will immediately recognize what you are saying, and may even sympathize with it in their hearts, will they feel a duty to rebuff you? Will this jeopardize your future relations with them? On two similar occasions I came down on different sides of this dilemma.

Or what, to take another example, do you do when negotiating a visit to the United States by a delegation of Chinese philosophy professors—membership on which is extremely coveted—and Chinese officials propose a delegation list including persons who are second- or third-rate professionally, or even entirely unknown, but, you find, are in line for rewards on the basis of seniority or personal connections? And what do you say about the "nonnegotiable" nominee, always included in such delegations, who is not even nominally a scholar but a "delegation companion" whose primary function is surveillance and whose full expenses you are asked to cover just as if he or she were a scholar? Do you go along with the official list, to ensure that the trip gets approved, or do you hold out for higher-quality delegates, at the cost of long and unpleasant negotiations, and perhaps the ultimate failure of the project?

Your balancing task is further complicated because the "sides" in negotiation can sometimes subtly shift, obliging you to play different games at different levels. At the explicit level you represent "the American side" in negotiation with "the Chinese side" over issues such as scheduling, visas, and the crucial one of money. But when intellectual issues are involved—concerning such matters as personnel, topic, and agenda—you often find yourself between Chinese officials on one side and the intellectual community as a whole, both Chinese and American, on the other. This may not be a position you seek, but it falls to your lot. For example, Chinese and American historians of philosophy can agree fairly easily about who their outstanding Chinese colleagues are—or at least that the official nominees are not among them. When you propose higher-quality candidates in negotiations, you may be stating the position of the American side but expressing the views of the Chinese intellectual community as well. Your counterparts in the negotiation are aware of this fact, and at an unspoken level even seem to welcome it. They judiciously distance themselves from their own intellectual community—which is something they occasionally need to do anyway—and use you as the pivot for achieving the distancing. Chinese intellectuals are cleverly abandoned, and it is made clear that if anyone is to support their interests, it must be you. For example, if a distinguished Chinese scholar is to replace a party-picked nominee on a delegation, the Chinese officials "regretfully" announce that the logistics they normally handle—such as permissions for leave, passports, and travel tickets, all of which can be difficult to obtain in China—will have to be taken care of either by the individual scholar or by you, the American representative. Yet all of this communication is done through a language game that scrupulously observes the fiction that Chinese officials represent the whole of the Chinese side on all issues. The terms of your multiple-role, level-shifting negotiations might become convoluted to the point of choking. But to allow an explicit break in the fiction of "the two sides," parallel in all things, including dignity, would be even worse. It would cause a loss of face that could paralyze discussion entirely.

Even if you could figure out the ideal combination of principle and practicality for every circumstance, and moreover master the language game perfectly, there would be the further problem of unpredictability. This problem looms especially large in exchanges with China. In March 1989, CSCPRC had a wide range of activities under way, and by June, because of the Beijing massacre, all were either canceled or suspended. This is an extreme case, but there are many more-ordinary ones as well. You can be ironing out the final details of a group's itinerary and then suddenly learn that the Chinese leadership has decided that it would be better not to go. There is no good defense against such surprises. Short of simply quitting, which has its own costs, a group like CSCPRC has no alternative but to accept unforeseen disappointments and just keep on trying. CSCPRC's record in China since 1978 shows that repeated efforts, based on consistent principles, will yield the desired results *on the average*, although there can be no certainty of what will happen in any one instance.

Several times during my year of work for CSCPRC, I had to remind myself of this "rule of averages." But I never felt doubt about what I saw as the overall, long-term goals of my office: quality and efficiency in scholarly exchange. These were the very goals that led me to "draw close to" leading Chinese intellectuals in a variety of fields, whom I saw as natural and important allies despite the difficult and complicated relations between them and their state. I believe I share with my academic critics, for the most part,[12] a definition of the goals of the CSCPRC

12. I say "for the most part" because some in American academe would include support of Sino-American state relations as a third goal of scholarly exchange and, indeed, give it a higher priority than intellectual quality and efficiency. This view grows out of the late 1970s, when the Carter administration's diplomatic breakthrough with

office; we differ in our judgments about where best to strike the necessary balance in reaching those goals.

Beginning in late May 1989 and extending until June 9, when I left China, "quality and efficiency of scholarly exchange" became impossible goals for the CSCPRC office. Martial law had been declared, dark rumors were circulating, a massacre took place, and a harsh crackdown began. On June 5, I received a telex from CSCPRC's head office in Washington requesting that I notify all the Americans on our programs that it was now official CSCPRC policy that they leave China as soon as possible. I took it as my task to help with logistics where I could— by securing air tickets or finding rides to the airport.

But I could not avoid concern for Chinese colleagues as well as Americans. Foreigners in Beijing were not really in much physical danger during those days, notwithstanding all the excitement and spectacular publicity. The same could not be said of Chinese, including the intellectuals with whom I had worked. Several who feared that they had been targeted by their government asked me, as early as May 24, for help of various kinds. At first I did nothing in response, but as the situation grew uglier, the question of what to do became harder to ignore. I began to wonder about the analogy of the bystander who watches a crime on the streets of New York and does nothing. Does it matter that I am in a different country? Does it matter that I wear an "official hat"? How does it matter? How much? Which of a person's "identities" entails which responsibilities? In the end I found my efforts to reason about such things supplanted by a more intuitive perception that, for lack of a better

China called for academic and cultural exchange as a way of demonstrating progress in the Sino-American rapprochement. For the ice-breaking academic delegations in those early days, the scholarly quality of exchange was considered largely beside the point, which was to arrange successfully the exchange of something other than Ping-Pong delegations. By the late 1980s Sino-American relations, both diplomatic and scholarly, had developed well beyond the point where scholarly exchange needed to serve diplomacy in this way. The great majority of American China scholars had begun to measure exchange with China by its intellectual payoff. But a few persisted in conceiving scholarly exchange as a modality of state relations and remained ready to argue that intellectual quality should be a subordinate goal to the greater good of smooth relations between the two governments.

explanation, I can attribute only to the extraordinary situation I was in. The claims of poets and seers that shared humanity is the most fundamental of human identities can seem other-worldly, or even a bit embarrassing, within the confident bustle of "normal" life; but in that peculiar situation in Beijing the intuition began to seem almost absurdly straightforward. I doubt that it sprang from any abnormality of my own, and find it hard to imagine that another person in my position would not have sensed it. By now those unusual days have receded in my memory, and my daily life has returned to more ordinary patterns. But I find myself carrying a new appreciation of the concept of "human rights," and for that I am thankful.

In any case, I did begin to help Chinese intellectuals where I could. I helped five reach safety immediately before and after the massacre. Two of these were Fang Lizhi and Li Shuxian. The Fangs' decision to take refuge inside the American embassy, unlike that to trek through the Beijing streets on February 26, was something they had time to contemplate several days in advance. On May 26 their son Fang Zhe came to the Friendship Hotel and invited me outdoors for a walk. His parents were out of town at the time, but he was worried about what would happen when they returned to Beijing. He asked my opinion of their moving either to a foreign embassy or to a tourist hotel—where the international press could at least record an arrest or, because such a scene would embarrass the regime, possibly even deter it. From then until June 5, when the Fangs entered the American embassy, they struggled with the implications of accepting or not accepting foreign help.

About noon on June 4, some hours after the shooting had begun, I rode my bicycle to their apartment in order to make it clear that, if they did want help, I was ready to do whatever I could. When Li Shuxian met me at the door, she was fitfully repeating, in a hoarse whisper, "They're mad! . . . They've really gone mad." Like the rest of the city, the couple were reeling from the horrible stories that had reached them. But they declined my offer of help. Fang was, typically, reasoning from the broadest principles: "This is my home; I have done nothing wrong;

why should I leave?" As I left, however, Li Shuxian whispered that, if they decided they did need my help, she would telephone to "invite the children over to play." During the afternoon they received a stream of calls from friends, relatives, and students who were concerned that they were in great danger and who strongly urged them to leave home. At about five I received a call inviting my children over to play.

I took the Fangs to a tourist hotel, where they spent the evening; the next day, after further difficult weighing of options on their part, we took a nerve-racking car trip across Beijing to the American embassy. I was worried that we might be intercepted, as we had been the night of the Bush banquet, and feared what might happen to the Fangs in such an event. My best explanation for the fact that we were not stopped, or even harassed at the gate of the embassy, is that the top Chinese leadership itself must have been in frenzied disarray the day after ordering one of the most visible massacres in modern history. It very likely had not had time to give specific orders about Fang Lizhi, in the absence of which no underling would risk an initiative.[13]

Inside the embassy we talked with two high-ranking diplomats for about four hours about what to do. The first, chilling interruption was a volley of rifle and machine-gun fire from troops parading up and down the street directly outside. Fang explained that he wanted to stay in the embassy just a few days "until the situation became clearer." He also requested that there be no publicity or notification of the Chinese government, so that the matter not blow up and become a question of diplomatic "face." The Americans explained that secrecy was impossible, because of surveillance by the Chinese staff in the embassy and because bugging devices were presumably already at work.

13. The overseas Chinese press later published several kinds of speculation that the Deng regime had purposely allowed Fang to enter the embassy—or even plotted the event—because having him there subtly served its interests. Such conjecture is far-fetched. It probably overestimates not only the degree of Deng's forethought on June 5 but his cleverness as well. The supposition that Deng would judge Fang's presence in the American embassy to be in his interests is also dubious and tends to contradict the attribution of cleverness to Deng.

Fang then began to consider carefully the political costs of requesting refuge: the Deng regime would almost certainly denounce him for seeking protection and the United States for harboring him. By themselves these criticisms could be shrugged off; but Fang worried that the government could vilify the whole protest movement by charging that it was backed by foreign forces. Although anyone involved in the movement would know such charges to be absurd, the many Chinese whose only source of "information" was the government could easily be misled and could have their native patriotism channeled into opposition to the democracy movement. At the end of the long afternoon Fang turned to me, eyebrows lifted high as if to suggest, "I guess there's no choice," and said, "We'd better not stay. Let's go." His casual manner belied the palpable danger to him of simply walking back out on the street. But that is what we did.

Outside the gate, Fang commented, "I think it would be good if the American embassy gave protection to some ordinary people—a worker, a student, or just a regular townsperson like the ones who were killed last night. It would be a good statement about human rights—better than taking in a famous person." We went to the nearby Jianguo Hotel, had dinner in its Cantonese restaurant, and then went to a room that a friend of mine had vacated and was willing to lend to the Fangs. Dusk was falling, and I was eager to get back to my own family, which had not heard from me since morning, because telephone calls were practically impossible that day. I said good-bye to the Fangs and promised to try to call them the next day. I did not see them again until they arrived in Princeton, New Jersey, nineteen months later. When we met again, they told me that later that night the same two American diplomats with whom we had talked in the afternoon came to see them in the hotel. The American officials invited them back to the embassy as the "guests of President Bush."[14] Fang accepted this invitation but remained

---

14. Although the offer of refuge to the Fangs was the only significant public statement that the Bush administration made in support of Chinese human rights in the wake of the massacre, even in this gesture it remained worried about embarrassing "our Chinese friends" in the regime. A year later, when the Fangs were released from the

deeply ambivalent about the decision. Two days later he went so far as to request a car in which to return home. Li Shuxian, who believes Fang's arrest would have led to his death—whether officially or "by accident"—was instrumental in dissuading him.

The next day, June 6, tanks on Beijing's main street assumed battle formation, and rumors of civil war circulated. Until that moment I had remained convinced that foreigners who lived in tourist hotels and avoided the areas of violence were in no real danger. But civil war was another matter. Jean and I decided that she and the children should leave right away. They headed for the airport without tickets or reservations. Many other foreigners had obviously made the same decision; the Beijing airport was in chaos. I spent the day trying to help other Americans on CSCPRC programs find ways to leave. In the afternoon I called the Fangs' number at the Jianguo Hotel, but there was no answer. That night I went to sleep not knowing what had happened to them, or where my own family was, or the condition of many other colleagues and friends both Chinese and American. There were no news media in Beijing at the time, and both fax and overseas telephone service had been cut off at the Friendship Hotel.

The next day I heard by telex that my family had arrived in Hong Kong, having barely been able to get tickets on a British Air charter. Two days later, after packing our family's personal effects and closing the CSCPRC office, I left for Hong Kong myself on a regular flight of the Chinese airline.

In Hong Kong I was again surprised, as I had been after the Bush banquet, to hear the commentary on my "performance." To me it had all felt terribly grueling, and of course the circumstances had been highly unusual; but the personal choices I had made seemed to me commonsensical and in fact rather ordinary. To the Hong Kong media I had once again become an improbable hero. They wanted interviews. I received a fax from

embassy and began to describe what had happened, including the invitation to be the "guests of President Bush," a high administrative official approached a friend of the Fangs to request that the detail of association with the president be omitted.

Frank Press, who as president of the National Academy of Sciences was my ultimate superior at CSCPRC, thanking me for "courageous service . . . valiantly done" and asking me not even to consider returning to the dangerous situation in Beijing. On the other hand, one of my fellow China scholars at CSCPRC was enraged beyond control that I had helped Fang Lizhi enter the embassy. For its part, the official New China News Agency published a story in *Reference News*, China's largest-circulation newspaper, informing Chinese readers that I had been fired by the American State Department for meddling in China's internal affairs.

My sincere thanks go to Liu Binyan for planting the seed of this book and to Andrew Nathan for giving the sapling a subsoil fertilization—although I must insist that the blame for any crooked limbs or misshapen leaves is mine, not theirs. I am grateful as well to Merle Goldman and Marsha Wagner for helpful comments and to my editor, Steven Forman, for his advice and expert editing. I also wish to thank the National Academy of Sciences and CSCPRC for the opportunity to work in China, for their support during difficult times, and for their excellent work over more than a decade in promoting Sino-American scholarly exchange. I am also grateful to the National Endowment for the Humanities and to the Program in East Asian Studies at Princeton University for support during the writing of the book. I alone am responsible for the content that follows, which in no sense is intended to represent the views of any of the above groups. Finally, I wish to thank all the fine people whose views I *do* try to represent, but cannot name. The concerns expressed in their "evening chats" during 1988–89 regrettably resonate far beyond that particular year. In May of 1966 a courageous writer named Deng Tuo was hounded to commit suicide after daring to remonstrate with Mao Zedong in a series of essays he called "Evening Chats in Yanshan [another name for Beijing]." And more evening chats are continuing as I write, and will continue as you read, until the time when repression in China finally ends.

*P.L.*
*Princeton, N.J.*
*May 1991*

# One

# SOCIAL WORLD

When Deng Xiaoping "opened" China to the outside world in the 1980s, he did not adequately appreciate the impact that the comparison with the West would have on the Chinese populace. The effects were by no means limited to those Chinese who actually traveled abroad. Stories about life abroad that were passed along orally, images from foreign films and television, and the increased presence in China of foreigners and overseas Chinese all contributed to the impression, as China crept slowly out of its Maoist isolation, that the Chinese were "way behind." Chinese who have not been to foreign places, but have only heard about them, sometimes find it hard to grasp that the Western world itself has big problems. One evening in 1980, a senior professor in Guangzhou was in my apartment watching an American television report on poverty in U.S. cities—a report that the Chinese authorities had apparently approved because it showed the dark side of life in the capitalist West. As we watched the TV crew interview a family in a plain-looking New York tenement house, the professor said impatiently, "Just look, that family has a couch, a TV set, a refrigerator, and carpeting. If they were in Guangzhou, their problem would be not 'poverty' but how to avoid other people's jealousy. I'm a full professor, and I don't have those things."

The comparison with other Chinese societies—especially those of Taiwan, Hong Kong, and Singapore—was especially galling. "Why is it," one of China's most brilliant young academics asked me in late 1988, "that Chinese people do well everywhere in the world—*except* in China? The Chinese people are not lazy. They are not stupid. *Something's wrong.*" A novelist focused on the comparison with Taiwan. "We share a cultural tradition with them," he said. "So you can't say Chinese culture is the main problem. Obviously, the problems lie in our social system. Sure, our living standards have improved in the 1980s, mostly because of the government's reform program. But these improvements are basically just a matter of catching up to where China was before the Cultural Revolution. The party doesn't know how to reform any further without cutting back its own power, and it will never do that. We're stuck. The pressure is building. Something's going to happen."

The mounting pressure was being brought about by problems vast in effect and deep in causation. These problems are so intricately interconnected that they resist disentangling. We will rely on the analyses of Beijing intellectuals themselves to begin.

## Corruption

Shortly after I arrived in Beijing, a senior literary scholar told me about a friend of his who, on opening a carton of cigarettes he had recently bought from a street-side hawker, found inside not cigarettes but three thousand yuan[1] in Chinese currency. The two friends had tried to puzzle out what had happened. Someone must have wanted to deliver a bribe and used the

---

1. In 1988–89 one U.S. dollar was worth 3.174 Chinese yuan at the official exchange rate, which would make 3,000 yuan equivalent to about $945. The figure is more meaningful, however, if put in the context of daily Chinese living: the average worker's income in Beijing in 1989, counting salary and bonuses, was about 180 yuan per month. Food for one person cost about 80 yuan per month, and rent averaged about 5 yuan per month. A new bicycle cost about 250 yuan, a monthly bus pass 5 yuan, a television set about 2,000 yuan, and admission to a movie .50 yuan.

cigarette pack as a disguise. But the intended recipient, not guessing what was inside—or perhaps not a smoker, or perhaps not fond of that brand of cigarettes—had either sold the carton, or passed it on to someone who sold it, to the unknowing hawker who had put it out for resale. "Just think," said the scholar, "of the misunderstandings that must have been caused between the giver of that bribe and the 'recipient' who never received it. The former surely thought the latter terribly ungrateful; the latter must have thought the former unpardonably pushy. They may have been just small people. The big bribes in our city are much more than three thousand yuan."

The many stories that circulated about large-scale corruption tended to focus on the offspring of top leaders, including Deng Xiaoping, Zhao Ziyang, Yang Shangkun, Wang Zhen, He Long, Song Renqiong, Peng Zhen, Bo Yibo, Ulanfu, and many others. How much these stories were embroidered is hard to say, but they were widely repeated and believed, among common people as well as among intellectuals. Because such stories are indispensable background for understanding China's public mood, we need to look at an example, even if the repetition of rumor may seem ungraceful. I choose below a story I heard repeated many times in the late 1980s. I have done my best to give a substantially true version, by checking the details with some well-placed sources. But in choosing this example I do not mean to imply that the family in question is unusually blameworthy.

Hu Qiaomu, the highest authority in the Deng Xiaoping regime in matters of Marxist ideology, and a man widely feared among intellectuals for his record as a bully, has a son named Hu Shiying. In the early 1980s some people in the Chinese air force obtained pornographic videotapes and showed them in the gymnasium of the air force command compound at Gongzhufen, in western Beijing. As service personnel of both sexes watched, they "combined theory and practice," as one raconteur put it. Hu Shiying was among the revelers. Unfortunately for his father, the incident came to light just about the time of the "anti–spiritual pollution campaign" in fall 1983, when Hu senior was riding herd on intellectuals for allowing decadence to seep into China. When he heard about the pornographic videotape party, Hu Qiaomu demanded to know which air force woman was responsible for "seducing" his son.

Some time later Hu Qiaomu sought to elevate his son to membership in the Communist party, putting the best face on things by proclaiming that his son should be "held to the highest standards." At the time, Hu Shiying was editing a magazine called *Human Talent (Rencai)*, published by the Workers' Publishing House, which in turn was affiliated with the National Labor Union. His application to join the party therefore came before the labor union, which rejected it because of the well-known, and basically unchallenged, story about the videotape party. Hu Shiying then transferred his party application to the Academy of Social Sciences, where his father had been president and still wielded considerable personal influence. This application was successful.

But Hu Shiying's troubles were not over. In the mid-1980s, seeing a rising public interest in the study of law, he announced the founding of a correspondence law school to which many unsuspecting people sent "tuition" payments. The destination of this money became clear when Hu Qiaomu's house on Nanchang Street in Beijing underwent renovations: construction workers were surprised to discover gunnysacks stuffed with cash hidden in the walls. An investigation, ordered by the Communist party general secretary, Hu Yaobang, produced evidence of the embezzlement of three million yuan. Hu Shiying was arrested and detained in fall of 1986. The minister of public security said the evidence of his guilt was incontrovertible.

These events predictably triggered an angry response from Hu Qiaomu. Hu's protests were supported by several other top leaders, who joined in, according to the popular accounts, less from sympathy than from the panic that came from knowing that their own offspring were similarly vulnerable. Hu Yaobang, reportedly holding fast to the view that no exceptions could be made "no matter whose son was involved," deputed Qiao Shi, a central party secretary, to give a speech that set forth this principle and cited the Hu Shiying case as an example.

In January 1987 Hu Yaobang was ousted as general secretary. Many factors contributed to this event, but on the grapevine in Beijing, Hu Yaobang's prosecution of the Hu Shiying case was prominent among them. In any event, shortly after the sacking of Hu Yaobang, Hu Shiying was given a token reprimand and released from custody.

Chinese who could remember the 1940s indignantly proclaimed that corruption was even worse than it had been during the last years of the Guomindang[2]—a time long regarded not only as a low point for China but as the "lowest possible" point. In 1988, I heard Fang Lizhi chided for his suggestion, made two years earlier, that idealistic young people should join the Communist party in order to make it better. "Fang was too optimistic when he said that," one of his fellow scientists told me. "This party is beyond saving. I am a member myself, but stay in only to await the moment when my resignation will have maximum impact."

Corruption in the 1980s took many forms: bribery, nepotism, smuggling, trading of favors, eating and drinking on the public dole, taking goods home to "test" them, "borrowing" money and not returning it (on the threat of political retaliation). The mode of corruption that provoked the most comment and anger, however, was called *guandao* ("official profiteering"). In *guandao* an official or a member of his family buys commodities at low, state-fixed prices and then sells them—with huge, unearned markups—on the free market. This kind of corruption was born of China's transitional economy in the mid-1980s, in which Soviet-style central planning and a market economy were awkwardly juxtaposed.[3] It especially drew people's ire not only because it involved millions of yuan but also because access to *guandao* was limited to very high officials

2. The Nationalist party, which ruled much of China from 1912 to 1949. It is also romanized as Kuomintang and known as the KMT.

3. In 1989 China's total national income was about 1,500 billion yuan, of which about 600 billion was personal income. The portion of the domestic economy that was vulnerable to *guandao* (it is impossible to measure how much, without this sector, was actually corrupted) was between 200 billion and 300 billion yuan annually. These figures do not include any corruption connected with foreign trade and investment.

and their families—the very ones whose morality, in Chinese tradition, is supposed to guide the country.

"Have you seen all those buildings going up on the Beijing skyline?" a graduate student of economics asked me. "It looks pretty impressive to you foreigners, doesn't it? But you don't know how much of the capital is simply siphoned from the public wealth through *guandao*. What you see is not economic growth; it's self-consumption, the tiger eating itself. What's more, you'd be surprised how many rooms in those new buildings are *empty* in spite of the severe housing shortage in Beijing. Why? Because they're 'reserved' for the relatives and children of officials—sometimes even for unborn children! The doors are padlocked and may remain that way for years, while the little ones grow up. Just take a look some evening at how many rooms in those new buildings are not lit."

The Mercedes Benz became a symbol of *guandao* throughout Beijing society. It was said that officials were spending hundreds of millions of yuan on the luxury cars. One of the commonest slogans of the spring 1989 uprising (among workers more than among intellectuals) was "Sell the Benzes to Pay the National Debt!" I once asked a friend whether he thought it was true that China was selling arms to Iran and Iraq. "Of course it's true," he said. "Everybody knows it." He went on with an animated account of which children of which leaders in what places were involved in arms deals, how many Mercedes they got in return, to whom those Mercedes were parceled out, and even which leaders were miffed because they hadn't gotten a car.

Much talk, all negative, was spent on the real and imagined family connections of top leaders. The "four big companies" (Kanghua, Guangda, Sitong, and Zhongxin), all headquartered in Beijing, were said to be connected to the "four big [political] families." Many stories focused on the ways in which the companies used political connections to amass unearned profits or commercial advantages. Kanghua, created by China's State Council and headed by the retired minister of mining Tang Ke, was the largest, most diversified, and—to judge from the tenor of popular opinion—most thoroughly corrupt of the four com-

panies, specializing in the use of political connections to procure commodities and licenses in the state sector for resale in
the market economy. Deng Xiaoping's son Deng Pufang was
one of many family members of high officials prominently
involved with Kanghua, whose name literally means "health for
China." Zhongxin was headed by the elderly Rong Yiren, the
party's model capitalist in the 1980s and the son of a textiles
magnate in prerevolutionary Shanghai. The company engaged
in some foreign trade but specialized in bringing foreign investment into China. Zhongxin recruited two kinds of personnel—
experts in finance and people with pull, including the son of
China's vice-president, Wang Zhen. Guangda was founded by
Wang Guangying, brother-in-law of Mao Zedong's rival and
former president of China, Liu Shaoqi; it began by trading
between the state and free markets in automobiles and other
secondhand equipment and later moved into capital investment in Hong Kong. Sitong, famed for its computers and type-
writers, was run by Wan Runnan, who started the company
with the help of his father-in-law, Li Chang, former party secretary of the Chinese Academy of Sciences. Wan fled China
after the Beijing massacre and eventually became a leader in
China's overseas democracy movement.

Many observers interpreted political appointments as nepotism: Premier Li Peng is known to be Zhou Enlai's adopted son;
Deng Xiaoping was rumored to be the former lover of the mother
of Li Tieying (commissioner of education); Li Tieying was said
to have been Li Peng's classmate; in June 1989 the (false) rumor
spread very quickly that the new party secretary, Jiang Zemin,
was the son-in-law of former President Li Xiannian. China's
intellectuals, although sometimes concerned to separate truth
from fiction on the rumor mill, generally shared with the populace at large the assumption that nepotism was to be taken for
granted. "Deng Xiaoping runs China," said an economist, "the
way a patriarch runs a family business; 'so-and-so is a good boy—
he can do x. So-and-so's an old friend—he can take care of y.' "
The burden of proof seemed to be on anyone who denied such
an analysis.

Some did, however. "Personally I do not believe that people like Deng Xiaoping, Hu Qili, and Li Peng are corrupt," a well-respected senior social scientist told me in January 1989. "I think they want the best for China, just as I do. But many of the people right below them are out-and-out scoundrels, and the system as a whole is rotten to the core. It is beyond reform." A middle-aged computer scientist said, "We intellectuals, including me, are full of bitter complaints; but sometimes if you imagine yourself on top, trying to get something done, you can also appreciate how hard it would be to try to be an honest leader."

Many said that no leader could survive without partaking in the corruption. "If a leader is too clean, he loses out," an archaeologist told me. "Although I didn't agree with Hu Yaobang's every sneeze, I do believe he was axed because he was too honest. Some people in Xiamen[4] arranged for his daughter-in-law to be deputy mayor, and Hu wrote a letter protesting that she wasn't qualified." A senior art historian said, "In China, politics is at the bottom of everything, including corruption. Every leader is jockeying to strengthen his own position. Just look how they feed dirt on one another's factions to the Hong Kong magazines.[5] Of course, they appoint their own friends; they would be silly not to. That's why we Chinese intellectuals are so envious of Mr. Gorbachev's *glasnost.*"

The widespread perception that the top leadership was corrupt made it seem not only natural but almost justifiable that lower levels be corrupt as well. As one popular ditty had it,

> Central officials are busy politicking,
> Provincial officials are busy emigrating,
> County officials are busy eating and drinking,
> Local officials are busy gambling.

A survey in 324 cities in 1988 showed that between 69 and 85 percent of the intellectuals thought their local leader would

4. A major city in Fujian province, on the south China coast.

5. She was referring to monthly news magazines in Chinese, such as *Zheng Ming, Jing Bao, Ming Bao Monthly,* and *Nanbeiji.* Only those that generally serve the interests of the ruling authority are allowed to be sold in China, and then only in hotels for foreign tourists. As of fall 1988, these were *Jing Bao* and *Ming Bao Monthly.*

hire a relative in preference to a better-qualified candidate.[6] Banqueting was viewed as an especially common way in which people would "eat from the big public pot." A dinner party at a good restaurant could cost several times a person's monthly salary, yet Beijing supported hundreds of well-filled restaurants in 1988. Functions held to welcome or send off visiting officials became occasions for sumptuous meals that guests otherwise could never afford. My own presence in Beijing was several times used as a pretext for such banquets, the beneficiaries of which included some of my intellectual friends. The irony of complaining about corruption after imbibing wine purchased on public funds seemed to be dulled less by the effects of the wine than by the confidence that, because the whole system is so corrupt and the abuses at the top so massive, we little people would be blockheads to balk at a free dinner, which a just system would afford us anyway.

"Why should I report all my foreign exchange certificates?"[7] a taxi driver asked me. "The state leaders are pulling them in by the net load. Am I supposed to report the small amounts I get? Besides, if I did hand them in, the money would just get swiped by someone higher up. Do you think it would ever get to the bank? Hah!" Another popular ditty went,

> Speculators and middlemen get rich,
> The honest and law-abiding get poor,

6. Ye Jianmin, "Lixing de huanghun: Dui Zhongguo zhishifenzi chujing he xintai de liang xiang diaocha" (The dusk of reason: Two surveys on the predicament and mood of Chinese intellectuals) *Ming Bao Monthly* (Hong Kong), February 1989, p. 16.

7. In order to maintain control of its foreign currency reserves, the Chinese government has ruled that ordinary Chinese currency (*renminbi*, or RMB) cannot be exchanged for foreign currencies. Foreigners who exchange money in China receive "foreign exchange certificates" (FEC) in the same denominations as regular currency—yuan, jiao (dimes), and fen (cents)—but the two currencies are easy to distinguish in appearance. In theory, only foreigners can spend FEC; when they use them to pay for goods and services, Chinese shop clerks and taxi drivers are supposed to channel the FEC to the Bank of China in exchange for RMB. But the Chinese people covet FEC, because they are worth more than RMB on the widespread black market (where, in 1988, it took 7.5 or 8.0 RMB to buy a U.S. dollar, compared with only 3.17 FEC per dollar at the official exchanges). Moreover, FEC are accepted at the special stores where foreigners—or anyone else holding FEC—can buy goods unavailable elsewhere.

Liars and hypocrites get rewarded,
Sycophants and toadies get promoted.

But it was not just cynicism that led ordinary people to join in the corruption themselves. For many, especially urban residents facing 30 percent inflation on fixed salaries, economic necessity required cutting every possible corner. Qian Jiaju, a widely respected senior member of China's Political Consultative Congress, argued in April 1988 that without some graft, some "squeeze," some private use of public equipment, and so on, ordinary people simply would not be able to support families.[8]

In the same speech, Qian Jiaju courageously raised in public the problem of corruption in a justice system that shows undue leniency to the privileged. Qian cited the example of a provincial leader who was sentenced to two years in prison for spending several thousand U.S. dollars on a call girl, while the same court imposed life sentences on some "bad elements" who had been caught stealing watermelons. Chinese people generally consider courts to be tools for use by the authorities, not as instruments of justice for the citizenry. Citizens seeking redress must appeal to someone with authority, using personal connections and gifts as necessary; if that fails, they usually absorb their grievances, with some frustration, until there is an opportunity to act.

Meantime, they trade stories about injustice, which are extremely common. In Beijing a senior professor at the Academy of Sciences told me about one of his graduate students whose pretty girlfriend worked as a waitress in the Great Hall of the People, where the top leaders hold their official banquets. The couple wanted to marry, and the waitress approached her group leader to ask for the required permission. The group leader refused, offering no good reason, and leaving the couple with the impression that he simply wanted to keep a pretty girl near him. The couple appealed to the law, as well as to every person they could think of approaching, but found that no one

8. "Qian Jiaju tan wujia, jiaoyu he shehui fengqi" (Qian Jiaju talks about prices, education, and the public ethic), *Wenhuibao* (Hong Kong), April 4, 1988, p. 2.

would risk taking on the well-connected leader, who could exercise tyrannical power in his own duchy. At least for the time being, the couple had no way out. Theirs was an example of a much broader problem, inherent in China's "work units."

## The Work-Unit System

The leader of an urban work unit (*danwei*—a general term for any factory, office, school, or other organized workplace) has a broad range of powers in matters that concern everyone in the unit. This leader, usually a party secretary, not only determines a worker's rank, salary, and job description but also controls his or her housing, children's education, permission to travel, access to rationed goods, and political reputation. So important to every aspect of daily life is one's unit leadership that most people simply cannot consider offending their leadership in any way. It is possible to gain leverage against a local leader if one has a strong personal connection with a higher official. But few people have such a connection. The resulting relationship between workers and leaders is what one sociologist has aptly termed "organized dependence."[9]

For most urban Chinese, securing an assignment to a work unit is itself a difficult process. Ordinary graduates of elementary or high schools do not receive work assignments, and many must remain unemployed while they search for a job. Local units that need workers send requisitions to the higher levels of their bureaucracies, where officials formulate comprehensive plans with job quotas. These are distributed back down the rungs of another bureaucracy to city districts, and finally to the "neighborhood committees" that make individual assignments. Both the neighborhood committees and the hiring work units can test a candidate's eligibility for a job, but it is widely assumed that personal connections and gift giving are the crucial factors in hiring decisions. Parents often try to pass their positions to

9. Andrew G. Walder, "Organized Dependence and Cultures of Authority in Chinese Industry," *Journal of Asian Studies* 43, no. 1 (November 1983): 51–76.

their children and sometimes accept early retirement in order to assure that this happens.

Graduates of universities and other postsecondary schools are more fortunate in that they all receive job assignments, which are based on quotas issued directly to their schools. But there is still much anxiety over the distribution of assignments. The quota for a university department of foreign languages, for example, might include positions for a high school English teacher in a remote town (undesirable) and for an interpreter with a trading company in Shanghai (highly desirable). Normally a single party official in each academic department distributes all of its job assignments, amid much speculation about personal connections and favoritism. It was this issue that caused protesting Beijing University students, in spring 1989, to march to Tiananmen with the freshmen and sophomores in the more visible front rows and the seniors in the rear: with job assignments soon to be decided, the seniors were most vulnerable to reprisal through punitive assignments. Later that summer, as the crackdown proceeded, authorities recalled seniors to campus and had them write criticisms of the "counterrevolutionary rebellion." Very few students balked at this, because they all knew that to refuse would not only cost them their job assignments but also make them ineligible for any at all—leaving them social pariahs.

Although intellectuals spoke most excitedly about the problem of corruption when they reflected carefully on why China seemed so "stuck," so incapable of a major breakthrough to a happier, wealthier, more modern society, they often pointed to the work-unit system as the cause. Leaders of work units are themselves beholden to leaders at higher levels within a huge bureaucracy whose trappings include laws and regulations but whose real social glue is personal authority. The prominent political scientist (and refugee of the June 1989 crackdown) Yan Jiaqi claimed in early 1988 that the system was not only unfair but inefficient.[10] This kind of "personal authority" sys-

10. Yan Jiaqi, "Zhongguo ruhe qiangda qilai" (How China can become strong and wealthy), *Dagongbao* (Hong Kong), March 23, 1988, p. 9.

tem, said Yan, demands a great number of ad hoc decisions; and, since the borderlines of authority are never clear and punishments for mistakes can be great, it becomes excessively common to *qingshi* ("request instruction") from higher authorities, even on relatively minor or routine questions. This tendency concentrates power at the top even beyond the degree those at the top might want.

An investigative journalist put it this way: "In our work-unit system, if a manager hires an engineer, he has no incentive to make the engineer happy. His only incentive is to make his bureaucratic superior happy. If that is done, nothing else matters—not efficiency, not the engineer, nothing. If the manager does do something for the engineer, that counts as 'bestowal of a favor,' as something for which the engineer is supposed to be thankful—as if he hadn't earned it. Now, I know that in the Western competitive system, the manager *has* to be good to the engineer in order to keep him happy and in place, so that the enterprise will be competitive. The Chinese system makes workers feel like *beneficiaries* of the leadership, when actually it's the other way around. Actually it's the leaders who live off the workers."

Some pointed out that the work-unit system could be difficult from a leader's point of view as well. What if a well-intentioned unit leader really wanted to raise efficiency and productivity? Such a leader would have to worry not just about work efficiency but about medical clinics, about schools from the nursery level through junior high, and about countless other details concerning workers' welfare. I was given an unintentional demonstration of the extent of these responsibilities one morning while interviewing the director of a scientific research institute in her office. We were interrupted six or seven times by knocks on the door or by telephone calls from people in the institute inquiring about various errands. Was the institute going to buy duck eggs today for its members? Was the driver of the school bus ill? Why was the clinic not open? The director told me she once lost nearly a whole summer of research time because of the unexpected death of one of the faculty, and the consequent need for attention to the funeral, the relatives, and the refutation of rumors about the cause of death.

A reporter who worked on these questions told me that a factory's welfare activities may consume as much as half its resources. If the workers are unsatisfied with the benefits they receive, morale and production will suffer. Moreover, the leader cannot choose whom he will work with. Managers of state factories cannot hire or fire workers, and a child normally has the right to inherit a parent's position. A leader at a large technical institute told me that he sometimes has trouble with new employees who are freshly returned from study in the West. "They are full of bright ideas," he said. "But they have forgotten—or never knew—how hard it is to make any changes under our system. How, for example, do you get people to work eight hours a day? Some people in my institute come to work at ten, leave at three, and have a lunch break in between. But if the leader complains, he might offend them, and they will do even less. They have 'iron rice bowls' [job security]. The top manager can send a message to all the department heads, but what will motivate the department head? The task before him is unpleasant, it might cost him some good relations, and in any case he's paid the same whether anything happens or not."

"In the unit system," a sociologist told me, "keeping good 'relations' with people becomes much more important than doing one's work well. Only the relations, not the work, count when it comes to promotions and welfare. But even these relations are a veneer, only a set of appearances that people maintain. Beneath the veneer everyone busily calculates personal interests and manipulates both the official jargon and the social relations in order to maximize personal benefit. The leaders, naturally, have by far the most leverage, and that explains both why they live best and why everyone else must toady to them or pay a stiff price."

"After all," he continued, "the leadership's leverage comes not just from things that the unit does for the worker. Even things that you Westerners take as natural rights—where you live, whether you can travel, when you can marry, or have a child—are controlled by the unit leaders in China. Your leader also makes records in your personnel file, which you are not allowed to see. If you offend him or her, the comments stay with you forever. If you move, they move. At worst, your leader can recommend that you be 'transferred' to a remote area somewhere. And if that happens, well, then that's it—and probably for the rest of our life. You may never get out."

For years it has been said, in the Beijing dialect, that when a leader harasses someone under him by withholding various bureaucratic permissions, he is making the person "wear small shoes"—making life uncomfortable. By 1989 the phrase had appeared in a new version—to "wear small *glass* shoes"—in which "glass" refers to the invisibility of the harassment. In public a leader will smile and dispel any sense of ill will, but behind the scenes he will block one's road as firmly as ever.

The inordinate personal power of party secretaries is a major cause for the favoritism in hiring discussed earlier. The director of one of China's provincial academies of sciences told me that fully half of the people on her academy's permanent payroll simply should not be there. They were not suited to do their jobs. They had gotten there through "back door" connections with party officials in the academy. Not long after she had been on the job, the provincial party leadership "recommended" that she hire the young wife of one of the provincial leaders. When the woman came for an interview, the academy's only openings were those of (a) assistant chef and (b) director of research programs. The party leader's wife was unwilling to consider the chef's post, which was beneath her, and was completely unqualified to manage research. The director, knowing she would have to have a reason for not taking the official's wife, asked her to write an essay on her beliefs about scientific research. She could not manage to write anything. "All right," said the director, "then just write about your past experience." Still nothing. Not a word. ("She probably was not illiterate," the director observed to me, "but just afraid of looking bad.")

When the director announced the decision not to hire the "candidate," she was subjected for several weeks to pressure and "advice" from the provincial party committee to reconsider. They used various channels; even the head of the academy's automobile fleet (a powerful person in a culture in which access to automobile transportation is a coveted privilege) came to warn her of the possible consequences of "poor judgment." Finally, people began approaching the scientists in her academy privately, saying "XXX [her name] is not in good health, you know. If she should step down, whom would you like to see take over?" As it happened, she actually was not in the best of health at that time. But when she heard this rumor, she resolved to persist.

A young researcher at the Chinese Academy of Sciences in Beijing described similar problems there. "In my institute," he said, "fully one-third of the people on salary do absolutely nothing. There's another third who really *do* want to do something. The final third are in charge of ensuring that the ones who do want to do something can't." His ironic suggestion that the final third are "in charge of" obstruction was a widespread complaint. It refers to those who manage personnel and administration: people chosen not for their professional credentials—because normally they have none—but for their political reliability. For functionaries in the system, political reliability consists in maintaining a "clean record" of having made no political mistakes. But under a regime in which the "correct" line has flip-flopped so often and abruptly, the surest way to avoid "mistakes" is to avoid initiative of any kind. Those who survive the system do so by honing the skill—which at its best is remarkable to behold—of adapting their language and actions to fit any political requirement and at the same time leaving behind no visible trail of responsibility.

Intellectuals frequently express frustration at being "led" by such people. A senior researcher at the Academy of Sciences told me, "My party secretary is ignorant. He's not a bad man; he would never want to see a political persecution campaign against us. But he doesn't know the first thing about science, and he also just isn't very smart. All he does is pass down the 'guidelines' from the top leaders, who also don't know the first thing about science. The 'guidelines' only make our work harder. And when we really *do* need something—like equipment, books, or invitations to experts in our field—there is simply no way that these 'leaders' can understand us."

A graduate student in physics said, "The leaders want only two things from scientists: technology and face. They want us to build and run machines to make China 'modern'; they also want some big, glory-producing projects like a proton accelerator, which only a few countries have. [Party General Secretary] Zhao Ziyang goes to 'visit' the proton accelerator and gets his picture on the front pages the next day. What does he know about physics? Does he know what actual good the machine does for our work? Does he know, does he care, that we have many, much simpler needs that prevent us from getting anywhere near the level of needing that machine? [Premier] Li Peng wants a big dam on the Yangzi River. Does he understand the scientific questions? He's not even interested in listening to the scientists! He just wants pride. The leaders at all levels don't know what science is. They only want quick results from a 'magic box.' "

Many intellectuals would like to be able to change work units, but this is hard to do. They are bound to their job assignments, and both they and their leaders know it. "If I am at Beijing University and want to transfer to Qinghua University," a young scientist told me, using a hypothetical example, "I can't afford to let this be known at Beijing University, because the leadership would kill the initiative, and then punish me (make me 'wear tight shoes') for wanting to leave in the first place. I would be worse off than when I started." A senior professor of history was only a bit less pessimistic: "Changing work units in China is an art. The key is to appear unremarkably mediocre, ensuring that the leaders neither like you nor dislike you very much. If they like you, they will insist on keeping you. If they have something against you, they will wreck your deal out of spite, and keep you under them where they can punish you. You also have to be careful about the *timing* of the matter. You must pick a time when your unit can afford to see you go, and when the other unit is ready to receive you. Because if you try and fail, you lose face in your own unit."

The immobility of the work force can frustrate a manager as well as an employee. I was surprised one day to learn that the core editorial staff of a major literary magazine consisted of only four people. They were overwhelmed with work. "Can't you get someone else?" I asked. "Yes," an editor answered, "we can get someone, but not someone *good.* There are good people, and we do have the money, and we know they would like to come. But their present units won't approve. And if they live outside Beijing, it's almost impossible to bring them here even if their units permit it, because we have no local registry [*hukou*] slot to offer."

Moving to a major city like Beijing is especially difficult because the demand is so great, and the supply of slots is fixed by the government through a household registry system. Without proper registry a person has no legal access to housing, schools, hospitals, or rationed goods. Although an increasing number of single people were traveling to China's cities in the late 1980s to live "without registry," it was virtually impossible to raise a family with this status. It is possible to "exchange registries"—one must find a person at one's desired destination willing to switch, and both leaderships must approve—but in such cases the exchanged positions must be of roughly equal desirability. It would be highly exceptional to trade residence in Beijing for that in a small town.

The rigid authoritarianism of the unit system gives rise to metaphors of human bondage. "In theory," said a history professor, "China uses a contract system to bind employer and employee. But that's simply false. In reality it's more like ownership. Yes, they *own* you. My wife actually uses that term, just to stick up for the truth." His wife expanded, "In China, people are not hired; they are, in effect, *bought.* When I 'buy' you, I take care of your housing, health, education, and so on and give you a little bit of food money. You have no alternative. You can't change jobs. If you complain, I punish you. I own you." A legal scholar described the bondage as appropriation of familial powers by the state. "The unit leader has all the powers of a patriarch; you oppose him at great risk, and you can't change families."

A journalist who had been to the West found it ironic that China's unit system, which had originated in socialist ideals of fairness and egalitarianism, in fact caused people to become more selfish and petty. "When everybody starts eating out of the same big pot, they begin to notice very carefully who else is taking how much and how to get as much as possible for themselves. This problem pervades China. But it doesn't come from Chinese character. It's in human nature. In the West, people in department stores don't always peek at each other, jealous of what the other one is getting. That's because they're all buying different things at different prices, and calculating separately how much they want to spend. But if those same Western people all pay twenty dollars to share a buffet, with only a certain amount of food on the buffet table, then they start watching each other, getting envious, and squeezing for position. *Everything* in a Chinese unit is like the buffet—except that in China there is one man on top deciding who gets what. Why should we be surprised that people in Chinese work units are constantly jealous of one another? Any people would be the same."

Can the unit system be modified or abolished? I asked. "Have you heard," answered the journalist, "of the Four Basic Principles,[11] the bedrock that cannot change while other things reform? 'Leadership of the Communist party' is one of these unmovables, and in daily life the unit system is exactly what that principle means. The party has a big vested interest in it and will

11. Viz., (1) the socialist road, (2) dictatorship of the proletariat, (3) leadership of the Communist party, and (4) Marxism-Leninism-Mao Zedong thought. These were originally set forth on March 30, 1979, in a speech by Deng Xiaoping. See "Jianchi sixiang jiben yuanze: Deng Xiaoping zai dang de lilun gongzuo wuxu hui de jianghua" (Uphold four basic principles: Deng Xiaoping's speech at the party's meeting to discuss ideological principles in theoretical work) *Deng Xiaoping wenxuan (1975–82)* (Selected works of Deng Xiaoping [1975–82]) (Beijing: People's Publishing House, 1983), pp. 150–51. The Four Basic Principles were later written into the preamble of the Chinese constitution.

not let go at any cost." I pressed him by pointing out that with the economic reforms of the 1980s, the growing authority of the market had allowed some Chinese to gain at least some independence from their work units. From peasants who could work on private plots or in "sideline" industry to urban youth who were "individual entrepreneurs" *(getihu)* and to performers who could now sell tickets to their own shows, several groups of Chinese were more economically—and therefore perhaps politically—independent. But my friend was not convinced. "The strength of the unit system is shown precisely by the fact that it has frustrated those market forces that you have noticed. The leadership favored economic reform in order to make China wealthy. But when the reforms advanced to where they encountered the iron teeth of the unit system—I mean especially the key question of *ownership* of the units—then the reforms ground to a halt. The party would not give up power. That explains much of the standoff and stagnation we see today."

## Money First, Education Last

Throughout the 1980s, as more and more goods appeared in China's stores, Chinese consumerism rebounded from the forced austerity of the Cultural Revolution period. But it was not just the shortages of the past that fueled consumerism; it was also uncertainty about the future. For how long will we have this opportunity to buy things? Deng Xiaoping is an old man; will state policy change again when he departs? The unpredictability of party policy in the past had encouraged in people a "get what you can while you can get it" approach to the market and, indeed, to life generally.

To these pressures were added those of inflation, which in mid-1988 was running as high as 30 percent in major cities and bringing unaccustomed difficulties to people on fixed incomes. People were fearful, and occasionally even panicky, at seeing prices rise faster than their salaries and the interest on their savings. The psychological impact of the inflation was all the greater because of the stability fixed prices for many staples had afforded since the 1950s. In late summer 1988, when rumors spread that further price reforms might push inflation even higher, urban residents rushed to convert their savings to any durable goods they could find—bicycles, tape recorders, furniture, watches, pots and pans, even salt—as hedges against inflation. The buying sprees were especially spirited in Shanghai and Guangzhou, where the People's Bank was rumored to be running out of cash.

Intellectuals generally acknowledged that the inflation resulted from the release of price controls. Some pointed to excessive capital investment as a factor. On the popular rumor mill, and among some intellectuals as well, official corruption was also considered a cause: "with all that eating and drinking on the public till, and no productivity in return, the value of our currency is bound to fall"; or "the big, unearned markups in 'official profiteering' [guandao] push prices up by leaps, and when the officials go spend the profits, they drive up prices even more."

For many, especially the young, it appeared that one way to cope with the inflation was to get rich oneself. The great rush to "look toward the future" (xiang qian kan, with a pun on "look toward money") began to dominate the pubic mind. "To get rich is glorious," as Deng Xiaoping had said, and, indeed, stories spread about people who made millions by founding a trucking company in Jilin province or by selling a special kind of smoked chicken in Guangzhou—and were then welcomed into the Communist party as exemplars of the new ethic. China's new capitalists seemed to listen to political pronouncements selectively: does it affect my money-making? If so, how? If not, then I'll ignore it if possible. Peasants began to plant cash crops in place of basic grains, and by winter 1989 China was already beginning to feel the pinch of a grain shortage that the government predicted would worsen. But there were also stories of peasants suddenly grown rich. A popular ditty captured the spirit of the 1980s this way:

If you weren't a "rightist" in the 1950s, you'll probably never make it;[12]

If you didn't starve to death in the 1960s, you're not the kind who starves to death;[13]

If you weren't beaten to death in the 1970s, it'll probably never happen to you;[14]

If you don't get rich in the 1980s, you're just not the money-making type.

To many of China's intellectuals, especially the middle-aged and elderly, the rush to get rich was cause for worry. "The Chinese people are poor," said a senior professor of aesthetics. "So, of course, I am happy if they can live better. But this new capitalism seems 'raw' to me—uncivil. I didn't have this feeling when I visited the United States, where your capitalism may be too big, but at least is governed by law. Here it is 'raw.' In Wuhan, people were caught selling 'powdered milk' that wasn't milk at all and that in fact contained poisonous ingredients. People don't care, as long as they make money." A young professor in Beijing made the same point, telling a shocking story whose truth I do not doubt, because I know him well, but which must be viewed as an unusually extreme instance: "A couple who live downstairs contracted with a private 'day care service.' But they found their child not sleeping at bedtime—indeed, remaining wide awake late into the night. Eventually they discovered that the toddlers at this 'day care' began their day by taking 'candies.' These actually were sleeping pills, used to keep the tots drowsy or asleep and, therefore, easy to manage. The parents were furious, but there was nothing they could do except withdraw their child. In some countries you can sue. But what can you do here?"

Another consequence of the unbridled money-making that was especially disturbing to older intellectuals was the popular

12. Referring ironically to the Antirightist Campaign of 1957, when over half a million people were punished as "rightists."

13. Referring to the severe famines of the early 1960s, which followed Mao Zedong's catastrophic Great Leap Forward.

14. Referring to the later stages of the Cultural Revolution.

devaluation it brought to education at all levels. The educational system had collapsed during the Cultural Revolution, and the priorities of the 1980s were doing little to revive it. At stake was not only future productivity but China's "cultured society." In early 1989 a writer named Xiao Sike substantiated these worries in a piece of literary reportage entitled "The Twenty-first Century Will Have Its Revenge."[15] Xiao showed that, as of 1988, one-quarter of China's primary school–age students had dropped out. Most gave as their reason "to make money." Many were drawn to unlawful activities such as gambling, smuggling, and prostitution. An alarming proportion disappeared from their homes and neighborhoods. And the phenomenon was by no means limited to disadvantaged children; the offspring of officials and intellectuals were involved as well.

If primary education was in decline, higher education was doing no better. An archaeologist from Shanghai patiently explained to me the following peculiar situation in her city: ten years ago, students at high schools in Shanghai excelled in competition for college admission. But by 1988 the proportion of Shanghai students going to college declined and the number admitted from outlying areas grew. Why? "Because the value of big-city residence had surpassed the value of a college education," she explained. "If you went to college, you ran the risk of being assigned to work in the provinces after graduation, and thus losing your permit to live in Shanghai. Shanghai students began purposely scoring poorly on the nationwide college entrance examinations. By 1987 a score of only 300 was sufficient to put a Shanghai student into college, whereas a score of 500 was necessary for a student from the provinces. We know that the difference was artificial, because when the students got to college, the ones from Shanghai who scored 300 did at least as well as their provincial classmates who scored 500."

The perceived value of graduate education was plummeting as well. Graduate schools, including even medical schools, often

15. "Baochou zai ershiyi shiji," *Xibei junshi wenxue* (Northwest military literature), no. 1 (1989), abridged by Chen Li in *Wenhuibao* (Wenhui daily) (Shanghai), April 9, 1989, p. 4.

had fewer applicants than spaces available. In 1989 the Institute of Linguistics at the prestigious Chinese Academy of Social Sciences received only 3 applications for 5 available spaces, whereas in 1978, the first year after the Cultural Revolution in which the Institute accepted graduate students, there had been 280 applications for only 1 spot. In 1988 a group of Shanghai universities organized an "open house" to introduce young people to various careers. "The tables for business and foreign trade were crowded," reported a historian. "But the tables for history and culture were *deserted.* The students weren't interested, and it was hard to convince them that they should be. Who needs historians? A few schools and libraries? The party's propaganda department?"

"Ten years ago," said a young literary critic, "graduate students in Beijing were at the top of the list as prospective marriage partners. Now they're near the bottom. Now overseas Chinese or foreigners are at the top, followed by people who work in joint ventures, or foreign trade, or other businesses that make money and perhaps can help employees to emigrate." "Professors are not respected," said a physicist who could remember the 1940s. "We were poor during the Guomindang years, but the common people always respected a professor. You might still find that respect among older people today. But not among the young. It's been destroyed."

There is almost complete consensus among intellectuals that the decline in respect for education is related to the series of devastating anti-intellectual political campaigns mounted by the party since 1949. A further problem in the 1980s was the government's low investment in education. "Why is it," argued Fang Lizhi, characteristically saying in public what others said only privately, "that a country like China, which has stressed education throughout its history, should now be among the *lowest in the world* in its investment in education, as a percentage of GNP?"[16] Shortages of funds diminished the quality and avail-

16. Abbreviated in Fang's article "China's Despair and China's Hope," *New York Review of Books,* February 2, 1989, p. 3. See also the *Free China Journal,* November 10, 1988, p. 5. China's 1988 investment in education of 2 percent of GNP compared with

ability of education at every level. A ditty circulating in Beijing held that "a good nursery school is as hard to find as a good graduate school." This was substantiated by published research showing that 86 percent of all children in Henan province, or 7.2 million, were not receiving proper education as of the mid-1980s. In Guangzhou the school dropout rate was increasing by one-third each year. Even as general living standards had risen by 30 to 40 percent during the 1980s, illiteracy, for the nation as a whole, had risen by 10 percent. Only 68 percent of all primary school students were advancing to high school.[17] Only about 1 percent of the high school graduates went on to college (compared with 9 percent in India and 20 percent in South Korea), and about 1 percent of the college graduates continued in postgraduate school.

The overall budgets of major universities, such as Beijing University, were frozen through the 1980s. As costs rose sharply with inflation, central-government authorities told university presidents to find ways in which their own institutions could make up the difference. Some schools and departments, including even the prestigious Academy of Sciences, began to go into business in various ways. Engineering departments did consulting work on computers; foreign-language departments opened extension courses in English for the public; a fine arts school in Guangzhou set up its own company to produce art for commercial advertisements. On the other hand, many academics felt humiliated by these commercial pressures and some actively resisted. The physics department at Beijing University refused to sell its name by offering night courses and watered-down degrees to the People's Liberation Army. As a consequence its members accepted lower incomes than faculty in other departments were getting.

China's intellectuals have been virtually unanimous in their antipathy to the hugely expensive Yangzi Gorges Dam project that was conceived by Mao Zedong in the 1950s and promoted

an average 3.3 percent among countries with an annual per capita income of U.S. $300 or less.

17. Xiao Sike, "Baochou zai ershiyi shiji" (note 15).

again by the top leaders in the 1980s.[18] "If they were to put that money into education, the benefits to our country would be *enormous*," commented a literary scholar. "But the benefits of education aren't immediately visible and don't support their pride. So they don't consider it. This year the central government is spending five or six times more on preparations for the 1990 Asian Games than on preparation for the twenty-first century through education. The Asian Games bring China 'glory,' they think. But how can we feel glory when we know our house is not in order?"

Many intellectuals saw the government's low investment in education as a case of misplaced priorities. But I was surprised at how often I heard a more radical view—that it was a conscious technique of rule, a recrudescence of the "policy of keeping the populace ignorant" (*yumin zhengce*) used by Chinese tyrants in imperial times. At first I resisted this view, finding it hard to imagine even a government like China's capable of such a policy. But I do not believe that my doubts swayed my conversation partners. "Our leaders' view," explained a historian, "is that they know the truth. The purpose of education is to share that truth with the masses, but even education of this sort is not terribly important. What is important is that the masses be properly led. There is no need for people to think for themselves—in fact, independent thought, as they see it, can lead to chaos and trouble." Young intellectuals who had returned to China with a Western education sometimes expressed doubts that their government really wanted them back. "Of course, they have to *say* they want us back," one explained. "It would be impossible for them to say otherwise. They would appear ridiculous. But in fact they make life hard for us when we return. Their actions, not for their words, tell what they really think." A young literary scholar told me very seriously one night that, "at the most highly classified level," the ideologue Hu Qiaomu has said, "If these foreign-trained students choose not to come back, then so be it. They're digging our graves." I felt, and still feel, unsure about what Hu Qiaomu might originally have said,

18. For some of the reasons for this opposition, see below, pp. 208–9.

if anything; but there is no doubt that this young man regarded the quotation not only as authentic but as revelatory of the "true face" of the leadership.

It was a virtually unanimous view that Chinese education in the Communist period had systematically deemphasized "general education" and "learning to be a cultured citizen." This led to the related worry over how China could build a more modern and democratic society if the "quality" (suzhi) of the population remained so low. "How can we have democracy," a young writer asked, "if most people in the countryside don't read, and don't have much that they *can* read? Education is crucial."[19] Speaking at a meeting of literary intellectuals in fall 1988, two young researchers, who had recently returned from several weeks in the rural areas of China's poorest provinces, were visibly depressed. "The schoolteachers in the remote areas would have no notion whatever of anything we've been discussing at this meeting. Their heads still contain 'a complete set of Maoism.' "

"The problem we face," said a young journalist, "is not just inadequate funding for education, although that is very important. The other crucial need is to change the educational method. Are we to continue training people in how to be tools of authority, or should we teach them how to think for themselves? The aim now, as it has been for the last forty years, from primary school up, is to mold people. Study Lei Feng—imitate the model![20] In order to change this system, we need two things: first, freedom of expression in society as a whole; and second,

19. Liu Binyan, although he would certainly agree about the need for better rural education, points out that Chinese peasants have a much better sense for their political environment than many, including Chinese intellectuals, give them credit for. After two years of living in the United States, Liu concluded that, if given a chance, Chinese peasants would have greater interest in local elections than do American voters.

20. Lei Feng, a People's Liberation Army soldier famous for his dictum "Whatever Chairman Mao says, I will do," has since the mid-1960s often been held up as a model for Chinese schoolchildren to emulate. Intellectuals in Beijing were enthusiastic when, during the glory days of the student movement in May 1989, Deng Xiaoping announced that his greatest regret about the reforms of the 1980s was the "insufficient stress on education." This elation was matched by anger and disgust when, a month later, after the bloody suppression on June 4, Deng allowed that what he actually meant was that *ideological* education had not been stressed sufficiently. Shortly thereafter the party resurrected Lei Feng as a model for Chinese youth.

better people in the educational establishment. The second problem, getting better people, is especially difficult because of the way work is assigned in China; school principals can't get the good people they need. And then there's the problem of the school administrators themselves, who have all grown up in the system that molds people. They wouldn't recognize a good teacher if they saw one."

Fang Lizhi argued for education not only to rescue China from disaster but to promote human progress. "I have a 'theory of determinism by physics,' " he once observed, playfully but also quite seriously. "Americans didn't abolish their slave system; agricultural technology did. Now computers are abolishing secretaries. This is liberation. The more people who can be freed from serving others, the more brains will be available to help humankind advance. This is the most basic reason why Chinese have to get out from under a premodern governmental system—so that more brains can function."

Fang was not alone in tying the decline of education to the problem of persecution of intellectuals. Many pointed out that the Communist party has never trusted intellectuals and has launched one after another humiliating campaign against them. Some made the point that problems of commercialism and materialism, even material hardship, were not as important to intellectuals as intangible values such as freedom of expression. "To use a material yardstick," argued the eminent literary theorist Liu Zaifu,[21] "the current situation of intellectuals is indeed bleak. Too many of our younger intellectuals use only a material yardstick, which is essentially a businessman's yardstick. If you use an intellectual yardstick, the 1980s have seen considerable progress. Look what we can say now, read now, and publish now, compared with ten years ago! There's no comparison. But there still are limits and threats to this freedom, and *that* should be worrying us, not this silly commercialism."

---

21. For a brief sketch of Liu, see below, p. 129.

# *Repression*

"Our old, Long March generation of leaders," said a senior Beijing editor, "have two incurable shortcomings. The first is that they won't let other people talk. The second is that they cling religiously to their own crusty version of 'the truth,' no matter how farfetched it has become in today's world. The two shortcomings are related, of course: if they have the truth, why do they need to let other people talk? But if they don't let other people talk, their 'truth' stands up even as it grows feebler." A young literary critic said, "Even now in 1988, when we are as free as we have ever been, the top leaders can't keep their hands off intellectuals. Vice-President Wang Zhen has to deliver his opinion that 'River Elegy'[22] is 'extremely reactionary.' Even the 'enlightened' Zhao Ziyang says intellectuals have dangerous 'centrifugal tendencies.' " A young physicist agreed, adding, "They come up with these opinions without understanding what we are actually saying. They don't really hear us—sometimes because they think they have nothing to learn, but also because of the way in which information is channeled to them. I know some of Zhao Ziyang's advisers. They tell him what he wants to hear. They compete to get their own advice accepted, and to do this their 'information' has to be palatable to him. If it's this way for Zhao Ziyang, I'm sure it's worse for the older conservatives."

22. "River Elegy" is a controversial six-part video production that was broadcast on Chinese national television in the summer of 1988. It addresses issues such as Chinese xenophobia and national pride, isolationism and wall building, authoritarian rule, and the contrast between a backward hinterland and a thriving, outward-looking coastal economy. The authors, Su Xiaokang and Wang Luxiang, criticize "feudal" traditions of the past in order to convey criticisms of the contemporary political system that would be taboo if stated more directly. They assail party dictatorship by criticizing imperial rule; they raise recent persecutions of intellectuals by mentioning pogroms against scholars in the ancient past. The text was first published in Beijing in June 1988 by the Modern Publishing House. For a translation and commentary see Richard W. Bodman and Pin Pin Wan, *Deathsong of a River* (Northfield, Minn.: Department of Russian and East Asian Languages, St. Olaf College, 1991). For more on "River Elegy," see below, pp. 156–58.

A senior historian concurred. "The leaders want the channel between us and them to be a one-way road. They have no use for our thinking, but insist that we accept theirs. Over the years, we have learned through bitter experience that we have to submit. By now the strongest censorship, by far, is our own *self-censorship*. Every time I write, I seem to feel a shadow peering over my shoulder—'shouldn't say this' . . . 'mustn't phrase that point quite that way.' But even when I force myself to be conscious of these insidious pressures, I go along with them anyway, because I want to be published. It would be even worse if I couldn't be published at all." As the historian continued, I was impressed by the ways in which his battle with self-censorship seemed to condition his whole project of writing and thinking. The wish to find a "best way of putting things," which is observable in so many aspects of Chinese culture, was for him thoroughly dominated by the question of how to accommodate—and yet resist—the demands of party orthodoxy. Ironically the dominance of this question, its unpleasant side notwithstanding, seemed to clarify and strengthen his self-conception as a writer. Would his bearings be as firm, I wondered, if orthodoxy and repression weren't there to inspire every feint and spar? (The question takes on practical significance for Chinese intellectuals who leave China in search of freedom in the West, only to find, after arriving, that "nothing much comes out.")[23]

This scholar's field, modern Chinese history, was especially sensitive. "The shadow over the shoulder" had to be considered at almost every sentence. The problem has generally been less severe in other fields, where "political cover" can sometimes be taken in fairly simple ways. A scholar of linguistics (a compar-

23. The quotation is from Su Xiaokang, the well-known author of "River Elegy" and several important works of literary reportage. Su was speaking in early 1991 of himself and other refugee intellectuals at Princeton University who had found that when the lid of censorship was lifted they did not, after all, have large reservoirs of "free thinking" overflowing into prose. Czeslaw Milosz, writing about Poland in the late 1940s, observed the same problem: "A poet muses over what he would write if he were not bound by his political responsibilities, but could he realize his visions if he were at liberty to do so?" See *The Captive Mind* (New York: Alfred A. Knopf, 1953), p. 80.

atively apolitical field) who published in the highly politicized 1960s and 1970s described how she and her colleagues made their essays on grammar politically acceptable. "We would begin by quoting Marx or Engels or Mao. Then we wrote, 'From these universal truths it follows that . . . ,' and would proceed with our technical discussion. At the end we would again quote the political sages and express our thanks. In Chinese this is called 'wearing hats and boots.' "

In fall of 1988, when controls on expression were especially loose, this kind of sardonic disdain for political intrusion upon scholarship was expressed often and openly. In fact, it was so frank that I was moved to ask why controls were perceived as a problem at all. "Because," explained an art historian, "we all know that the limits remain, even if they are currently in retreat. The Communists have a history of being merciless when they want to be, and it would be naive to think they are different now. The knife could drop at any time. If there were demonstrations here like those in South Korea . . . in the streets with Molotov cocktails . . . we would simply be mowed down by machine guns. In the Cultural Revolution, if you disagreed with Mao, or if they just *thought* you disagreed with Mao, you could be carted off and shot in the back of the head." From time to time in the post-Mao period, sabers have been rattled to remind people of the ultimate limits. In fall 1988, when word spread through the intellectual community that Deng Xiaoping was threatening a libel suit against Fang Lizhi (which no one doubted Deng would win, if he wished), one of Fang's fellow scientists at the Academy of Sciences told me, "The real threat is pointed less at Fang than at the rest of us, us scientists and all intellectuals. The message is 'Don't be like Fang, or else . . . .' "

"Dictatorship is internally weak," said a news reporter. "It must limit speech because it truly fears collapse if exposed to free criticism. When the leadership 'opens up' and encourages you to talk, this is after it has made a calculation that the benefit of appearing to be magnanimous and open-minded will outweigh the damage that the free talking will bring. But when the limits are reached, then *that's it*—no more talking."

Fear of punishment for "incorrect" expression is firmly planted in the memories of intellectuals old enough to remember the campaigns of the 1950s and 1960s. An archaeologist who was labeled an "active counterrevolutionary" during the Cultural Revolution remembers that the first signs of his "crimes" were that co-workers avoided eye contact and then began to shun him. Quietly he became a pariah. Then the charges against him were announced, suddenly and spectacularly, in "big-character posters" throughout his institute. In the 1980s he had returned from disgrace to become an institute official. "But even now," he told me in 1989, "I have sudden flashes of fear in which I suspect that people are whispering behind my back, or looking at me strangely."

The memory of oppression and the party's continuing use of implied threat have had far-reaching effects on the people of China. These effects have accumulated over many years, seeped into the texture of language and interpersonal contact, and become a permanent part of daily life. These conditions are not obvious to the short-term foreign visitor, nor are they often noticed by ordinary folk in China, who have come to accept them like the air they breathe. But Chinese intellectuals notice and are disturbed.[24] To take just one illustration for now, when the Chinese speak in public, they often add the proviso "This is my own personal view." This innocuous-looking statement provides them double protection. First, it distances the speaker, at least a bit, from responsibility for perfect "correctness"; second, it preserves the fiction that "we are now engaged in free speech," which, as a political fiction, the state very much needs to preserve and therefore wants its citizens to acknowledge. Yet, in public, "personal views" are still delivered with great care; speakers strain what they want to say through their own internalized sense of what is expected in the political environment. When a speaker does offer a glimmer of his or her independent

24. In this they are like intellectuals elsewhere who have lived under long-term repression. A recent account of Soviet intellectuals, Vladimir Shlapentokh, *Soviet Intellectuals and Political Power: The Post-Stalin Era* (Princeton: Princeton University Press, 1990), reveals many parallels to the Chinese case in the relations of "public" and "private" spheres of life, modes of manipulating language, the psychological defense mechanisms of the repressed, and many other questions.

thinking, it is often deeply embedded within formal language and discernible only to those who are properly attuned. Yet such glimmers can be vitally important to both speaker and listeners. They represent more than the particular thoughts they express; they attest to the continuing possibility of a public truth that lies outside the official "line." It is for this reason that truisms and other seemingly bland statements can signify exciting things to a Chinese audience.

Through my own experience in China, I learned how difficult it can be to insert a bit of unofficial truth into the official arena. One day in an exercise room at the Friendship Hotel, I happened across a copy of *Flowers of Friendship,* an in-house newspaper for service workers. Inside there was a little story about an American guest who had had a problem with his hot-water supply. He called for repairs, the story said, and was so elated with the results that he asked the hotel manager to give the repair crew a commendation. The guest's room number was listed in the news story, and I used this fact to identify him a few days later when we happened to meet in the snowy courtyard. When I told him about the news story, he was at first incredulous and then outraged. His hot water had been off for ten days. It was still off. He had complained every way he knew, and had even threatened to withhold rent. A repair crew had come, spent an afternoon "investigating," and left saying the problem was insoluble. The American asked me for the news clip, got it translated into English, and then went to the hotel management with an additional demand: publish a correction and an apology. But this never happened.

My Chinese friends were amused by the story, but unimpressed. What did you Americans expect? That they really would publish a correction? The following month another example presented itself, this time from the highest levels of the press. On March 20, 1989, the Chinese magazine *Outlook (Liaowang)* carried an article, which was also run in *People's Daily* and other newspapers, on the "true story of Fang Lizhi and the Bush banquet."[25] The article said that Fang, Li Shuxian, Jean, and I had

25. Yu Mu, " 'Fang Lizhi fuyan fengbo' de beihou" (Behind the "Tempest over Fang

showed up at the hotel door that evening and that, because Fang refused to show an invitation, we were turned away in the normal manner. It said the four of us then boarded a taxi and circled around toward a back entrance but, in doing so, broke traffic rules and were stopped by a policeman on routine patrol. The article had obviously been worked on carefully, because its extended narration, although highly imaginary, was as internally consistent as a true account might have been. The overall point was to establish that Fang Lizhi had plotted in advance with foreign forces (me) to cause trouble.

When I asked Fang about the article, he chuckled and said, "Shameless! But what can you do?" I thought it would be interesting, at least, to run an experiment: what would happen if I did try to correct the record? I selected five points of fact on which the *Outlook* account was most spectacularly errant. I telephoned the magazine's editorial offices, identified myself, and asked if I could speak with the editor. "Hold on," came the answer. I held on for fully five minutes, during which I could hear, but not make out, a flurry of agitated talk in the background. Then the voice returned to the phone and said, "He's out of town." I asked if I could speak with Yu Mu, the name listed as author of the *Outlook* article. "Yu Mu is a pen name!" came the answer, almost shouted. "Well, then," I asked, "could I come over and just talk with you comrades who are there?" "We're not in charge of manuscripts!" he replied. I pressed a bit further, until the poor man on the other end finally said, "We're on vacation here!" and hung up.

I decided to try again by mail, writing out my five points of fact and addressing them to the editorial board. No response. I wrote again, this time by registered mail with return receipt requested. No response. No returned receipt.

A few weeks later, while in town on an errand, I dropped in

Lizhi and the banquet") *Liaowang zhoukan* (Outlook weekly), March 20, 1989, pp. 46–47; "Toulu 'Fang Lizhi fuyan fengbo' shimo" (Disclosing the whole story of the "Tempest over Fang Lizhi and the banquet") *People's Daily (Overseas Edition)*, March 18, 1989, p. 4; " 'Fang Lizhi fuyan fengbo' zhenxiang" (The true story of the "Tempest over Fang Lizhi and the banquet") *Jiefang ribao baokan wenzhai* (Liberation daily digest of periodicals), March 28, 1989, p. 4.

at the *Outlook* editorial offices on my way home. A nervous staff sat me down with a Mr. Li Qin, chief of the political editorial section. Smiling unctuously, Li told me that the chief editor was still out of town. I asked if I could speak with the person who uses the pen name Yu Mu. "Yu Mu is Yu Mu, but Yu Mu is not here," Li answered. (Several months later I learned from friends that Li Qin himself had written the Yu Mu article, in response to pressure from above. The editors at *Outlook* were ordered to publish it, but expressed their reluctance by putting it on the very last page.)[26]

Again my Chinese friends, although interested in the details of this story, took its denouement for granted. Listening to their comments gave me new insight into the ways in which they understand the political "line" and its related "news" stories. They generally saw the line neither as description of fact nor as advocacy of social policy but as an expression of what the top leadership takes to be in its own interests.[27] "Of course, such stories are not *true*," said a young reporter. "But we don't even think of them as lies, as you foreigners do, because we don't expect truth in the first place. We read the official statements in order to understand the changing 'wind direction' from the top. And these facts, like them or not, are very real. They can touch the life of every Chinese." A senior fiction writer, who was also a longtime party member, expanded on the point: "There is truth in Chinese newspapers, but you have to know how to find it. This often means reading upside down. If they say great strides have been made against corruption in Henan, you know

26. I eventually published my corrections in the Hong Kong magazine *The Nineties* (*Jiushi niandai*), June 1989, pp. 78–80. But I viewed this as basically a failure. My aim had been to correct the record for the huge readership inside China that is not allowed to read magazines like *The Nineties*. The Hong Kong and overseas readership of such magazines was already familiar with the basic facts of the banquet incident and would be bored by my simple list of corrections. So I shifted the focus of my piece—which I called "A House of Cards inside a Greenhouse: *Outlook*'s 'True Story' of the Banquet"— to emphasize the frustrations of trying to make a correction through China's invisible wall of press control.

27. I say "takes to be" because the question of whether the line *actually* serves the interests of the rulers is problematic. Irony and other complications in the way messages are read and heard prevent any simple equation of the line's intended and actual effects.

that corruption is especially bad in Henan. If they say dozens of police were hurt in a clash with students, you know hundreds of students were injured if not killed."

After the bloody crackdown at Tiananmen on June 4, 1989, a news blackout in Beijing prevented the populace from hearing any official or systematic account of what happened. Yet the thirst for information was insuperable, and rumors, many of them false, sprang up everywhere. It was said that Li Peng had been shot in the thigh by a bodyguard; that the army was going to invade all the university campuses; that sidewalk gratings had been wired to deliver shocks to passersby at the flick of a switch. When the government resumed broadcasting, one of its first acts was to issue warnings against "spreading rumors." Although the shocking massacre was still fresh in my mind, I thought that on this one point, at least, the government had done something right. But as the broadcasters continued and I realized what they meant, I was made to think of the old writer and his advice about "reading upside down." By "rumor" the government did not mean the welter of false stories that were circulating. It meant the news of the massacre itself—precisely the few kernels of horrible truth that were *not* in doubt: that troops had opened fire on unarmed protesters, that tanks had crushed others, and that violence and arrests were continuing. People who repeated any of these truths were now subject to arrest for spreading rumors.

Once again it fell to me, a foreigner, to find the official language use exceptional. The people on the streets of Beijing showed no puzzlement at the two entirely different referents for the word "rumor." They understood easily and began immediately to adapt to the new language game. They could also handle the reverse case of one referent being labeled by two very different terms. Before June 4 there had been a "democracy movement." Afterwards—at least in public—there had been a "counterrevolutionary rebellion." With the city in crisis, the bifurcation between official and unofficial language became especially clear and pervasive. A worker interviewed on television was speaking against the counterrevolutionary rebellion.

Was he trying to tell the truth or to deceive? It seemed to me farfetched to imagine either of these two motivations. This was not the salient question for him. The questions broadcast in the eyes of that frightened man were practical: What should I say to fit this situation? What effects are possible? What performance will best serve my interests?

But it would be a mistake to think that the label "counter-revolutionary rebellion" was used only cynically or that the term had no effect. It had, first, a considerable power to mislead, or at least to confuse, the large number of people outside China's major cities who had no direct experience of the demonstrations and who knew that one is always well advised to go along with the official version of events, especially faraway events. Second, even for those who were close to the actions, the official term took on a certain life of its own. Its "proper use" became important. It joined a long list of other terms whose appropriate use in official contexts constituted a discourse of considerable sophistication and weight, a discourse whose outcomes of "advantage" and "disadvantage" made its linguistic navigation complicated and, potentially, deadly serious.

In fall 1988 one of China's best young poets told me that the most painful job in China is to be a nursery school teacher. "What do you teach the little ones?" he asked. "To tell the truth? If you do that, you are dooming them. Do you have the right to doom them? But what, on the other hand, is your alternative? Can you teach them to speak falsely? Could you face yourself as a teacher if you did that?"

Only a small portion of China's intellectuals have the strength—as this poet has—to look squarely at the profound implications of the political language game. Its costs to public morale have been tremendous. People know that misplaying the game can bring lasting damage or even disaster to their lives. It becomes extremely important that unofficial talk not go on record at the official level. For many this means simply avoiding political comment outside the home—or, when playing the language game is unavoidable, playing it conservatively. It also means—and here the worst devastation begins—

that one's circle of trusted conversation partners must be severely limited. A general fear of being informed upon easily turns to suspicion that anyone—a colleague, a friend, a passerby—could become an informer. People who have shared an office for years often do not speak frankly to each other; a popular adage has it, "Do not make friends at work." Even a friend, under the pressures of a political campaign, can succumb to the temptation to save himself by denouncing you. Routine contacts among strangers are even more vulnerable to destruction by mutual suspicion and ill temper. And the most pernicious fact about plainclothes agents is not that a few of them may be in any crowd but that they make *everyone* in the crowd into a potential enemy.

Humor has been one of the Chinese people's healthier responses to the debilitating effects of repression and the official language game. During the post-Mao thaw in the late 1970s, "comedians' dialogues" (*xiangsheng*) packed with political and social satire—including satire of the language game—were tremendously popular in China. For example, in a piece called "Here's How You Take a Photo,"[28] a man visits a photography shop to have his portrait taken. To do so is a rare and glamorous opportunity in China, so the man arrives feeling somewhat nervous. He encounters a shopkeeper who is being extremely defensive politically, explaining that everything in his shop must be "revolutionary": "Whatever revolutionary comrade enters the revolutionary door of my revolutionary photography shop to ask revolutionary questions about taking a revolutionary photo must first shout a revolutionary slogan. If the revolutionary customer does not shout the revolutionary slogan, then the revolutionary clerk will ignore his revolutionary request." Duly intimidated, yet not wishing to relinquish his chance at a portrait, the customer obliges, and this dialogue ensues:

A (customer): "Serve the People!" May I ask a question?

B (clerk): "Oppose Selfishness and Revisionism!" Go ahead.

A: "Annihilate Capitalism and Uphold the Proletariat!" Could I take a photo?

28. Jiang Kun and Li Wenhua, "Ruci zhaoxiang," *Tianjin yanchang* (Performing art of Tianjin), nos. 5–6 (1978): 17–20.

B: "Destroy the Private and Establish the Public!" What size?

A: "The Revolution Is Faultless." Three-inch size.

B: "Rebellion Is Justified." Okay, pay up.

A: "Stress Politics." How much?

B: "Criticize Reactionary Authorities." Sixty-three cents.

The rapid-fire exchange continues for some time and is doubly hilarious among people for whom the slogans have long carried stressful connotations. Such bold pieces could be performed openly and were sometimes broadcast in official media in 1979 and early 1980, when the Deng Xiaoping leadership saw them as debunking the former, Maoist regime and thus supportive of itself. But in mid-1980, the Deng leadership suddenly ruled that enough was enough and that *xiangsheng* henceforth could include only mild social satire. Public performances have been innocuous ever since—and hence poorly attended.

Jokes, however, continue to circulate unofficially. I heard more than one version of the following story about a man who wanted to test whether his mail was being opened. He writes a letter to his mother, telling her that he cannot come to see her, but adding that he is enclosing a hair from his head by which she can remember him. Then he seals the envelope *without* enclosing a hair. After several weeks he receives a warm return letter from his mother, who says she has received his letter and is keeping his hair as a precious memento. The friend who told me this joke offered a vivid pantomime of how he imagined the postal inspector to have panicked over the "lost" hair and to have plucked a substitute from his own head. The Chinese sense of humor, tested daily, clearly has great staying power.

# Two

# LIVELIHOOD

Not long after I arrived in Bejing, a middle-aged professor of Chinese invited me to dinner. This is what I saw. Two parents and a child inhabit two sparely furnished rooms totaling about 150–200 square feet. We have dinner on the small table in the front room, which when cleaned serves as a desk on which the child does her homework. When the child finishes, and goes to the back room where all three of them sleep, the desk reverts to the parents, both professors, for their own study. Their "home office" equipment is pen, paper, and one bookshelf apiece. The family prize is a new television. It has remote control, which its owners are eager to demonstrate for me even though the tiny room barely allows sufficient space to make the point. The kitchen is a dirty gas burner and sink, located in the public hallway of the dormitory-like building and shared with several other families. The communal toilets are down the corridor. The passageway also serves as everyone's pantry, laundry room, and storage space. It is cluttered to near-impassability with boxes, clotheslines, cooking equipment, bicycles, and other things. My friends, who in Chinese terms were accepting a considerable loss of face by letting a foreigner see their quarters, apologized to me for their "shabby conditions."

Chinese intellectuals complain bitterly about such conditions. A professor of medicine said, "We are underpaid, underprivileged, underappreciated, and overworked. That sums it up." Such statements are so recurrent as to seem like tiresome carping if one does not bear in mind their demonstrable grounding in fact. A 1988 survey in Beijing of two hundred university-level intellectuals found an average salary of 125 yuan per month, which was 11 percent below the average for the city's populace as a whole. These intellectuals also worked one hour and thirty-nine minutes per day longer than the average, slept fifty-one minutes per day less, and took about half the recreation time.[1] An obstetrician in the survey commented that he had to do an average of three to four Cesarean sections per day and prepare a written report on each.

The same survey found that 70 percent of all Beijing intellectuals suffered from one or more chronic diseases. A larger survey,[2] published in early 1989, found similar results nationwide: over 60 percent of all intellectuals suffered a chronic illness; their average age at death was 58.5 years, nearly ten years below the average for the Chinese populace as a whole; intellectuals between forty and sixty years of age died at a rate that was higher than that of people over sixty in the rest of the population. Even college students, the survey found, were "seriously underweight." Although the survey was conducted by people sympathetic to the intellectuals, the official press published the results under the headline "Intellectuals Must Pay Better Attention to Their Health."

## Daily Life

To understand the problems of daily life for Chinese intellectuals, we must first try to appreciate the broader living conditions that most Chinese people face. These conditions, which

1. Ye Jianmin, "Lixing de huanghun: Dui Zhongguo zhishifenzi chujing he xintai de liang xiang diaocha" (The dusk of reason: Two surveys of the predicament and mood of Chinese intellectuals) *Ming Bao Monthly* (Hong Kong), February 1989, p. 15.

2. "Zhishi fenzi yao qianghua jiankang yishi" (Intellectuals must pay better attention to their health) *Renmin ribao (haiwaiban)*, January 15, 1989, p. 8. According to the article, the survey was done in more than twenty high-level institutes in eleven provinces or municipalities.

only foreigners and very high-ranking Chinese rise above, and which generally are worse for ordinary workers and peasants than for intellectuals, often escape comment simply because they are so pervasive. One of these conditions is the difficulty of getting any task, even a simple one, done. At least in recent decades, the vaunted patience of the Chinese people has reflected less a philosophy of life than a practical—indeed, almost required—attitude toward the mechanics of daily living. Patience and perseverance are necessary in nearly every errand; if you cannot afford them, you do not even bother to begin. An ordinary person keeps a very short list of goals and marshals all possible resources, including time, toward their achievement. Setbacks that would cause a citizen of the modern West to give up and try something else seldom have that effect in China. The setbacks are expected and worked around—or outwaited. They might occasion a change of tactic, but not so easily a change of goal.

A professor of mathematical logic who spent nearly all his time huddled at home working at his scholarship was visibly unhappy one morning as he set out to buy a new electric hot plate. He had allocated a whole day for the task. "I hate shopping in Beijing," he said. "I dread it days in advance. The store clerks are rude. They always make me feel that they would like me to disappear. Asking to see a hot plate is like begging, and then you have to test the hot plate to be sure it works, because many don't. If you can find a place that's selling something good, the crowd to get it will be large, and you have to be pushy to get a chance, and I hate to be pushy, and . . ." The logician was becoming agitated just imagining what his quest for a hot plate would entail.

Larger tasks, such as getting a telephone installed, are easy only for high officials and their families. Others must choose between waiting in line literally for years (still with no guarantee of success) and going to great expense and effort in cultivating "back door" connections—by offering gifts or hosting banquets at several levels, from middle-echelon officials to the work crew that does the actual wiring. Liu Binyan tells an amusing story of his attempt to install a telephone in Beijing in the mid-1980s. After many fruitless initiatives by Liu, a colleague at *People's Daily* who was personally acquainted with the minister of posts and telecommunications offered to write the official a letter about the matter. The minister complied by himself writing a letter specifically directing that a phone line be installed at Liu's address. Despite this directive, the leader of the installation crew demanded an expensive Japanese cassette recorder, naming his preferred brand and model. This crew leader may not have known that Liu Binyan was the most notorious exposer of corruption in all of China; but he did know that Liu was a reporter for *People's Daily*, and this fact didn't matter in the least. "So what?" he asked. "Don't reporters make plenty of money?" Because Liu refused to be part of the bribery, the matter of installing his telephone remained at a stalemate for a few weeks. A friend of Liu's finally resolved the standoff by inviting the work crew to a banquet.

"To get something done here," complained a young writer who had lived for several years in Hong Kong, which he was using as a base for comparison, "you have to be a wind bag. First you have to 'raise a topic' with many people and talk, talk, talk. Everybody first responds by saying no, no, no; and then you have to go back and talk, talk, talk some more. It's exhausting! After a while it starts to get exhausting for the people who were saying no, no, no, and for this or other reasons— including gifts, personal connections, and so on—they might begin to soften. The people who give out the original noes might do so expecting that your request will come back again one way or another, but still their normal beginning is no. If it diverts you, fine; if it doesn't, at least their starting point was safe."

The struggle through the web of impediments in daily life is normally an intensely individual effort. Although the language of socialism calls upon group leaders and public officials to protect the interests of group members and citizens, these leaders seldom do so out of official responsibility alone. If they take action at all, it is based on personal ties that have been cemented by extra-official considerations. Otherwise people are left to their own devices. Although I had seen countless examples of this pattern during my stay in China, I still was surprised, one frigid day in January 1989, to see Professor Li Shuxian, wife of Professor Fang Lizhi, standing outside the door of her apartment building in Beijing. She seemed to be doing nothing—which was strange for such a lively person—so I inquired. "We've had a lot of burglaries in our building recently," she explained. "We have reported them to the police, but they do nothing. They care nothing for us 'citizens.' Last week another neighbor was robbed, so the whole building held a meeting. We decided that since the police won't protect us, we'll have to do it ourselves. We drew up a chart. Everybody takes turns standing guard. This morning it was Fang's turn. He was here all morning. This afternoon it's my turn."

"It's too bad your time has to be used this way," I said, not anticipating that this comment would strike a raw nerve.

"There's no lack of police in this country," Li fumed. "But it's not their job to help the people, and they know it. The police? They watch us all the time! They have [switching to English] *telescopes, telescopes . . . telescopes always pointing at my door . . . but they not care the people.* [Switching back to Chinese] We don't have time. But we must be our own police."

## Financial Squeeze

One of China's most outstanding young humanists, who in his early thirties had already reached the rank of full professor, spent nearly all his time reading and writing in his two-room flat, which consisted of a small study plus a living-dining-playroom-bedroom for his wife, their two-year-old son, and himself. The family hired a nanny to take care of the little boy during daytime hours. The professor's entire monthly salary, which was a bit over one hundred yuan, was used to pay the nanny. The rest of the family budget—food, clothing, transportation, and books—relied on the salary of the wife, who earned seventy yuan per month as a library assistant, supplemented by incidental royalties from the professor's publications. The little family budget did not—could not—balance; each month during 1988 their savings dwindled. They were hoping to emigrate to Canada.

Yet they were well off compared with some others. One day in late 1988, the middle-aged writer Shi Tiesheng received an unexpected visit from a college classmate who was now a high school teacher. The man appeared thin and haggard. "You're the most famous of our classmates," he said to Shi, "so I am coming to you for help. The new year is approaching, and people might send you calendars. I wonder if perhaps . . . well . . . if you could save some for me?" During the next few minutes the background of this strange request became clear: the man and his wife were sacrificing all they could to afford their son a good education. To send a child to the better schools in Beijing, parents periodically had to give the schools quasi-official "donations" that could amount to hundreds of yuan per year. This couple had cut all other expenses to a minimum in order to make the payments. They ate no meat except on weekends when their son came home—and even then the meat was primarily for the son. They normally ate noodles and bean paste, which partly explained the man's gaunt appearance. The man had requested calendars because his son's teachers had announced that each student should give every teacher a calendar for the New Year. Since the giving of calendars was a standard way to lubricate social connections at New Year's, the teachers themselves would find good use for the dozen or two calendars they might collect. But calendars cost several yuan each, and well-illustrated ones could cost twenty or thirty yuan. The son had eight teachers. The father had no alternative but to swallow his pride (in China it is important to give an appearance of wealth at New Year's) and go begging for calendars.

In his April 1988 speech to China's Political Consultative Congress, the senior economist Qian Jiaju pointed out that primary school teachers in China are paid about 1 percent, and university professors about 2 percent, of what their counterparts in Hong Kong receive. No teachers, at any level, get 10 percent of what they were paid during World War II (when the Nationalists ruled).[3] To be sure, the socialist system calls for direct provision of housing, schooling, and health care and for subsidized prices for food and other necessities; but these provisions are not always carried out, and the housing problem in the cities is especially severe. Moreover, China's intellectuals are quick to point out that direct provision of material benefits can exacerbate inequalities. "In our society," said one of Beijing's leading writers, "salaries are fixed by rank. Professors' ranks are defined on a scale that corresponds to officials of middle and upper ranks. But in real-life benefits there is no comparison. The officials and their families get better housing, better schooling, reimbursed travel, use of public cars, access to special stores, and, not least, gifts and favors from fawning underlings and fellow officials."

Administrators at universities and research institutes sometimes tried to imitate the special benefits afforded to officials by devising various kinds of "bonuses" for professors: holiday bonuses, clothing bonuses, school-fee rebates, cold-winter bonuses, hot-summer bonuses, and so on. But such measures could stretch only so far, because the overall budgets of most institutions were fixed. Beijing University's budget was held at a constant 45 million yuan annually throughout the 1980s, even as inflation reduced the real value of this figure. It became ever more difficult to supplement professors' incomes.

Among young intellectuals, especially the theoretical scientists, the most distraught were not those with low salaries but those with no jobs or salaries at all. Because of filled personnel "quotas" in the universities and institutes, some young scientists could not find places. A new Ph.D. in physics from Beijing University reluctantly abandoned his field to seek work in a computer company. His professor had also left his laboratory and was making ends meet by working as a computer technician—a job a college student could have done. A recent Ph.D. in chemistry from the prestigious Academy of Sciences, having

3. Qian Jiaju, "Qian Jiaju tan wujia, jiaoyu he shehui fengqi" (Qian Jiaju talks about prices, education, and the public ethic) *Wenhuibao* (Hong Kong), April 4, 1988, p. 6.

failed repeatedly to find work and having been denied permission to accept offers abroad, in fall 1988 took the unusual step of announcing a personal hunger strike in order to call attention to the sudden bankruptcy of his small family. Cases like his seemed to confirm the widespread complaint of intellectuals that, under the economic reforms of the 1980s, they were perhaps the least-favored sector of society. As a rhymed ditty had it:

| | |
|---|---|
| Peasants are free-marketized; | [sell produce privately] |
| Workers are bonus-ized; | [get cash incentives] |
| Officials are back-door-ized; | [gain through corruption] |
| Intellectuals are pauper-ized. | [sink into poverty] |

These, according to the ditty, were the real provisions of the official drive known as the "four modernizations."

## Housing Pinch

Among all items of material welfare, housing is the one that China's intellectuals—and urban residents generally—worry about the most. In 1988, according to official statistics that many said were optimistic, residents of China's major cities had an average living space of six to seven square meters per capita.[4] State officials receive their housing assignments directly from the state; for everyone else, including intellectuals, housing is built, maintained, and distributed through work units. The perennial shortage requires people to wait in long lines for housing assignments. There are no national guidelines for how work units are to make their allocations, but most employ a combination of the following formal criteria: rank or title, seniority in the unit, family size, and nature of current housing. (Families with less than 1.5 square meters per capita are sometimes classified as "in difficulty" and assigned a higher priority.) In

4. The average for Beijing was 6.8 square meters per person, for Shanghai 6.2, and for Tianjin 6.1. See *China Urban Statistics 1988*, China Statistics Series, State Statistical Bureau of the People's Republic of China, ed. William T. Liu (New York: Praeger, 1990), p. 218.

1984 many units began using a system that awarded points for various degrees of need and seniority.

But there are myriad stories about circumvention of the formal criteria through personal connections and gift giving. According to the stories, party officials in the work units encourage this corruption. A young scholar who had just been hired by the Chinese Academy of Social Sciences was advised to present a box of imported chocolates and a bottle of Scotch whisky together with his housing request. After accepting the gifts, the office head of the Institute of Literature raised another condition: the young scholar must give him $3,000 in U.S. cash in exchange for "the equivalent" in Chinese yuan. But the official was to pay for the dollars with RMB at the official rate of 3.2 FEC to the dollar, instead of the unofficial (black market) rate of 7.5 or 8.0 RMB to the dollar. Hence his demand was actually for a bribe amounting to about $1,775 in U.S. currency. When the young scholar balked, the official offered him an alternative: he could procure the official a "quota" for a video camcorder. (China uses a complicated formula by which overseas Chinese are allowed duty-free importation of a limited number of cameras, television sets, and other consumer goods as gifts for their Chinese relatives. These "quotas" are highly coveted and have black-market values of their own.)

As he worried over what to do, the young man heard advice from friends that he should look around for the daughter of a high official to marry. These friends pointed out that there were many such young ladies in the capital and that the connections they offered would ease his path. A quick housing assignment would be only the beginning. If he wanted to make a significant career in Beijing, he'd need a *kaoshan* ("patron"—literally, "mountain to lean on").

Another informal criterion that figured in housing assignments was simply squatter's rights. If a young person was assigned to a work unit and that unit could not provide housing, the young person could stay with his or her parents in their unit housing and even inherit their housing after they died. The presence of squatters could inconvenience others, however, and even create a chain of problems. I knew a middle-aged couple who had once taught at the Guangzhou Academy of Fine Arts, but now commuted every day across the city to teach at Ji'nan University. For years they had failed to qualify for housing at Ji'nan, partly because they already did have adequate housing, albeit in the wrong work unit. Ji'nan University, in turn, was crowded in part because its buildings housed squatters who worked at Zhongshan University and elsewhere.

In many work units, all of the formal and informal considerations that went into housing decisions would come to a head in periodic meetings. Some of these meetings were open, but the crucial ones were usually sequestered party conclaves. These tense meetings could drag on for weeks, and according to some, their decisions could lead to beatings and even murders of people who appeared to have jumped line by using corrupt methods. In work units for intellectuals, such as the Chinese Academy of Social Sciences, housing decisions were sometimes made through democratic voting procedures or by drawing lots. But these methods hardly reduced tensions: in late 1988 all the windows at the Academy of Social Sciences had to be closed on the day housing assignments were announced. In earlier years people had stood at windowsills and threatened to jump if they were not assigned housing.

One scholar at the Academy of Social Sciences, a man in his fifties, lived in a single room with his wife, his two parents, and his college-age son. He had been waiting for better housing for years, but now the question was becoming especially urgent. There was no toilet in the room; you had to go downstairs and outside to a public toilet. But the man's aging parents had become too ill to do that. He put a covered bucket in the room for their toilet and emptied it at the end of the day when he returned from work.

In Shanghai, I visited a young writer whose short stories I admire. He took me to his attic apartment, which he shared with six other people. We entered by climbing a ladder through a trapdoor. Inside there was only one area of a few square feet where we could stand erect. The residents slept in the spaces where the roof slanted down toward the floor. "Where do you write?" I asked. "Out here," he replied, showing me another trapdoor, which led out to the top of the slanted roof, where he could perch and write if the weather permitted.

In the mid-1980s a young pianist was assigned to work at the Beijing Academy of Dance. Her housing assignment was one tiny room attached to the wall of the academy's furnace room. She moved into the room amid a flurry of apologies from her leadership that the assignment was only temporary. During the winter the giant furnace ran up to twenty-two hours a day, causing the walls of the room to vibrate so much that sleep became difficult. When the walls cracked from the vibrations, the pianist just pasted paper over the cracks, because she believed she would soon be able to move. As the months dragged on, "pasting paper became the symbol of [her] daily life." After three full years in the room, she concluded that she had been misled from the beginning: "They can deceive me, using the word 'temporary'; but they can't make me deceive myself." She fled China to the West, where she remains today.

I heard many stories about young people who could not marry, because they had no housing assignment. Others in this predicament married but continued to live separately. I knew a young couple who were both scholars of Chinese literature and had recently earned Ph.D. degrees at Beijing University. Both showed enough promise that the university hired them out of graduate school as lecturers. In 1984 they married and applied for housing, but were denied it because they were "too young." Their only option was to continue living in the sex-segregated graduate student dormitories, where four people shared a room. (In China's undergraduate dormitories, seven normally share a room.) In 1986 the university's housing officials lifted the designation "too young" from the couple, but still could not assign them a place to live until early 1989. From 1984 until 1989 the couple's intimacy was limited to occasional weekends, when friends allowed them to house-sit.

I was told of a rare but illuminating case of a couple who had housing but whose marriage had gone bad. They finally decided to apply to the leadership of their work unit for a divorce, but their application was rejected on the grounds that no alternative housing assignment was possible. Two years later, after the couple's relationship had worsened and both had taken lovers, the couple went back to the leadership to "insist" on a divorce. This time it was granted, but their housing assignment remained the same. The pair had to endure another two years side by side, until the man remarried and left to live with his new wife in her parents' home.

Where could this man and his lover find moments of intimacy? Like many couples in Chinese cities, they resorted to parks and movie theaters. Chinese parks seem deserted at night, but, if the weather is good, this appearance is deceiving. Their nooks and shrubbery are often filled, sometimes to capacity. Theaters, for their part, feature two-seat booths bounded by small partitions resembling those of library carrels. These seats are sold specially as "corners of love" or "love places," which are names stylishly drawn from the titles of well-known contemporary short stories.[5] A young writer who had studied in the United States told me, "I didn't know that sex could include sound until I saw American films. In China, whether at home or not, sex is silent."

One couple who had conducted their courtship in public places were determined to marry even though they had no housing. The man was a specialist in environmental protection at the Institute of Agricultural Economics of the Academy of Social Sciences. The woman was a composer whose work unit was the Central Orchestra. After repeated refusals of their housing requests at both units, they made the bold decision to move into the piano practice room that the young woman used at the orchestra. The narrow room could accommodate only the piano and one mattress. For a kitchen they put a kerosene stove outside the door. When a child was born, they placed its crib transversely on top of their mattress and slept by sliding their legs into bed around the legs of the crib. Unable to sleep this way, the young man bought a monthly pass for the Beijing buses, which, although extremely crowded at rush hours, have some

5. That is, "Aiqing de weizhi" (The place of love), by Liu Xinwu, and "Bei aiqing yiwang de jiaoluo" (The corner forgotten by love), by Zhang Xuan.

empty seats during the relatively slack period of 9 A.M. to noon. He would slouch in the backseats of buses during those hours and doze from one end of the line to the other.

Officials at the orchestra, who had been miffed by the couple's decision to live as squatters in the practice room, were not easily moved by the suffering of this small family. Indeed, they seemed to feel a greater concern for any minor discomfort caused to foreigners. One day they complained to the couple that fumes from their kerosene stove were filtering through the window of the reception room for foreign guests, leaving a bad impression of China. This was but one of many examples I saw of the ways in which Chinese insulate foreigners, especially short-term visitors, from the conditions of daily life. But even after I counted myself fully savvy about such matters, I was occasionally surprised to learn how I had been misled by yet another layer of insulation.

On July 4, 1980, near the end of a year of research in China, another American scholar and I went to visit the famous novelist Shen Congwen and his wife at their apartment at 3 East Qianmen Avenue in Beijing. Their three rooms were spacious, brightly lit, and well furnished. Shen was relaxed and affable and, to my delight, took out his ink stone and writing brush in order to present my colleague and me with samples of his calligraphy. I left with a favorable impression of Shen's housing, and later mentioned this in my teaching about Shen. I did not learn until seven years later, shortly after Shen died, that he had been living at 3 Qianmen Avenue less than a month when I saw him there. He and his wife had just moved out of an eighty-square-foot wing of a broken-down Beijing courtyard, where their only furniture was a bed, a rattan chair, a stool, a miniature table, and an old bookcase.[6] They had lived there three years. Before then, from approximately 1971 to 1977, Shen had lived, separately from his wife, in a windowless room that could

6. See "Shen Congwen congwei xiaoshi: Wang Yu zhi Zheng Shusen" (Shen Congwen has never disappeared: [a letter from] Wang Yu to Zheng Shusen), *Lianhebao guowai hangkongban (United Daily News Overseas Edition)*, June 30, 1988, p. 4. A slightly different description of these quarters appears in Xin Qishi, "Shen Congwen yinxiang"

accommodate only a bed and his books. Without a kitchen, he would walk half a mile to eat meals that his wife prepared for him where she lived.[7]

These facts of Shen's poor housing had been legendary on the intellectuals' grapevine during the 1970s. His nephew Huang Yongyu, a distinguished painter and poet, had invented the phrase "a room without scenery" to describe the windowless room. In the 1970s Huang himself had lived in such a room and had painted a window with a view onto his wall to cheer himself up. The writer Bai Hua noticed this detail and incorporated it (without using Huang's name) in his filmscript "Unrequited Love." The script aroused little notice when it was published in a literary magazine,[8] but when the party leader Deng Xiaoping saw the resulting film, he and his lieutenants decided to launch their 1981 national campaign against Bai Hua and "bourgeois liberalization."

Popular indignation over the housing pinch was deepened by stories of the luxuries enjoyed by high officials. A retired department chief in the central government lived in an old-style Beijing courtyard (siheyuan) with more than ten rooms, including a spacious living room and quarters for a nanny. The furniture, rugs, heating, and air-conditioning were supplied at government expense. In the late 1980s the State Council's Commission of Organizational Affairs, which is in charge of housing for top government officials, oversaw the construction of new apartment buildings in the Cuiwei district, on the northwestern outskirts of Beijing. The buildings contained large apartments of three and four stories. Next to them stood another row of luxury apartments reserved for the leaders' children, who

(Impressions of Shen Congwen), Lianhe wenxue (Unitas), no. 27 (January 1987): 166.

7. Jeffrey C. Kinkley, The Odyssey of Shen Congwen (Stanford: Stanford University Press, 1987), pp. 273, 365. One of Shen Congwen's friends, Xiao Qian, has written a full-length "history of moving house" describing his own precipitous shifts in housing assignment to match the risings and fallings of his political fortunes. See Hsiao Ch'ien, Taveller without a Map, trans. Jeffrey C. Kinkley (London: Hutchinson, 1990).

8. Bai Hua and Peng Ning, "Kulian" (Unrequited love), Shiyue (October) (Beijing), no. 3 (1979): 140–71, 248.

it was said had to be nearby in order to "care for" the elderly ones.[9]

Like housing, food was much easier for high officials to procure. In fall of 1988, after inflation had driven the price of pork in Beijing from 1.8 to 3.6 yuan per catty[10] in the state markets and to more than 6 yuan per catty on the free markets, many Beijing residents had to stop eating pork. I heard many repetitions of a comment attributed either to Wang Zhen, vice-president of the People's Republic, or to Li Xiannian, chairman of the Chinese People's Political Consultative Congress. When told of the unaffordability of pork, the octogenarian in question is supposed to have responded by asking, "Then why don't they eat shrimp?" (Shrimp, like pork, is available to top leaders at subsidized prices.) The story is too wonderful to be taken as true, but there can be no doubt that it reflected widespread resentment.

Shortly thereafter I encountered a more concrete illustration of the inequities in food distribution. Every two weeks in the late 1980s, the Institute of Literature of the Academy of Social Sciences held an open seminar. One day a young man came to the seminar carrying a huge live fish. He was a former student at the institute who was now teaching at something called the Spare-Time University, a special school for the families of top leaders who live in the exclusive Zhongnanhai compound next to Tiananmen. He brought the fish to the seminar just to prove to his old friends what one could buy within the high walls of Zhongnanhai. The three-foot fish had cost him only one yuan per catty. In the public markets such a fish would never be seen. And if it were, one would have to pay at least five times as much for it.

Zhou Ruchang, China's leading authority on the great eighteenth-century novel *The Dream of the Red Chamber,* had lived during the 1950s in a comfortable room with a large collection of rare books, antique paintings, and other cultural treasures. During the Cultural Revolution, Red Guards drove him from

9. These two stories appear in an article by a well-placed witness in Beijing who sent the account to Hong Kong for publication under a pseudonym. See Sima Long, "Beijing zhufang de yuan yu hen" (Resentment and anger over Beijing housing), *Open Magazine* (Hong Kong), December 1990, p. 49.

10. One catty = 1.1. lb.

his room, raided it, and confiscated the treasures in compliance with Mao Zedong's campaign to "smash the four olds."[11] Zhou Ruchang later learned that his antiques had found their way into the private homes of Jiang Qing, Lin Biao, Kang Sheng, and others of Mao's Cultural Revolution associates. This happened because the Red Guards had turned their booty over to the State Commission on Preservation of Cultural Relics, which in turn had offered them at absurdly low prices in private sales to top leaders. After Mao died and Deng Xiaoping came to power, Zhou Ruchang made two requests: that he be reassigned to his former room and that his books and relics be returned. He died before the first request received an answer. The second request was partially fulfilled when the items that had gone to Lin Biao, Kang Sheng, and other discredited leaders were returned to him. But those in Mao's own former residence were still untouchable, as were those in the homes of leaders who remained in power—such as, Zhou believed, Li Xiannian.

Beyond the difficulties of making do with inadequate housing, and the biting criticism of the privileged elite, the looming question of population size seemed to haunt China's intellectuals in the late 1980s. They seemed always vaguely aware that there was just not enough housing to go around and that even a fair system of allocation would not enlarge the ordinary person's living space by much. Population control therefore seemed necessary, but its implementation was ever caught in the impossible dilemma of curbing the nation's growth without stunting individual families. Traditionally in China, family size was a measure of wealth just as important as money. Sons were necessary both to fulfill the sacred duty of continuing the family line and to provide material security to parents in their old age. It was safest to have several sons in order to ensure that at least one would survive to maturity. Although modern medicine has improved survival rates, especially in the cities, the confidence of rural people that a single son will survive to maturity lags behind, and the desire to have at least one son persists.

During the 1980s the government's policy of "one child per

---

11. The four olds were old ideas, old culture, old customs, and old habits.

couple" put pressure on local officials to keep birthrates within fixed quotas. The methods that local officials used—including private moral suasion, public criticism and humiliation, fines, and threats that "excess" children would be denied schooling, medical care, and housing consideration—were all highly unpopular. The collision between the one-child policy and popular attitudes generated a range of additional problems: abortions hastily performed at government demand, the flight of pregnant women or small children to distant locations in order to elude officials, a black market in children of both sexes, and even female infanticide by families desperate for a son.

Yet despite the problems, the one-child policy in the 1980s was basically successful, especially in the cities. Like most other Chinese, intellectuals were often critical of the methods of local officials; but they withheld criticism of the Deng Xiaoping regime regarding the overall policy. I sometimes sensed a subtle pressure to shun the population question when it began to come up in conversation. The issue may have been just too large, dilemma ridden, and depressing to be faced squarely. The inability to criticize the government may have drained the issue of zest, and the lack of a clear villain left it without an easy handle.[12] But when debate on the question did arise, it provoked intellectuals to express some ungenerous attitudes toward other segments of the Chinese population.

"The peasants are having two or three children again?" queried a botanist at a luncheon party in fall 1988. "Well, at least they can *afford* them. Peasants are making money these days. For us intellectuals, child rearing is beyond our means!" A historian chimed in, "That shows that our national policy is wrong. Look at Singapore. In Singapore they give bonuses to intellectuals for having more children. The average quality of their population gets better and better. In China the intellectuals

---

12. Some people did like to point a finger back at Mao Zedong in the 1950s, when the great leader insisted on encouraging population growth. Of his many blunders, they argued, this one has had the most disastrous long-term consequences. To make matters worse, Mao had pressed his policy in defiance of the advice of China's leading demographer of the time, Professor Ma Yinchu of Beijing University, and had purged Ma as a "bourgeois Malthusian" for good measure.

have fewer children and the peasants more; the average quality goes down. It's a backward policy."

Most at the table seemed to agree with these views, although I doubt any would have acknowledged a conscious bias against peasants. None, either, seemed to be aware of their shared assumption that the children of intellectuals would naturally be intellectuals and that peasants would produce peasants. During the post-Mao thaw of the late 1970s, the intellectuals had complained loudly—and legitimately—about the regime's persecution of their innocent children for the "crimes" of the parents. In that case the regime had assumed that class nature is inherited, and the intellectuals had derided this view as *xuetonglun,* "theory of the bloodline." Although they would never embrace the term *xuetonglun,* which bore the taint of the Gang of Four, intellectuals in the late 1980s showed that some of their basic assumptions resembled that theory.

I was startled in a subsequent conversation by the vigorous dissent of a young physicist skeptical of the motives behind intellectuals' criticisms of population policy. "Hah! Those intellectuals were being hypocritical. They say such things only because they, just like peasants and everybody else, want to have more children. Intellectuals can call the peasants 'feudal minded,' but if wanting sons is feudal, then it's in us as much as in them."

"I disagree," said another. "Intellectuals have always had fewer children—even before there was any population policy. Even then the proportion of intellectuals in the population was getting smaller. If the government gave good education, it wouldn't be so important. But it doesn't. Real education, if it happens at all, happens in the homes of intellectuals."

"And we [intellectuals] not only have fewer children these days," added another. "We have fewer homes."

## Morale

The connection between material conditions and morale seemed strongest among the younger generation of China's intellectuals. Older ones, claiming more freedom from materialism themselves, liked to recall the idealism they had felt decades earlier. "If our young people thought there was something they could live for, could get excited about," commented a historian in his fifties, "you would not hear so many complaints about material privation. They often say that it is hopeless to build lives and careers in China, that China is a sinking ship, and that the only hope is to go abroad. But the real problem is not that China is in bad shape but that they don't feel *engaged* in making it better. If they thought that somewhere, at least, there was a healthy movement to which they could contribute, then privation and sacrifice wouldn't matter to them. They would be happy, generous, and mutually supportive. This was true of young Chinese intellectuals from the 1920s to the 1940s, and again at the beginning of the Cultural Revolution—and it could be true once more." These comments came less than three months before students launched their demonstrations in the spring of 1989.

In Marxist theory, "alienation" characterizes capitalist but not socialist society.[13] In the early 1980s, Wang Ruoshui, then deputy chief editor of *People's Daily* and one of China's few serious readers of Marx, had the courage to point out that alienation was in fact widespread in China. For this he was criticized and relieved of his duties in 1983. But Chinese life continued to produce clear examples to vindicate Wang. One of the more dramatic from my own experience in China was this. A baritone, one of China's best singers of Western opera, had been to Europe, where he had won several thousand pounds in prize money. Of this amount, the party had allowed him fifty pounds, keeping the rest for itself. (At one point during his overseas trip, the party assigned two people to "accompany" him every moment day and night—whether to monitor his intake of money or to guard against a defection is not clear.) Back in Beijing,

13. "Alienation" in Marx's specific sense of the "alienation of labor" in capitalist production is understood and debated in China only among a few theorists. For others, the term *yihua* (literally, something like "separate-ized") has come to mean psychological alienation in a considerably broader sense, which actually resembles the common Western usage more than the Marxist one.

while the baritone was "awaiting assignment" to housing, he lived alone, on the outskirts of the city, in what can only be called a mud-floor lean-to constructed of metal sheets. The lean-to had no heat in Beijing's icy winter. One day he got a notice instructing him to report to the studios of Central Broadcasting for a recording session. The party leadership there had decided to make a tape of patriotic songs to send to Chinese students overseas. "You can make a fine contribution to our love of the motherland," the baritone was told when he arrived for the session. He then sang, without dinner, until late into the night. When the recording was finally over, at 1:00 A.M., he was dismissed, still without dinner, and with no transportation home. The buses had stopped running, and he was miles from his suburban lean-to. By chance he met a sympathetic person, a scholar at China's Academy of Social Sciences, who brought him home to sleep on a couch. This scholar, a friend of mine, told me that story and added his own bitterly caustic commentary: "Motherland? . . . Love? . . . Nonsense!"

It was not only cynical treatment such as this that caused intellectuals to feel isolated, unappreciated, and even irrelevant. Society at large, bent on making money and cultivating "connections," seemed to value knowledge less and less. Even the intellectuals' own children and students tended to favor work in business or foreign trade.

The combination of material hardship and loss of respect created a growing sense of desperation among China's intellectuals in the late 1980s—a feeling that the crackdown after June 1989 only worsened. Although complaints about China's predicament were widely shared, the sense of urgency at having one's own back to the wall often seemed to be a lonely experience. People appeared generally to guard their survival strategies from one another. As a foreigner associated with an exchange program, I was viewed as potentially useful in various strategies for leaving China, and thus could hear a larger sampling of them than—I believe—people generally shared with one another.

More than once I was impressed by the hard-bitten determination that lay quietly beneath people's plans. For example, a fairly well-known literary scholar in his fifties came from a distant city to visit me in fall 1988, presenting me with some of his works on East–West literary relations and requesting "to learn from me." I could not possibly help him in his special field, where he knew far more than I did, and told him so. He followed up, not very relevantly, by praising my book *Mandarin Ducks and Butterflies* in florid terms and asking my permission to translate it for publication in China. I tried to point out that translation of my book was not worth his time, since the task could easily be done by a lesser scholar. I made this point many times, and in several ways, in an effort to get around his persistent response that I "shouldn't be so polite." I thought I had perhaps won the argument when I pointed out that, even if a translation of my book were done, such books were almost impossible to publish in the financially difficult times that Chinese publishers were experiencing. In the end the effort would be wasted. As he left, I repeated, firmly but politely, that I was withholding my approval of his proposal. A few months later I received a large package containing the draft of his translation. His accompanying letter asked my help in sponsoring him to be a visiting scholar in the United States.[14]

I had seen comparable cases before and was quite aware of the deeply rooted tradition in Chinese culture of using favors to incur and reciprocate obligations. Nevertheless, I felt a peculiar combination of surprise, irritation, and poignancy on reading this scholar's letter. His example seemed more stubborn, more desperate, than ones I had encountered among Chinese overseas or in countless works of Chinese fiction. A friend in Beijing interpreted the case for me. "That professor is perfectly clear about what he is doing. His goal from beginning to end was to try to make you feel indebted so that you will have to help him get out of China. He knows that he is burdening you. He knows that you don't want the burden. He may even feel sorry toward you for doing it. But he *just doesn't have any alter-*

14. I received the package in March 1989. After the June crackdown the chance for publication of the manuscript in China went from slight to nil. The scholar's chances of leaving China also declined to about zero, but I do not imagine that these setbacks have killed his patience, determination, or strategizing.

*native*. You may be the only hope he can see, so he pushes as hard as he can. It's this way for many of us. It's why so many students line up three days in advance to register for the TOEFL [Test of English as a Foreign Language, which is generally required for study in the United States or Canada]."

This and similar experiences deepened my mistrust of the surface equanimity of many intellectuals. The ability of people to "perform" in public contexts can be noted in any culture, but in China, and perhaps especially among intellectuals, masks can be more than usually misleading. Liu Binyan once described the typical Chinese intellectual as a victim of a kind of ray that crushes bones without hurting the skin or affecting most technical functions of the brain. "In the end he looks normal, can still see and analyze, and can pronounce regular sentences. He can fit in, and function, but is devastated inside."[15] While Liu basically sympathizes with intellectuals whom he describes in this way, a young physicist in Beijing was less charitable. "Intellectuals themselves must share the blame for their own weakness and dependency. Look at the workers. They go on strikes and work slowdowns a lot—much more than our official press admits. They are like a horse, which will buck you. Intellectuals are like a cow: eat grass, give milk, eat grass, give milk. No complaints. We should be more like the workers. We should buck."

I heard others complain, somewhat similarly, of a "loss of internal standards" in aesthetic matters, including daily housekeeping. "We have forgotten what taste is," observed a middle-aged literary scholar. "Beijing used to be proud of its elegance. Intellectuals used to keep nice old things—vases, paintings, carpets—in their homes. Now the nice things, if they exist anywhere, are all in the homes of foreigners! The homes of Chinese intellectuals are broken-down, neglected—usually a mess! We're busy competing for opportunities for our children, or for better housing, but we don't even take time to make our apartments pleasant."

Another young man, who had returned from study in Can-

---

15. Lecture at Princeton University, Department of East Asian Studies, December 6, 1989.

ada, outfitted his room in Guangzhou with some modern (but not outlandish) art, a carpet, and a tape deck. Afterwards he was visited by a senior writer who was an old and close family friend, and a hero in the eyes of the returned student. The older man criticized him: "I never thought you would change so much overseas. You've forgotten your roots." The younger man said he didn't think his decorations reflected anything as serious as "roots"; he just enjoyed living a bit more comfortably. Why not? Whom did it hurt? This reply eventually led to a heated argument, from which the younger man (who was my only source in the matter) drew the following conclusions: "I had never realized how thoroughly the older generation was browbeaten in the 1950s and 1960s. He [the old writer] was unfairly accused of 'bourgeois tendencies' in 1957 and has suffered ever since. I thought he would like my new things and would be the last to call me 'bourgeois.' I thought the reason why his own apartment is still so run-down is that he couldn't make it much better. But now, obviously, he really identifies in some sense with the run-down life-style. For this I don't blame him personally. But I also don't think it's because he really likes to live so poorly. I believe it's because his life is nearly over now, and he doesn't want to face the fact that a life of poverty was not the best life. He wants me to follow in his footsteps just to prove that his path through life was honorable."

The problem of maintaining morale, and some source of nonmaterial values, was a private struggle for many. It became even more difficult when one stepped into public—where a generalized fear of strangers, compounded by competition for scarce goods and services, generated a pervasive contentiousness that itself was a drain on morale.

## Public Incivility

A graduate student who had returned in the mid-1980s from four years of study in the West told me of her many-layered "reverse shock" upon returning to China. One problem was readjustment to Beijing street behavior. While bicycling along a street in the city one day, she was suddenly struck by a bicycle that was out of control. The fingers on one of her hands were mashed in the collision, and she was thrown to the street. Picking herself up and expecting perhaps a word of apology from the other cyclist, she heard instead a shrill attack: "Got no eyes, bitch?!" She was even more surprised to look and see that it was no scruffy hoodlum shouting at her, but another young woman, "well dressed and with a pretty face." Still wincing in pain, the graduate student decided not to pursue the matter but simply to gather up her bicycle and go her way. But later she wondered, "How can this be? What has happened to our people? What makes them this way?"

An elderly professor and lifelong resident of Beijing allowed, "Every once in a while I have to go out shopping. But I hate it. People in the shops are so rude, so harsh. I was in a shop the other day and saw a sign on the wall: 'Eight Points for Attention for the Model Service Person.' The sign said be polite, give correct change, and so on. Point number 7 was 'Do not curse or beat the customers.' I thought to myself, 'Look, simply to refrain from beating the customers has become model behavior in our society.' For me the saddest thing is that fifty years ago Beijing was the politest city in the world. There were problems of inequality, yes, but most people still felt personal pride and integrity and behaved toward others with civility and consideration."

Many of the reasons for this incivility seem rooted in the structures of society: jealousies are bred by the work-unit system, mutual suspicion springs from fear of informants, and the hypocritical language game builds cynicism. But I was interested to note how many of my Chinese friends, proceeding from the essentially Confucian notion that leaders should be moral exemplars, pointed to corruption among the leadership as the reason for ill temper among all. The use of the pronoun "they" (*tamen*) to refer to the leadership had more bite to it than I had noticed in 1979–80. In that year it had signaled a sense of distance from the decision makers, as well as an identification with the implicit "we" who are powerless. By the late 1980s, however, people were using *tamen* to express not just distance but utter scorn. "The people are fed up and 'they' are just brazen," a senior biologist told me. "Nobody, neither 'they' nor the people, gives a damn about public affairs unless it relates to their own personal welfare." He followed the standard practice of not bothering to provide an antecedent for "they" in this sense.

The conversation was joined by a middle-aged newspaper editor whose opinion of the leadership was similarly low, but who spoke more calmly. "The leader of our office," she explained, "wants to go to Oregon. A year ago he got an invitation to a conference in Portland, Oregon, and that's all he cares about. He has begun giving gifts and pulling strings to get his permissions. He is saving up money to spend and trying to change it to foreign currency. He is making promises to some people and collecting promises from others. It's hard work to get to Oregon. He spends all his time on it. He uses our office for it. He instructs his staff to help him. He doesn't care a whit about our magazine. He doesn't care if it's terrible or if it doesn't come out at all, just as long as nobody who can help him get to Oregon gets mad about it. When you ask about the magazine, he puts on a smile, says a few harmless words, and then walks away, thinking about Oregon. All this is clear to everybody in the unit."

I shared this story with others, fishing for a sense of its typicality. "The problem is everywhere," said a philosophy professor from a southern city. "It's extremely common. Of course, there are other goals than trips abroad. There are housing, bank accounts, vacations, job assignments and foreign study for one's children, foreign goods . . . all kinds of things. They *[tamen]* all regard their offices as property, as capital, that they can use to advance their private interests. That's the way they are." A moment later this man, who had joined the Communist movement in the 1940s, reflected wistfully, "It wasn't always this way. In the 1950s and early 1960s, most local officials basically did try to do what was right. The slogan 'Serve the People' meant something to them. Now it's an empty shell . . . doesn't mean a thing . . . except to use as leverage for some other goal. Both officials and the common people think that the system doesn't work, so they might as well just grab what they can. There are exceptions to this pattern, but very few. These days, if you really try to speak and act in the public interest, you're viewed as a fool."

I found such views everywhere and among all generations of intellectuals. Although usually reserved for securely private conversations, the disaffection occasionally appeared, in abbreviated form, in public. In April 1988 the respected elder democrat Qian Jiaju pointed out that in 1982 the party chief Hu Yaobang had called for a "fundamental turn for the better within five years" in the economy, in public ethics, and in party discipline (that is, avoidance of corruption). Yet, Qian asked, now that five years have passed, "Have we made any progress? Are there any grounds for optimism at all?"[16] By the end of 1988 Fang Lizhi had concluded that "there is no rational basis for a belief that this kind of dictatorship can overcome the corruption that it has itself bred."[17]

A computer scientist who had lived several years in the United States found a number of ironies in the theory and practice of socialism and capitalism. "In socialism, people are supposed to be concerned about each other, and public ethics should be strong. In capitalism, which is explicitly based on self-interest, you would think private connections would be everything and public morality weak. But never mind the labels; if you just look at the two societies, it's basically the opposite. People on the street in China are rude and pushy with each other, whereas Western people naturally form lines, and sometimes even say, 'Excuse me.' On the other hand, private connections in China can be very strong and solid, whereas Americans often don't have good friends and don't even know their neighbors. I know the reasons for all this are complex, but it's worth noting that

16. "Qian Jiaju tan wujia," p. 2.
17. "China's Despair and China's Hope," *New York Review of Books,* February 2, 1989, p. 3.

the practice of socialism contributes to the opposite of what the theory calls for, and the practice of capitalism also does things you wouldn't expect." The same young scientist-philosopher also had a view on the U.S. crime rate. "You Americans think your murder rate is too high. But that's because you can own guns. If the Chinese people could own guns, *can you imagine* how many killings there would be? Compared with what would happen here, your murder rate is shockingly low."

For some of China's intellectuals, the only harbor in what they saw as a sea of cynicism was the possibility of personal integrity. The Confucian ideal of "acting as a [proper] person"—together, in some cases, with concepts of individualism from the post-Enlightenment West—became the basis for claiming that I, anyway, will not be false in my ordinary daily life. "But character can be hard to achieve in China," a well-known writer explained to me. "Integrity is not just a personal matter. It assumes a certain context, certain rules, in order to have any expression at all. But there are no rules in China. You can't assume anything. Right to the highest levels of authority, you can't assume anything. Let me tell you a story.[18] A few weeks ago Vice-Premier Wan Li gave a speech in which he made some comments about corruption in high places. Some young reporters at *People's Daily* took notes and prepared a story on it. Deng Xiaoping heard about the news story and called Wan Li to demand, 'How could you say such a thing?' Wan Li went to *People's Daily* and said, 'How could you say that I said such a thing?' *People's Daily* summoned the young reporters and demanded, 'How could you say that Vice-Premier Wan Li said such a thing?' The young reporters stood their ground: 'Because he did say it. We were there.' The *People's Daily* officials demanded proof. Luckily, the young reporters remembered that friends of theirs from Central Broadcasting had also covered the speech and had used tape recorders. They went to ask their friends for the tapes. Sure enough, the tapes clearly vindicated them. But before the reporters were allowed to borrow the tapes,

18. I have no independent confirmation of this story and offer it here as an illustration of the disillusionment of intellectuals, not as an account of fact. I should also say that I have no particular reason to doubt the account.

the party leadership at Central Broadcasting intervened: 'Why do you want these tapes?' The leaders took the tapes, checked with *People's Daily,* and then returned the tapes to the reporters with the key comments erased. 'Vice-Premier Wan Li did not say that,' they explained. The young reporters at *People's Daily* were then chastised for 'spreading rumors and causing trouble.' " The man who was telling me this story paused to scowl. "So you see, in China even the facts can change if the leader wants. Nothing is reliable. How can 'integrity' get a foothold?"

"They tell us to 'help the country,' " a university student complained to me. "Fine. But how do you do it? Whatever you try gets you nowhere, and then you get punished for trying. Why do almost all my classmates want to go abroad to study? The attraction of the West is part of the reason. But the other part is that *you can't do anything* here . . ." A friend interrupted him: "China is one word—impossible."

There was, fortunately, a bit of posturing involved in such comments. As time went on, I learned that the most cynical speakers were not as nihilistic as they wanted to seem. Those who were utterly disillusioned concentrated on leaving China or making money, without bothering to complain; those who complained—however bitterly—still did so from a submerged idealism, from a sense that China simply must do better. This latent idealism can be seen in some of the caustic self-satire of Beijing University students. In fall 1988 one group took to calling themselves the Nine-to-three Club because they got up at 9 A.M. and went to bed at 3 P.M.—implying that six hours of consciousness per day is enough for a life like this one. Another group called themselves the Ma Faction, meaning "Marxists," but with a pun on "Mah-jongg," the gambling game in which they passed their daily lives. Another were the Tuo Faction, meaning "Trotskyite," but with a pun on "TOEFL"—the test of English for study abroad. The irony in these names was obvious: to the students Marx and Trotsky were not relevant; mah-jongg and the TOEFL were. But later I realized that the irony had deeper levels. The students were alienated from both Marx/Trotsky *and* mah-jongg/TOEFL. They sought identification with something better than either. Marx and Trotsky were thoroughly dead, but mah-jongg and the TOEFL were also ridiculous as ideals.

In spring 1989 these underlying ideals burst to the surface. When students painted banners and put up posters calling for an end to corruption, for truth in journalism, for human rights, and so on, there was no irony, ambiguity, or sullenness. There was still great cynicism about the adversary, but spirits were high among the demonstrators. The goodwill gradually spread to the rest of the populace and was solidified by a sense of common cause. For a few weeks the characteristic grouchiness in public behavior substantially disappeared. People smiled, flashed "V for victory" to one another, and even apologized after bicycle collisions. No police were in sight, yet traffic moved normally, if not better than normally.

This brief but remarkable change in the public mood reinforced my feeling that at least some of the usual civic sourness in China is generated by mutual suspicion—which during those heady days had been overridden by the camaraderie of us-against-them. Normally people are isolated within their particular work units. They enter the streets only to join a sea of strangers, who reflexively regard one another with suspicion. There is no free press to allow these strangers a forum for sharing ideas. They have no way of knowing—except with remarkable breakthroughs like the Tiananmen protests—how much natural agreement already exists among them on issues such as corruption, lack of basic freedoms, and alienation from their leadership. The discovery of this natural consensus was one of the most important results of the 1989 protest movement. Although public street behavior quickly reverted to normal after the movement, the memory of another way almost certainly lingers.

## No Way Out

From the descriptions I heard in fall 1988, China's problems seemed so severe, and so complexly intertwined, that I made a point of asking each of my interviewees, "If you could choose, where would you start toward a solution?" The answers were almost as varied as the range of perceived problems. Some thought that no real reform could come until the "unit system" was dismantled; others said political competition would have to be allowed, if not through multiple parties, then at least through explicit recognition of the factions within the Communist party; some thought that freedom of the press could be a key to unlock doors and produce a concatenation of beneficial effects; some despaired that any key existed, except for patience and education. "China's problems are a giant ball of tangled strands," said a young reporter. "No matter which strand you tug, you won't pull the tangle free and may only tighten other knots. I wish I knew where to start, but, to be honest, I have no idea."[19]

Whether or not people thought they had possible answers, nearly everyone felt the pressure of time. "China's just falling further behind," commented a young humanist who had studied in the West. "In America, waste is a big problem; I have read that Americans produce, on the average, four pounds of waste per person per day. In China we don't waste material things. But we waste people—human talent. Here we put people in dead-end jobs, give them no incentives, allow leaders to bully them—and stifle, or even punish, their creativity. China is in trouble and needs help, but wastes the human resources that could help the most." A literary scholar recalled the famous metaphor, from the first chapter of the early-twentieth-century novel *The Travels of Lao Can,* in which China is a rickety, leaking, sinking ship, from which all those who can are trying to jump. "That's the attitude of young people today," he said. " 'It's hopeless! Abandon ship!' And the children of the high officials are the first to jump—to the West."

Some comments in this vein were, I felt, designed to shock listeners into a new view of things. Occasionally I sensed the device being aimed at me, the foreigner; but I also noticed it in use among Chinese, especially by the young against the old.

19. See below, pp. 278–83, for more on the suggestions of Chinese intellectuals about how to begin effective reform.

"China would be better off today," said a young man, overturning one of the few moral certainties in Chinese views of their modern history, "if England had colonized it after the Opium War. That would have been a great blow to Chinese pride, I know. But who needs Chinese pride? Are we supposed to be proud of China today? It's easier to be proud of Hong Kong!" Another young man, even more heretically, suggested that China would be better off if Japan had won World War II: "If that had happened, China today would be unfree but modern. The reality of China today is that we are unfree and unmodern." Speaking of the population problem, another youngster offered the rhetorical point that China would have hope only if it lost half its population—"whether by famine, atom bomb, or AIDS doesn't matter." Such statements from the young were hyperbolic—even for them. I felt that if you were to get such a youngster alone, shake him once, and ask, "Now, what do you *really* think?" you would quite likely get an admission that he or she had made these statements for their shock value. But that would not detract from the sincerity of the bold questioning that underlay them.

Older intellectuals, who understandably found it painful (if not impossible) to jettison solidly learned lessons, were sometimes hard-pressed to answer the irreverent challenges of the young. Where, after all, could they point to a better hope? By cultural habit they would look to a public ideology, of which there were two unappealing possibilities. One was reform ideology, but the reform movement had stalled, and its leader, Zhao Ziyang, was by 1988 already in deep political trouble. The introduction of market reforms into the structure of a planned economy had created a beast that was neither fish nor fowl, that was running the fever of inflation, that was hemorrhaging from massive corruption, and that the old men at the top had little idea how to feed or harness. "They are frantic, panicky," a university economist said. "They call on this expert and then on that one, but they don't really understand and don't know what they're doing." The other "ideological" alternative, however, was the thoroughly discredited language of Marxism-Leninism-

Maoism,[20] whose only live vestige—the Four Basic Principles—now seemed thoroughly reactionary.

"The Four Basic Principles," said a young political scientist, "might sound like empty rhetoric. The average man in the street will not even be able to list the four. But don't be fooled. Behind the puffery are real teeth. Listen: (1) *The socialist road.* Translated, that means there will be no private ownership of major property, which means that the people who actually control and enjoy China's wealth—the officials—will continue to control and enjoy it. (2) *Dictatorship of the proletariat.* That's a well-known euphemism for the police system. We even joke that when Public Security comes for you, it's 'the dictatorship of the proletariat in action.' (3) *Leadership of the Communist party.* That means that the work-unit system, in which the party secretary can be so autocratic, will not be changed. There are plenty of interests vested in this principle. (4) *Marxism-Leninism-Mao Zedong thought.* That means: don't raise other ideas. Any talk of democracy and so on is out of bounds." Another youngster went further: "The four principles boil down to just one. And really it's so simple you don't even need words to express it." At this point he stood up, imitated the bearing of a pompous official, and put his index finger to his nose, which is where Chinese point to indicate "me."

The bankruptcy of party ideology could be painful to intellectuals who had once been ardent members. The senior writer Wang Ruowang, expelled from the party in 1987, wrote four months before the bloody crackdown of June 1989, "The Chinese Communist Party is in the process of accelerating its own decline."[21] Six weeks before the crackdown, a poet who was still a party member and still felt attachment to what the party

20. When I say that Marxism was "thoroughly discredited," I refer to widespread popular contempt for the term as well as to the equally widespread hypocrisy of its use by officialdom; I am not speaking of the handful of Chinese thinkers—such as Su Shaozhi, Wang Ruoshui, and Liu Binyan—who have truly studied Marxism and once took it very seriously. It is a significant fact that China's most erudite Marxists have all been forced into foreign exile or internal alienation from the Chinese regime.

21. Quoted in Kyna Rubin, "A Chinese Half-Century of Satire and Dissent," *Los Angeles Times,* February 5, 1989, Opinion section, p. 1.

had once stood for, said that if the students' blood was spilled, that event would mark the final act of self-destruction by the party. After that it would have no moral authority at all and would be able to rule only by force.

The pervasive sense of dead end—of there being no path for China and no one capable of forging one—led many intellectuals to speak and think in terms of the "end of a century." In the spring and summer of 1988 the literary theorist Liu Zaifu raised, in a number of speeches, the issue of "fin de siècle consciousness." Liu's theme was the degeneration of ideology and public ethics, especially among officials, but his younger readers were also taken by the sense of stultification and "looming end" the speeches conveyed. I often heard the phrase *mei jin* ("no zest"—listless) used to describe the mood and situation in fall 1988. "There's no spark, no inspiration, no movement, no nothing," a young man complained. "If you try to do something, you waste your energy; if you get mad, you waste your energy; so you just keep to yourself—and thus still waste your energy." There was almost an implied wish that the conservatives in the party would launch a political attack on someone; then, at least, there would again be "zest" in life.

# Three

# HISTORY

China's intellectuals have spent much time in recent years worrying over how to reevaluate Chinese history, especially the history of the Communist revolution. In the free conversations I audited during 1988–89, revolutionary history was probably second only to corruption in the attention it received. Part of the appeal in discussing history was the relief that could be had by assigning blame for past disasters, large and small. But something else, more difficult and important, was also motivating these discussions. Intellectuals still assumed that, however bad things might be, it was their duty to *help* China. In order to help, they felt it necessary to understand clearly how the country had arrived at its present state. But such understanding was impossible if they relied on the standard version of the past— the version that continued to be taught in schools, that had seemed, at least in part, to grow out of their own life experience and that only a few years earlier had still appeared a basically serviceable interpretation. Now they found that the question "How can China be saved?" entailed the question "What *really* happened?"

The first problem facing intellectuals in reconstructing Chinese history was how to get out from under the party's version of events.[1] However battered, the party's account of China's twentieth-century history still carried some prestige for being official; moreover, because alternative views had been prohibited for decades, on many points the official story was accepted uncritically, just because it was there. Realizing this, some intellectuals, especially younger ones intent on escaping the conceptual prison of "received history," took as their starting point the extreme assumption that all official interpretations were necessarily false. Yet even for these people, the problem of official historiography would not go away. Where could one turn for sources? For alternate theories?

A second characteristic of the effort to rethink history was that, like the party version, it nearly always linked the past to the present. The need to understand the present lent an edge to historical questions, but also imposed on them a certain teleological cast. Intellectuals seemed to stand in the present and peer backward, probing into the murk of a particularly chaotic historical period in an effort to pinpoint the seeds of today's undoing. When they felt they had found something, they would sometimes speak of "awakening" to a new historical understanding. But their discoveries, and the accompanying metaphor, raised another major question: how long had they been "asleep"? If one awakens in the present and realizes that previous impressions were a lie or a dream (even official histories called the Cultural Revolution a "nightmare"), *how far back* does one have to go in order to get beyond the falsity and to reconnect with Chinese history as it existed before the "dream" intruded?

The probing backward seemed to go layer by layer, as if by pushing down a series of fabricated walls. In the late 1970s it

1. The Communist party's version of history is monolithic at any given time, but it does change. In the writing of party history, when push comes to shove, the question "What happened?" always yields to the question "What *should* have happened?" Of course, answers to the latter question can differ as the Great Helmsmen rises, the Gang of Four falls, and so on. Party historians need to be nimble. For more on this problem, see Simon Leys, "Closed for Repairs: A Note on Museums in People's China," in *Broken Images: Essays on Culture and Politics* (London: Allison and Busby, 1979), pp. 90–97.

was enough to say the Gang of Four was evil, and nearly every-one did. Next, people wanted to talk and hear about the truth of the whole 1966–76 Cultural Revolution. (The period was known as a "disaster," but how it had all happened remained essentially a mystery.) Mao, of course, was the next subject whose nefarious part in history had to be squarely faced and reassessed. Even Zhou Enlai, the premier who had appeared as the intellectuals' hero in the late 1970s because of his relative moderation in comparison to Mao, seemed by the mid-1980s much less a hero and more an accomplice of Mao. That Mao himself had from the beginnings of the revolution viewed intel-lectuals with deep distrust and antagonism was a lesson that most intellectuals resisted as long as they could. Some attributed Mao's attitude to his peasant background; others, to the "anti-intellectual" tradition of tyrants in Chinese history. One his-torian commented, "The basic problem with Mao was that he felt insecure in front of intellectuals. Zhou Enlai felt comfort-able among us, but not Mao. Mao had to knock us down to banish his hidden fear of inferiority."

But to look at the lives of Mao and Zhou was to look, in stages, well earlier than 1966. Writers like Liu Binyan and Su Xiaokang began pointing to the 1957 Antirightist Campaign against intellectuals, and the 1959 Lushan plenum—where the head of the military, Peng Dehuai, challenged Mao's policies of the Great Leap Forward—as critical turning points in the collapse of the revolution.[2] In the late 1980s, a number of works of "literary reportage" pushed the frontiers of the new truth tell-ing into the early 1950s (What really happened to Hu Feng, the literary theorist purged in 1955 for "anti-Marxist ideol-ogy"?)[3] and even into the prerevolutionary Communist base

2. In late 1986 Liu Binyan, Fang Lizhi, and Xu Liangying (a distinguished historian of science) planned, but were forbidden from convening, a major conference to study the 1957 Antirightist Campaign and commemorate its victims. Su Xiaokang, together with his coauthors Luo Shixu and Chen Zheng, in 1988 published a detailed factual account of the clash between Peng Dehuai and Mao Zedong over Mao's Great Leap Forward policies, which led directly to the largest famine in modern history. See *"Wut-uobang" ji: yi-jiu-wu-jiu nian Lushan zhi xia* (Memorial to "Utopia": Summer in Lushan, 1959) (Beijing: China News Press, 1988).

3. Hu Feng, a friend and young admirer of Lu Xun in the 1930s, was purged in

areas of the 1940s (What really happened to Wang Shiwei, who disappeared after an ideological campaign in 1942?).[4]

Older intellectuals, most of whom had supported the revolution in the 1940s and 1950s, began to reassess their experiences. At a dinner party in early 1989, a retired editor recalled how he had infiltrated the Nationalist government in the 1940s and worked as an agent for the Communists, only to be arrested and jailed by the Communists in the 1950s for having served as a Nationalist official. "Even as I sat in jail," he recalled, "I did not blame the party. I thought they had made a mistake in my case, perhaps just a clerical mistake. Gradually I learned that there were many other cases like my own, but I still didn't really object. I felt this was the price of the revolution. When the Communists released me, I continued to work for them, as a representative of the 'democratic parties' loyal to the new government. But now I have begun to see those years differently." This admission by the senior editor set the topic at the dinner party for more than two hours. It seemed to break a dam that released a small flood of similar stories and speculations about intellectuals who had been used, betrayed, and discarded in the 1940s and 1950s.

As this revisionist historiography pressed deeper and deeper into the past, the nature of people's interests in truth telling gradually changed. Everyone seemed ready and willing to denounce the Gang of Four. There was joy in *jiehen* "releasing [pent-up] anguish," as Chinese who had lived through the experience could suddenly say openly what they had long been wishing to say. But as the reevaluations reached as far back as

1955 as the head of a "counterrevolutionary clique," following which he spent most of the next twenty-five years in prisons, until his "exoneration" in 1980. When he died, in 1985, his case was still politically sensitive, but a young journalist named Li Hui nevertheless produced a sympathetic and richly detailed biography published under the title *Wentan beige* [Mourning song on the literary scene] *(Baihuazhou)* (Land of the hundred flowers) (n.p.), no. 4 (1988): 4–193. For more on Hu Feng, see Merle Goldman, *Literary Dissent in Communist China* (Cambridge: Harvard University Press, 1967; paperback, New York: Atheneum, 1971), pp. 129–57.

4. See Dai Qing, "Wang Shiwei yu 'Ye baihehua' " (Wang Shiwei and "Wild Lilies"), *Wenhui yuekan* (Wenhui monthly) (Shanghai), May 1988, pp. 22–41; also in *Ming Bao Monthly* (Hong King), May 1988, pp. 3–16, and June 1988, pp. 24–33.

the 1950s and 1940s, they resonated less with personal experience. The many Chinese who eagerly read the published reportage on this period by writers like Dai Qing and Su Xiaokang did not already "know the answers"; instead, they were driven by an appetite to learn more and, in particular, to discover how far back, and into which corners of the past, their revisions of history would have to extend.

Beneath this eagerness lay the faith that *somewhere* they would locate the points where the ersatz history began, move beyond those, and rediscover a more authentic Chinese history. There was a great hunger to get the *whole* story out, to discover the full extent of deception by the party—and of self-deception. In early 1989 a history professor at Beijing University who had supported the revolution in the 1950s plaintively recalled, "I *still* don't know whether my optimism in the early 1950s was appropriate, or was already being manipulated. There are party archives that would answer this question. They would show what Mao was really thinking in the 1940s and 1950s. But even we history professors are not allowed to see them."

For some the revisionist history, while necessary, was also disturbing in a way not always easy to articulate. The underlying questions seemed to be these: How much of modern Chinese history, including our own lives, now seem a waste? If the whole Chinese revolution looks like a disaster, what is left of us? Who are we?[5] These questions put a damper on the enthusiasm of some in the middle and older generations for digging out facts too fast or facing them too squarely. The generation under thirty was generally free from such worries, but only because its members identified the overall trajectory of their lives with a future they expected to be better.

Historical reevaluation involved efforts to reclaim language in ways reminiscent of the Confucian belief that the world is right only when words properly fit their referents. The revolution of 1949 had always been called "proletarian"; but, as the Shanghai writer Wang Ruowang pointed out, "the Chinese

5. For more on this topic, see chapters 4 and 5.

revolution was not actually proletarian at all. The proletariat has not obtained any of the rights [due it]."[6] A young literary scholar refused to use the word "People's" in official terms like "People's Republic," "People's Post Office," and *People's Daily.* "It is *not* the people's government; it is *not* the people's newspaper," she said. "These are simple, plain facts that anyone can see. Why should we misuse the words?" On the same principle she referred to *minhang,* the "People's Airline," as *guanhang,* the "Officials' Airline." "My term describes the actual fact," she explained. "I use it on purpose. It startles people who hear it, of course. But most people then chuckle in agreement, and even the ones who don't chuckle know that I am right. I know my little exercise won't change the airline. But I like to remind people of the manipulation that's embedded in our language."

## May Fourth

One of the issues that recurred in the process of historical reinterpretation was the "legacy" of the famous May Fourth movement of the late 1910s and early 1920s. That movement, in its narrower sense, consisted of a series of Chinese student demonstrations in 1919 protesting the inability of China's warlord government to protect China's territorial interests after World War I. In a larger sense, the term came to stand for a cultural "enlightenment" that included radical criticism of Chinese tradition and eager experimentation with various foreign ideas.[7] The values of "individualism" introduced through the May Fourth movement brought the possibility of a modern identity that could free them from traditional notions that they should serve the state, and allow them to stand independently.

6. Quoted in Kyna Rubin, "A Chinese Half-Century of Satire and Dissent," *Los Angeles Times,* February 5, 1989, Opinion section, p. 6.

7. On the May Fourth movement, see Tse-tsung Chow, *The May Fourth Movement: Intellectual Revolution in Modern China* (Stanford: Stanford University Press, 1967); Leo Lee, *The Romantic Generation of Modern Chinese Writers* (Cambridge: Harvard University Press, 1974); and Vera Schwarcz, *The Chinese Enlightenment: Intellectuals and the Legacy of the May Fourth Movement of 1919* (Berkeley and Los Angeles: University of California Press, 1986).

By the late 1980s many intellectuals were saying that this new, independent identity for intellectuals, which had appeared tentatively to take root in the 1920s, had been trampled in the rush of subsequent history. A leading proponent of this view was the renowned literary critic Liu Zaifu, a man who seemed to try consciously to embody his ideals, which were an unusual combination of Western-influenced "May Fourth integrity" and the moral cultivation of a Confucian gentleman. Every time I visited Liu—even if it was only to pick up his daughter, who would occasionally baby-sit our children—he would sign one of his books and present it to me. I could persuade him to stop only by showing that he had begun to give me duplicates. His manner was intense, and he worked long hours—two facts that helped me understand why he insisted on a daily nap after lunch, even falling asleep in meetings if he could not find a place to lie down. In interviews he had a way of probing deeper and deeper into a topic without being pushed to do so. I sometimes had trouble understanding his Fujianese accent, but was often hesitant to say so for fear that my interruptions would break his momentum.

"All kinds of ideas popped up during May Fourth," he said one day. "But later they all got channeled into a single funnel and came out as one thing: nationalism. This happened, first of all, because of our *wangguo yishi* ['perishing-nation conscious-ness'—the sense of being on the verge of extinction as a nation]. During May Fourth people spoke of Darwinism among nations and feared that China, as a 'weak' country, was ready for 'selective elimination.' There was a frantic casting about to find 'the way out.' For many the attraction of the Russian revolution, and Russian literature, sprang from the hope that Russia could be the model that would save China.

"*Wangguo yishi* increased dramatically with the Japanese attacks on China in the 1930s.[8] The call to save the country was so

8. On September 18, 1931, Japanese troops attacked China's northwestern prov-inces, overran them within five months, and set up the puppet government of Man-chukuo. On January 28, 1932, Japan opened a second front in China by bombing Shanghai and on July 7, 1937, launched a major invasion of north China. This recent history causes many contemporary Chinese, including intellectuals, to harbor a deep resentment of Japan.

strong that it simply had to come first—for everybody. It pushed everything else aside. The May Fourth spirit of 'individual nature' *(gexing)* for intellectuals completely surrendered to 'collective nature' ( *jitixing).* That this should happen seemed so necessary, so correct, that no one even thought of questioning it. The crisis mood continued during the civil war in the late 1940s. Then, in the 1950s, the series of campaigns against intellectuals[9] forcibly established the dominance of 'collective nature' over 'individual nature' as a principle of state orthodoxy. So you see, from the 1920s through the 1950s, history conspired to frustrate the growth of a modern independent identity for Chinese intellectuals."

A much younger man, a journalist and historian, put it more bluntly: "The years 1949–57 are sometimes called the golden age of the Chinese revolution. But for intellectuals, that is exactly when the 'flowers' of the revolution, which were ready to bloom, were trampled. The anti-intellectual campaigns of those years were the historical negation of May Fourth. After 1957 there was, essentially, *no* free speaking any more. Shao Quanlin [who in 1961–62 called for realistic 'middle characters' in Chinese literature, not just stereotyped heroes and villains] and Deng Tuo [whose articles entitled 'Evening Chats in Beijing' were indirect but powerful indictments of Mao Zedong's autocratic rule] were rare exceptions."[10]

An art historian who had enthusiastically supported the party

9. Detailed in Goldman, *Literary Dissent,* chaps. 5–10.

10. Shao Quanlin was a deputy director of the party's propaganda department whose plea for a literature of "people in the middle" was, although he could not label it as such, a challenge to Mao's "revolutionary romanticism," in which the heroism and villainy of literary characters had to be apparent in virtually all respects—from philosophy to life to the appearance of their teeth. In summer 1964 Shao was attacked as part of a socialist education campaign aimed at eliminating "middle characters." For more, see Merle Goldman, *China's Intellectuals: Advise and Dissent* (Cambridge: Harvard University Press, 1981), pp. 47–50, 101–4, and elsewhere.

Deng Tuo was a high official in the Beijing municipal party committee and also a journalist who in the early 1960s began, in concert with a few allies, to publish a series of barbed criticisms of Mao and his policies by using Aesopian language and stories from China's imperial past. Mao's counterattacks on Deng and his friends became the opening salvos of the Cultural Revolution. See ibid., pp. 25–38, 118–24.

in the 1940s and 1950s recalled that the first campaigns against intellectuals had seemed to make sense to him. "Hu Shi, Yu Pingbo, Hu Feng [all targeted between 1951 and 1955][11]—I thought each of them probably should be criticized, and if some of the criticisms were mistakes, well, those were just accidents. The overall trend of the campaigns had to be right. Now when I look back at those years, I see a very different trend. I see the teeth systematically sinking in. Now I think Hu Shi was right. He was right all along."

I found admiration of Hu Shi surprisingly widespread. In 1951 Hu, while living in New York, became the target of a political campaign in China. He was targeted because of his association with the Nationalist Chinese government, which had fled to Taiwan in 1949, and was denounced specifically for his advocacy of detached scholarship during the May Fourth period, a time of intense crisis for China. But by the late 1980s mainland intellectuals had come to see Hu's "detached" stance as an example of independence and integrity and his advocacy of democracy and human rights, which had been ignored during the 1951 campaign, as farsighted wisdom.

It was almost a set view to regard May Fourth intellectuals as belonging to three camps: those allied with the Communists, those attached to the Nationalists, and the "liberals"—the ones who cherished "independence and integrity." Members of the third group had been targets during the campaigns of the 1950s, and now they were heroes. In the late 1980s a few famous cases were repeatedly cited, reverently if somewhat mechanically: In addition to Hu Shi, there were Chen Yinke (a preeminent scholar

---

11. Hu Shi, an influential literary reformer and pragmatic social thinker in the late 1910s and early 1920s, later served in important diplomatic and academic posts for the Nationalist Chinese government, including that of ambassador to the United States from 1938 to 1942. See Jerome Grieder, *Hu Shih and the Chinese Renaissance: Liberalism in the Chinese Revolution, 1917–37* (Cambridge: Harvard University Press, 1970). Yu Pingbo was a student of Hu Shi and a scholar of the great eighteenth-century Chinese novel *Dream of the Red Chamber*. In the early 1950s Yu showed himself unwilling completely to change his interpretation of *Dream* to fit Marxist theory, and thus he became a target of attack in 1954. For more on Yu see Goldman, *Literary Dissent*, pp. 115–19. On Hu Feng, see above, note 3.

of Chinese classical history and culture who refused to let modern politics distort his work and who turned down the Communist party's assignment to be director of the Institute of History at the Chinese Academy of Sciences in Beijing); Qian Zhongshu (a writer and a scholar of both Western literature and classical Chinese literature, who stood scornfully aloof from all politics after 1949, including the "reformist" leadership favored by many intellectuals); Liang Shuming (a Confucian educator who refused all involvement with official activity after Mao Zedong coarsely insulted him at a public meeting in 1953); and Shen Congwen (a gifted writer of fiction who abruptly abandoned creative writing in 1949, failed at suicide, and then devoted himself to "research on ancient Chinese clothing").[12] These, it was said, had kept their intellectual integrity intact throughout their lives. They were the few surviving links to May Fourth times.

Some intellectuals in the late 1980s tried to revive the May Fourth theme of individualism. In 1985 Liu Zaifu published an influential article on "subjectivity" (*zhutixing*) in literature, in which he stressed the importance of the author's moral autonomy.[13] For a few years *zhutixing* became a catchword among humanist intellectuals, who used it not only to oppose the conformity that the political regime imposed but, more important, to challenge themselves to shake off the moral sloth that years of uncritical "group nature" had produced.

"It's harder than it looks to cultivate *zhutixing*," said a young historian eager to do so. "The habit of submitting to the group, or the leader, is too deep within us. A few days ago we had a seminar in our institute, where we talked excitedly about democracy and individuality for a whole morning. The institute agreed to pay for our lunch that day, and our leader said, 'Let's

12. On Liang Shuming, see Guy S. Alitto, *The Last Confucian: Liang Shu-ming and the Dilemma of Modernity* (Berkeley and Los Angeles: University of California Press, 1979). On Shen Congwen, see Jeffrey C. Kinkley, *The Odyssey of Shen Congwen* (Stanford: Stanford University Press, 1987).

13. "Lun wenxue de zhutixing" (On the subjectivity of literature), *Wenxue pinglun* (Beijing), November–December 1985, pp. 11–26, and January–February 1986, pp. 3–19.

be democratic; let's have a vote about where to have lunch.' No one could say anything. Everyone just looked at the leader. There were no suggestions. Finally the leader mentioned a few restaurants we could choose from and asked for opinions. Then a few opinions came out, but I still don't think they were individual preferences. They were just guesses at what people thought the leader wanted."

"In my opinion," he continued, "this happens not primarily because of deference to group opinion or concern for group interests. If that were the case, I wouldn't mind. The problem is that deference specifically to the *leader* is ingrained in us. And fundamentally, the leader has his authority because he represents the state. We can dislike the state all we want, but, you see, it's still there—it still defines how we think about things. The state leaders still occupy the emperor's seat, 'the authority of heaven (*tian*).' A few years ago some of us young people noticed this problem and debated whether to 'repair heaven' (*butian*) or 'dismantle heaven' (*chaitian*). Most of us favored repair, although recently there have been more and more dismantlers. But the problem with *all* of this is that it assumes we must define our thinking in relation to *tian*. Why? The independent thinkers of May Fourth were 'outside of *tian*' (*tian zhi wai*). We need to recover that independence; it was the most precious legacy of May Fourth."

The Chinese Communist party, which was itself founded during the May Fourth period, expressed its own concerns about the movement's legacy as the seventieth anniversary of May Fourth approached, in spring 1989. Official meetings, conferences, and newspaper articles spoke of the "patriotic, anti-imperialist" tradition of May Fourth. "The party stresses the patriotism of May Fourth," said a literary editor, "and we intellectuals stress the individualism. May Fourth was a complex movement that included both of these ideas. But now neither side can afford to accommodate the other, because what the party means by 'patriotism' is *precisely opposed* to our vision of individual integrity. They want no distinctions among country, government, and party when it comes to 'patriotism'; they ask us to accept all these things as the same and to 'love' them together. But to 'love the party' means to hand over individual judgment and integrity, which we refuse to do any more. Both sides know what is really at stake, so there are going to be two very different kinds of observances of the anniversary."

When May 4, 1989, did arrive, there was a large commemorative conference at the official Chinese Academy of Sciences. The drama of the Tiananmen demonstrations just a few blocks away cast an eerie irony over the dry, ritual praise that elderly party spokesmen pronounced for a student demonstration that had occurred at the same site seventy years earlier. Meanwhile, elsewhere in Beijing, at the universities and at some second-rate hotels, intellectuals organized four "rump" conferences on May Fourth. The atmosphere at the two that I visited seemed live enough to charge a battery. Very little of the talk had directly to do with the historical May Fourth movement. It was all about China's contemporary crisis. When the events of 1919 were mentioned at all, it was for the lessons they bore for today.

"Learning from May Fourth" could be frustrating for people old enough to have tried it before. "In May Fourth times," the senior playwright Wu Zuguang commented in late April 1989, "our slogan was 'Science and Democracy'; today our slogan is *still* 'Science and Democracy'! Where has seventy years gotten us?"[14] A senior literary critic put it this way: "China keeps 'learning' the same thing over and over. Look how many times in the last century, but especially in the Communist period, a 'new' China has been announced. Everybody gets excited for a while, until things end in a big mess, and then we all wait for another announcement of another 'new' China. Enough! I think the best lesson of May Fourth for Chinese intellectuals is to be completely independent of politics, including 'save the nation' politics. We can achieve more—and even save the nation better—by staying apart."

14. At "China Symposium '89," Bolinas, California, April 27, 1989, quoted in Perry Link, "The Intellectuals and the Revolt," *New York Review of Books,* June 29, 1989, p. 40.

## "Peasant Consciousness"

Intellectuals old enough to remember the 1940s could also recall that the Chinese Communist party was then known as "the peasant party" and was associated with "peasant values" such as simplicity, honesty, and frugality. By the 1980s many intellectuals were struggling to reevaluate the "peasant consciousness" (*nongmin yishi*) they had earlier regarded as an ideal. Peasants recruited into the Communist movement in the 1940s and 1950s were in leadership positions in work units all around the country, and intellectuals had now come to see "peasant consciousness" not as an ideal to emulate but as a narrow, hidebound outlook that was a serious impediment to progress. The problem for intellectuals was not just to revise their earlier impressions of the peasantry but also to understand the seemingly total inversion of these views. "Simplicity" had come to mean ignorance and closed-mindedness; "honesty," a stubborn and blunt conservatism; and "frugality," a self-defeating stinginess.

The director of a botany research institute in Shanghai explained her first impressions of "peasant consciousness" in the 1940s: "I was raised in Shanghai, but my father came from Anhui. When we went back to our countryside home, the peasants seemed so simple and honest (*laoshi*); most of all, they were *good* to us. They were dirt poor. For them to eat an egg was a rare treat. Once when I went home, during my college years, they brought me *four eggs* for my noon meal. I couldn't eat; I just wept. When I first learned about the Communist party, 'the peasant party,' I thought of these farmers. To me they seemed the exact opposite of the Nationalists, whose greedy profiteering during and after the war was so disgusting to us college students. Later, when the Communist party marched out of the hills, wearing straw sandals, telling the truth, and promising a 'new' China, naturally my heart went out to them. I felt guilty in front of them. Who was I, an urban college student, even to question them? I had always wanted to study medicine. But the party said it needed botany. So I did botany. I had no question about it."

"Some of the urban intellectuals did not hand over their allegiance automatically," said a young journalist who had studied the revolution in the 1940s. "They wanted to maintain their independence and their own standards. Mao knew this, and that is why he launched his series of anti-intellectual campaigns in the 1950s. He wanted to uproot their independence, which he called 'bourgeois,' and establish 'party consciousness'—which was really 'peasant consciousness'—in its place. Even as the intellectuals were being purged, peasant cadres were being promoted all across the country. We're still living with the consequences of that big change. The petty despots who 'lead' the work units are either peasants or people who have learned 'peasant consciousness.' "

Liu Zaifu described the uncomfortable turnabout this way: "During and after the May Fourth years, the intellectuals were the bearers of enlightenment *(qimengzhe)* for the rest of society; this was the basis for their sympathy for the common people. But in the 1950s it was turned around, and we became the 'ones enlightened' by others *(beiqimengzhe)*. Now, there is all the difference in the world—in terms of your feelings, your self-respect—between sympathizing with the peasants because you want to and 'learning from' them because you're ordered to. In both cases, presumably, you regard the peasants with respect; but in the first case you are implicitly higher than they and in the second lower. When Cai Yuanpei [president of Beijing University during the May Fourth period] said to the Chinese common people, 'Your labor is noble,' his implicit assumption was that we who say such things already 'know' nobility and thus in a sense already have it. But Mao's idea of 'learn from the peasants' carried exactly the opposite connotation—that intellectuals entirely lack nobility."

"To put the same point another way," Liu continued, "the May Fourth intellectuals' sympathy with the common people was a generous impulse, undertaken voluntarily; but in the 1950s the sympathy was mandated and the generosity gone. The very *possibility* of generosity was gone. How can a forced act be generous? Intellectuals wanted to support the revolution; but the spirit was killed as soon as they were forced. Soon the sense of peasant 'nobility' was killed as well. What looked like nobility, while intellectuals peered down from an 'on high' point of view, turned out, when they were forced into a close-up look, also to include ordinary ignorance, prejudice, and superstition. I still feel respect for Chinese peasants, because of their daily struggles with poverty. But nobility?—that was an illusion."

The turnabout in attitudes toward "peasant consciousness" seemed to some so complete as to demand serious introspection. What had happened? Why were we so naive in the 1940s? What was it *in us* that allowed us to be so misled?

Some blamed the deceptive rhetoric of the party. "I was misled," said the director of the botany institute who had abandoned her plans for medical school to suit the party. "Many years later, after the Cultural Revolution, I discovered that the same party people who had been advising me to be altruistic were themselves, at that very time, being selfish. I began to blame myself for being gullible. I sifted through my memories again and recalled that the values I had learned in primary school in Shanghai were all 'liberty, equality, and fraternity.' It was from that background that I was first attracted to the Communists. Weren't they for equality? For the common person? It wasn't until much later that I understood the difference between rhetoric and reality and perceived the manipulation."

"What happened to her was quite common," observed a history professor. "In the late 1940s there was a widespread view among intellectuals that the morality of the Communist party had been so thoroughly tempered—by the Long March, by years of frugal living—that it was somehow impervious to corruption. There was no need to question its integrity."

A younger historian, born in the 1950s, went further in probing the psychology of his elders. "Intellectuals who were attracted to 'peasant consciousness' in the 1940s were still 'stooping to appreciate.' We should be clear about the two levels involved here. After the May Fourth movement, urban intellectuals idolized the 'pure, honest' peasant and the 'untrammeled' countryside, as intellectuals in the modern West have also done. But this could happen only because the intellectuals still enjoyed the security of the superior position. It was very different from sharing 'peasant consciousness' unconditionally. The intellectuals could agree that 'the peasants are lovable'; but this was always more a moral statement than an intellectual one. The attitude persisted even into the 1950s, after the campaigns against the intellectuals had already begun. Liu Binyan's love of the peasants has always been colored by it.[15] Lao She, who spent his life admiring the common folk from 'on high,' never really perceived the other side of 'peasant consciousness,' even when it eventually killed him.[16]

A still younger person, a writer born in the 1960s, thought that both versions of "peasant consciousness," the positive and the negative, were partially accurate. "There are all kinds of Chinese peasants, and they also differ greatly from place to place. They can be good and wholesome, but also crafty and vicious. The countryside can be peaceful, but also the site of bloody feuds. These two sides of peasant character are brought into especially sharp focus in peasant attitudes toward us urbanites. Both sides are there simultaneously. They look at us and are polite, deferential, and respectful; but they are also mistrustful, jealous, and ready to flare up. This is very similar to the way most Chinese people look at foreigners—the common attitude has the same two sides. So I feel that when my elder generation gets all wrought up about which 'peasant consciousness' is the real one, that's just because history has buffeted them around too much. Actually both kinds have been there all along."

To an outsider like myself, the intellectuals' two images of "peasant consciousness" seemed less like a contradiction than

15. Readers can judge this statement for themselves by reading Liu's autobiography, *A Higher Kind of Loyalty*, trans. Zhu Hong (New York: Pantheon, 1990).

16. Lao She, one of modern China's most famous writers of fiction, is known for humor, colorful Beijing language, and a Dickensian sympathy for the common person. See Lao She, *Rickshaw*, trans. Jean James (Honolulu: University of Hawaii Press, 1979). Despite his conscientious attempt to work with the Communist regime in the 1950s, Lao She was driven to suicide in 1966.

like two sides of a coin. "Simplicity" and "stubbornness" were perhaps not very far apart; nor were "frugality" and "stinginess," or "honesty" and the peasants' supposed "naïveté." Each pair of contrasting views shared an assumption of the intellectuals' superiority, which was implicit in the romantic view of the peasants and explicit in the resentful view. But my intellectual friends resisted this point. And even as I felt frustration at their reluctance to acknowledge their social assumptions, I was moved by their genuine anguish at having to live with the "peasant consciousness" of the officials who ruled in their work units. After a long talk one day with a professor of international relations at Beijing University, she looked at me and said, " 'Peasant consciousness' has soaked into our system, into our daily life. It's everywhere. When you fight it, it just becomes part of you. I've tried to be rid of it, but I'm afraid it has seeped into every cell of my body." She raised her hand slightly above the cafeteria table where we were sitting, shaking her fingers quickly back and forth.

## The Campaigns of the 1950s

Criticisms and campaigns against intellectuals have been part of Communist Chinese history since the 1940s. But the 1950s witnessed a quickly escalating succession of them, directed against selected individuals such as Hu Shi, Yu Pingbo, Hu Feng, and the novelist Ding Ling, who was accused of "one-book-ism"— the idea that a successful writer of fiction must publish a full-length novel, not just short stories.[17] These "targeted" campaigns were aimed to serve as warnings to intellectuals generally. They culminated in the great Antirightist Campaign of 1957, which directly targeted as many as 500,000 Chinese. This history of persecution had led Chinese intellectuals to pay especially close attention to the 1950s in examining such questions

17. See Goldman, *Literary Dissent*, pp. 207–16; see also Yi-tsi Mei Feuerwerker, *Ding Ling's Fiction: Ideology and Narrative in Modern Chinese Literature* (Cambridge: Harvard University Press, 1982).

as, Why did we cooperate in our own persecution? Why did it take us so long to realize what was happening?

Almost without exception, intellectuals who were criticized in the 1950s recalled their initial reactions as something like this: *Of course* I must be wrong. How could the party be mistaken? Who am I to question a party of such moral probity? "When we heard about 'ideological remolding,' at first we *wanted* it," recalled a prominent literary scholar who had been a college student in the 1950s. "We thought 'class standpoint' was a real problem, and we wanted dearly to have the right standpoint."

As "criticism" escalated into attack, and attack into society-wide purge, the intellectuals began tentatively to suspect their government of "making mistakes." But it was a reluctant conclusion; there remained a strong emotional need to wish the problem away, and thus to avoid facing it squarely. "As the campaigns against intellectuals in the 1950s arrived one after another," recalled an art historian, "I vaguely felt that each had misperceived the case somewhat. But—and how strange it seems to say so now!—I saw them only as flaws in a policy that was basically correct. I didn't see any systematic problem." A professor who had been close to the famous architect Liang Sicheng recalled Liang's reaction to the Communist party's criticism of his book *A History of Chinese Architecture.*[18] "To him the Communist party was beyond reproach. Even when they criticized his professional work, his position was still that 'the Communist party is fine in every way; it's just too bad they don't understand architecture.' "

The eventual realization that the anti-intellectual campaigns were not flaws but a long-term policy forced many into painful reassessment of their social position in the eyes of the regime. But even after accepting the fact that their government was forcing them into a lower position, Chinese intellectuals

18. *Zhongguo jianzhu shi* (Shanghai: Shangwu yinshuguan, 1955). See also Liang Ssu-ch'eng, *A Pictorial History of Chinese Architecture: A Study of the Development of Its Structural System and the Evolution of Its Types*, ed. Wilma Fairbank (Cambridge and London: MIT Press, 1984).

remained, on the whole, eager to help the regime if they could. They resembled, said one, those children's dolls with weighted bases which, when knocked down, pop right back up, smilingly ready to be knocked down again. Why? some wondered. Why do we always come back for more? One obvious answer is that they have rarely had alternatives. Any step into public affairs has to involve the party. Withdrawal—whether into a hermit-like position or into apolitical fields of study—has been possible only intermittently and to a limited extent. Support of the party has consistently been enforced in required study sessions, where poor performance can always result in social ostracism as well as in material penalties in daily life.

My brief mention of this lack of alternatives, in a group conversation among about fifteen people, drew several acknowledgments of the "of course" variety, and led to a few other comments that, in light of this, there is a temptation to surrender fully to the party and build a career on the basis of obedience. But this explanation was not fully satisfying to the group. There was something deeper in the psychology of "always coming back for more" that it wanted to root out. Why, despite everything, do intellectuals somehow feel "good" about serving the political authority? Why, careerist reasons aside, do we still *want* to do it?

Some pointed to enduring notions of the scholar's social-political duty—to "take responsibility for all under heaven," "be the first in the world to take on its worries," and so on, coupled with the assumption—which held in traditional times as well as now—that the state is the proper and most effective avenue through which to perform this duty. "During the worst years under the Nationalists," said a historian, "we could still try—at least try—to help. It took us a long time to learn that the Communists don't even want our efforts. Time and again we kept trying anyway, out of habit and a feeling of duty."

Some felt that for the older and middle generations, a sense of guilt about their "exploiting class backgrounds" lay behind persistent efforts to prove themselves loyal. Lao She, the acclaimed modern novelist, was cited as an example. Most

Chinese writers who emerged in the 1920s and 1930s simply stopped writing after 1949, finding the "guidelines" imposed by the new regime incompatible with their creativity. But Lao She, famous for his good-natured sympathy with the common folk, and perhaps feeling guilty about his "bourgeois" background, did all he could to "rethink" his position sincerely and to fit the new requirements. He wrote plays and comedians' dialogues praising the commune movement and the Great Leap Forward, and opposing counterrevolutionaries and American aggression in Korea. His last work, published in April 1966, was a clappertale in support of Mao Zedong's campaign to "raise a lot of pigs." The last line of this final work read, "Eternally uphold the great red banner of Mao Zedong thought."[19] But not even that could earn forgiveness for Lao She. Four months later he committed suicide. Similarly Fu Lei, a noted scholar and translator, wrote in his *Letters Home*, "It was right that I was labeled a 'rightist' in 1957." But having conscientiously sought to reform himself, Fu Lei was persecuted during the Cultural Revolution; at one point he was forced to kneel down and crawl across the street. Fu Lei also ended his trials by taking his own life.

A distinguished historian, who as a graduate student in the 1950s had been an enthusiastic supporter of the revolution, was still struggling in 1989 to regain his balance on these questions. "Most Chinese intellectuals desperately *wanted* to help the government in the 1950s. I think 99 percent of those who spoke out in 1956 [in response to Mao Zedong's call to 'let a hundred flowers bloom'] sincerely wanted to help. But they all got knocked down [in the 1957 Antirightist Campaign]. Nothing hurts more than to mean well and get kicked in the teeth. And it happened over and over, in all the campaigns from 1951 to 1957. And worst, there was *no need* for it. No need! The Communist party could have had our loyalty for free, and they just wasted

---

19. Wang Xingzhi, *"Wo lun Lao She"* (My views on Lao She), *Wenyibao* (The literary gazette), January 21, 1989, p. 3. Although most older Chinese intellectuals sympathized with Lao She, some younger ones derisively blamed him for his naive, even stubborn, readiness to cooperate with a repressive regime. "I hate to say it," claimed one university student, "but it serves him right."

it. They could have put our brains to good use, but just threw them away."

The historian exemplified a pattern especially common among the middle generation of intellectuals. Members of this group, educated in the 1950s when the Soviet influence in China was strong, had seen themselves proudly as the first generation of Chinese socialist intellectuals. When punishment came, their response for years was to declare their goodwill and their loyalty—an effort that even in the late 1980s was reflected in their views of the past.[20] The historian continued, "Why did they [the party leaders] treat us this way? Because they really thought— in fact, the handful of oldest leaders today still *really think*— that they have the exclusive truth. There was no need to ask about any other truth. It was like a religion. Their attitude was 'I can lead you to the promised land; just follow. What? You have opinions? I am leading you to paradise and you still have criticisms about it?' That was the mental trap that made them so blind and eventually led them to be so cruel.

"But if they never did change, we intellectuals finally did. Speaking for myself, I have felt three great disappointments since the revolution. After 1949, I was full of hope, and my hopes were smashed by the Great Leap Forward [1958–60] and the Cultural Revolution [1966–76]. With the 'smashing of the Gang of Four' in 1976, my hopes sprang up again, and I started

20. Virtually all of China's well-known writers of this generation—including Wang Meng, Liu Binyan, Zhang Xianliang, Zhang Jie, Chen Rong, Cong Weixi, Bai Hua, and others—exemplify this pattern in one way or another, at least until the late 1980s, when some became thoroughly disillusioned. See, for example, Wang Meng's 1979 novella *Bolshevik Salute,* in which a young party enthusiast (apparently Wang Meng himself) is sent into hard labor during the Cultural Revolution, all the while wishing he could deliver a "Bolshevik salute" to protest his innocence and the "mistake" of his punishment. As he suffers, he still sings Russian songs and reads Soviet novels, which he learned to love in the 1950s. See "Buli" (Bolshevik Salute, 1979), translated by Wendy Larson as *Bolshevik Salute* (Seattle: University of Washington Press, 1989). The same phenomenon is clear in Zhang Xianliang's labor camp novels, near the ends of which the long-suffering protagonist-inmate rededicates himself to serving the state in the way he had originally wanted. See "Lühuashu," translated as "Mimosa" in Zhang Xianliang, *Mimosa* (Beijing: Panda Books, 1985), pp. 13–181; and *Nanren de yiban shi nüren,* translated by Martha Avery as *Half of Man Is Woman* (London: Viking Press, 1988).

talking and writing about the 'new beginning.' But that euphoria eventually wore off. Then came Deng Xiaoping's reform program in the 1980s. Again I thought that, finally, China was on the right track. Again I invested my idealism. You can imagine how bitter I feel today to see the reform program blocked by political 'unmovables' and foundering in a sea of corruption. But this time it's different. I don't think I can trust them again. My attitude now is just to try to do my own work well. If I die in this disconnected state, at least I die clearheaded." He did not attribute his change in attitude entirely to his own disillusionment; he felt there had also been an actual decline over the years in the quality of the thinking emanating from the top levels in the party. "In the 1950s we used to read the political editorials in *People's Daily* with respect, even as literary models. But now the writing is sloppy. There are all kinds of mistakes. Paragraphs don't follow. Themes are unclear."

The experience of a "final break" with the party, after repeated stretchings to the limit, was expressed by a language teacher from Shanghai who said, "When they criticized us in the 1950s, we thought the purpose was 'remolding.' But they were severing our spines. We were stupid not to realize it. Now, battered into submission, our idealism still twitches, but needs an outlet entirely separate from the party. That is why we are interested again in the 'independent integrity' of May Fourth."

## The Revelations of Dai Qing

Dai Qing has been a major contributor to Chinese reassessments of the 1940s and 1950s. A specialist in "literary reportage," a genre that resembles investigative reporting in the West, Dai Qing began as early as 1979 to write pieces that exposed difficult and politically sensitive problems in contemporary Chinese society.[21] In the late 1980s her interests turned to his-

21. See, for example, her 1979 story "Anticipation," about the problem of spouses who are assigned to work units in different cities and therefore find family life nearly impossible, in Perry Link, ed., *Roses and Thorns: The Second Blooming of the Hundred*

tory. She began to probe publicly unmentionable questions in the history of the Communist movement with a boldness that stimulated many readers to undertake their own reexaminations of the same and related questions. In the spring of 1988 an article by Dai Qing, "Wang Shiwei and 'Wild Lilies,' " shocked intellectual circles by its revelation of the persecution and fate of Communist China's first literary dissident. The article explored the long-mysterious question of what had happened to Wang Shiwei, the Communist writer who had been criticized by the party after revealing the presence of abuses, including special privilege, bureaucratism, and repression, in the Communist base at Yan'an in the 1940s. By publishing Wang Shiwei's original articles along with her own, Dai Qing showed that he had not been a Trotskyite counterrevolutionary or a Nationalist spy, as Mao Zedong had charged. Nor had he merely "disappeared" after his criticism in 1942. He was held in a squalid prison for five years and then beheaded on the personal order of the Communist general He Long. (These were facts that even Wang Shiwei's widow did not know until 1978, thirty-one years after her husband's beheading.)[22] When General He's widow threatened Dai Qing with a lawsuit for revealing her husband's role, the effect was only to broaden the fame of the article and sympathy for Dai Qing among intellectuals. But the boldest move in Dai Qing's article was that it named and quoted those among Wang Shiwei's persecutors who were still living and in power: Yang Shangkun, who was president of the People's Republic of China when the article was published; Wang Zhen, vice-president; and Hu Qiaomu, a leading Marxist ideologue. It had been Wang Zhen, in 1942, who first raised the issue of punishing Wang Shiwei; Yang Shangkun and Hu Qiaomu had given speeches supporting the punishment.[23]

*Flowers in Chinese Fiction, 1979–80* (Berkeley and Los Angeles: University of California Press, 1984), pp. 146–67.

22. Dai Qing, "Wang Shiwei yu 'Ye baihehua,' " p. 33.

23. The details concerning Yang Shangkun were censored when Dai Qing's piece was published in the *Wenhui Monthly (Wenhui yuekan)* (Shanghai), May 1988, pp. 22–41, but the article was published in full in the Hong Kong *Ming Bao Monthly* (see above, note 4).

Dai Qing's piece on Wang Shiwei was followed, in winter 1989, by her account of Chu Anping, the editor of the official newspaper for intellectuals, called *Guangming Daily*, and one of the first targets of the Antirightist Campaign in 1957. The Chu Anping story, as Dai Qing told it, was far more than the narrative of one victim of the party's mass movement; it was a penetrating analysis of why liberalism in almost any form had been doomed to slow pulverization in the emerging "world of the party"—as Dai Qing subtitled her piece.[24] It was written in a steady, unemotional style whose restraint only heightened the power of the narrative. Dai Qing was also credited with an essay called "Liang Shuming and Mao Zedong"[25] about the face-off in 1953 between Mao and one of China's most independent intellectuals. (She did not in fact write most of this piece, but was willing to have her name put alongside the pseudonym of the elderly author who feared to use his own name.)

Whether one loved what Dai Qing said, as many Chinese intellectuals did, or despised it, as many party elders did, her words carried special credibility because of her unusual background. The orphaned daughter of a "revolutionary martyr" who died in the 1940s, Dai Qing (whose original name is Fu Ning) was raised in the family of Marshal Ye Jianying, who spent much of his life at or around the pinnacle of Communist power. Dai Qing grew up personally seeing and hearing many things, both trivial and momentous, having to do with the Communist elite at the highest level, and occasionally she would reveal them. At a dance party in spring 1989, for example, someone raised the topic of dancing at the Communist base in Yan'an in the 1940s, complaining that the young men who danced then were now old men who frowned when others danced. Dai Qing, with characteristic élan, suddenly leaped to her feet and offered a demonstration of how Mao Zedong used to dance. "He would

24. The words "and the world of the party" were censored when the piece was published in China in *Eastern Chronicle (Dongfang jishi)*, no. 1 (1989): 94–135. The uncensored version was published in Hong Kong, in *Ming Bao Monthly*, January 1988, pp. 36–47; February 1989, pp. 44–54, 64; and March 1989, pp. 54–64.

25. Dai Qing and Zheng Zhishu, "Liang Shuming yu Mao Zedong," *Wenhui yuekan* (Wenhui monthly) (Shanghai), January 1988, pp. 24–32.

grab the woman he wanted and then dance in a straight line, like this," she said. She then assumed a fox-trot position and began patting her hand rhythmically on the back of Mao's imaginary partner, saying, "*Pia!*" ("Whack!"), with each quick pat. She strode briskly straight ahead, pushing the imaginary partner directly backwards until she collided with a wall, then turned ninety degrees, like a machine gun on a turret, and stalked off *pia! pia! pia!* in another direction.

In the late 1980s, even as she dared to reveal extremely sensitive historical facts, Dai Qing still enjoyed a double protection: first because of her high-level connections, which required the observance of a certain "in-group" respect even for a renegade,[26] and second because the party elite knew, after all, that her information was solid. Hard facts, reported from her own memory as well as from documentary sources in her possession, would not be easy to refute, and to try to muzzle Dai Qing might only anger her into making more public revelations.

In an interview in early 1989, Dai Qing casually mentioned some events in Communist party history that she had not yet written about: between 1936 and 1946, Chinese Communists numbering as many as ten thousand and including "many excellent, independent-minded people," were accused of being "Trotskyites" or "Nationalist agents" and "eliminated" by drowning, burying alive, or death in squalid prisons. Dai Qing said that these facts should be brought to light and that she hoped to do it some day—indeed, that she felt a certain pressure to do it quickly, while the remaining witnesses were still available for interviews.

I asked her about her choice of the cases of Wang Shiwei and Chu Anping. Why were they interesting? "A case like Wang Shiwei's," she answered, "is interesting partly because it is a historical riddle. For readers finally to learn what really happened to Wang Shiwei has its purely intellectual interest. More important, though, is the interest that comes from shattering orthodox myths. What interested me about this case was that

26. This buffer could disappear when people acted anonymously. Dai Qing received telephone death threats in 1988.

everything I learned from historical witnesses contradicted what was in the textbooks. I felt a joy in 'waking up' from ossified beliefs and felt eager to share that joy with readers."

Why, I asked, did she think readers were so attracted to the "new viewpoint"? "In part," she answered, "I think it is just the spice of saying that the devil is good. Wang Shiwei was always officially evil, so people find it interesting when I praise him. Maybe they suspect that the one who is called evil by people who are evil is good. But they also take what I say, I believe, as a small beginning toward finding the truth, toward saying what really happened. There is a tremendous thirst for this in China. You foreigners, with your free press, will find it hard to understand this great thirst, because you are so flooded with newspapers and books. To appreciate why Chinese readers can be so interested in one little article, you should imagine living in a dark room with all the shades drawn. If one shade goes up—just a crack—the light that enters is suddenly *very interesting*. Everyone will rush to look. People in a normally lit room would find the same ray of light unremarkable. Or think of an emperor who has hundreds of concubines, and thus has lost interest in promiscuous sex, and compare him with a deprived man who rushes eagerly when a single opportunity arises.

"But this still describes a fairly superficial attraction of my articles. Their more durable interest, I believe, is in questions like, How did we end up in this mess? Where did we go wrong? These are complex questions, and readers use my articles to help study them."

Among Dai Qing's readers, there was a fairly clear divide along generational lines over this question of where China had gone wrong. To the middle and older generations, who had supported the revolution in the 1940s or 1950s, the question seemed crucial. Had the party always been arrogant and cruel, and we just didn't know it? Or had it "turned bad" at some point? How and when? But to the younger generation, whose earliest memories were from the 1960s or later, there was no real "turn" to explain. A writer in his late twenties said, "To me, history was filthy (*angzang*) from the start; the question

'Where did we go wrong?' is uninteresting. For me, to look back at the 1940s and find 'a dark side' in the Communist movement seems hardly something to get excited about."

Literally everyone with whom I discussed Dai Qing's works assumed them to have contemporary relevance. "The same things were going on back then that go on now," said one. "That may seem depressing, but it also cheers me. It helps to show that the problem lies with 'them'—a certain group, a certain work-style—and that is a relief." It is striking, said a young woman born in 1962, that "the *methods* they used in the 1940s are the same that they have used during my lifetime. Even some of the actual players are the same that Dai Qing talks about—like He Long and Wang Zhen. By looking into Dai Qing's historical mirror, we're not exactly learning from *other* times and places; we're looking at the other end of the same animal that's with us today."

## The Cultural Revolution

No historical question has loomed larger for Chinese intellectuals, or demanded of them more painful self-examination, than that of the Great Proletarian Cultural Revolution and its aftermath. What really happened? Where did the chaos and violence come from? What does this ugly experience say about us?

The great event had far-reaching consequences for every generation of intellectuals: for those educated in the 1940s or earlier, it shattered faith in the revolution; for those educated under the new regime of the 1950s, it was, as one put it, "what really educated us, after we had read all the 'new classics' of the revolution"; for the younger ones, whose education was disrupted by the events themselves, the morass left a strong cynicism that has persisted ever since and may mark their generation to the end. The events of the 1980s, including the massacre at Tiananmen, are frequently analyzed, directly or indirectly, as aftershocks of the Cultural Revolution.

The Chinese have written much about the Cultural Revolution, in memoirs, in reportage, and, most of all, in the short stories that proliferated as "scar literature" during the years 1977–80.[27] But all this writing, however sincere, has struck many Chinese intellectuals as superficial and immature. From time to time since, they have commented that they wish someone would really dig in, conceive it all grandly, and write a book whose magisterial vision matches the epochal significance of the event itself. They often mention *War and Peace* in this regard. But, widespread though the idea is, there is no sign yet of its realization.

Part of the problem in coming to grips with the Cultural Revolution is practical. So much happened to so many people, at so many places and levels, that the research required simply to establish the sequence of events is daunting. The painful memories that many Chinese carry, for all their drama and vividness, can seem narrowly personal. The larger picture—in particular, what really happened in the misty clouds at the very top—has not been easy to discern, even years later, under conditions of a controlled press.

But there are deeper reasons, some of them difficult to explicate, for the failure of Chinese to comprehend the Cultural Revolution. There has been, first of all, a reluctance to face squarely—meaning to face publicly or in print—the magnitude of the cruelty involved. " 'Scar literature' is fine as far as it goes," said an engineer from Guangzhou. "It tells about broken homes, forced divorces, and sometimes mentions prison life, rape, or hunger. But it stops short of the ugliest images—images that stick in my memory and, I assume, in the memories of others. I saw people lying on the street with their eyes gouged out. Parents were forced to 'reimburse the state' for the bullet that was used to kill their child. 'Scar literature' tells only two-fifths of the whole story."

27. For samples in English translation, see Lee Yee, ed., *The New Realism: Writings from China after the Cultural Revolution* (New York: Hippocrene Books, 1983); Helen Siu and Zelda Stern, eds., *Mao's Harvest: Voices from China's New Generation* (London and New York: Oxford University Press, 1983); Perry Link, ed., *Stubborn Weeds: Popular and Controversial Chinese Literature after the Cultural Revolution* (Bloomington: Indiana University Press, 1983); and Link, ed., *Roses and Thorns*.

I asked a professor of medicine about a "scar" story called "Fire," by Cao Guanlong.[28] This story seemed so horrible to me, and so unusual even for "scar literature," that I suspected it of exaggeration. It tells of a doctor who surgically removes the eyes of a prisoner right after he is executed, so that the corneas can be "donated" to a party secretary. Prior to the execution, the party secretary has "visited" the prisoner "out of concern for his health." Did this kind of thing really happen? "I'm afraid so," said the doctor, averting her eyes. "I know it happened, at least, for kidneys. Kidneys were harvested from prisons. Sometimes the 'donors' got special food in advance, to be sure the kidneys would be healthy."

Zhang Xianliang's novella *Mimosa* also stands out for its revelation of suffering. It tells of a "rightist" who was sent to a labor camp in the countryside in the late 1950s, and describes in minute detail the hunger he suffered. The story became well known for its "bold" realism. But Li Tuo, one of China's most prominent literary critics, flared up when I mentioned this set view of the story. "To call it 'bold' only shows the double standard between what we know and what we write. The man in that story suffered? Yes, he suffered. But he still *did eat*. And he could write. He even had a woman's love. You think that was the worst of labor reform? Nonsense! I know a man who went to a camp that held thousands. Only he and six others came back. Seven out of thousands. But nobody writes about *that*."

Censorship has, of course, been a formidable barrier to the publication of the ugliest truths. Neither "Fire" nor *Mimosa* was easily published, and neither was free from official criticism after it appeared. Another reason for quiescence regarding the Cultural Revolution was simply the emotional recoil that one naturally feels at the thought of spelling out horrible things. Literary accounts of the Holocaust, and of the dropping of atomic bombs on Japan, also appeared only decades after those events. Yet some of my friends in China thought that the widespread avoid-

28. Translated in Link, ed. *Roses and Thorns*, pp. 130–45.

ance of ugly truths was, at least in part, attributable to Chinese culture. "We have a long tradition of exalting our written language, and we still think there should be a certain decorum about the printed word," said one. "It is undignified *(butimian)* to put such awful things in writing." Another thought it had to do with national "face." "All the world can read 'scar literature,' " she said. "Chinese feel embarassed to admit to others that such uncivilized things happened in China. It doesn't matter that we intellectuals were the victims. We are still embarrassed for China to admit that it happened."

The question of whom to blame was difficult to disentangle from the events of the Cultural Revolution. For Chinese intellectuals in the late 1980s, it was much easier to attribute responsibility for the Antirightist Campaign of 1957 than for the Cultural Revolution. This was in part because, some thirty years later, the Antirightist Campaign stood out for them as the first decisive downward turn in the history of the People's Republic. But more important, the moral terms of the Antirightist Campaign seemed in retrospect relatively clear: on one side were basically well-intentioned intellectuals and on the other a harsh regime that slapped them down. Responsibility for the Cultural Revolution was much harder to sort out. To be sure, the party had officially blamed the Gang of Four, who then became, for a year or two after 1976, scapegoats upon whom the Chinese could vent their pent-up anger. For some this catharsis seemed enough and the Deng regime's admonition to "look forward" the best course. But for many of China's worrying intellectuals, the Gang of Four remained a flimsy answer to a problem that required a much deeper explanation. It was ridiculous to think that four people somehow did it all. Gradually, between 1977 and 1980, the party acknowledged that Kang Sheng, the widely feared chief of public security, had also been tied up with the Gang of Four, and that Lin Biao, for a time Mao's appointed successor and "closest comrade-in-arms," was just as bad; privately, intellectuals knew—and said—that Mao Zedong was one of the group all along. But still, could only seven people have brought about such a catastrophe? To a country of eight hundred million? What caused millions of others to take part in the violence?

Some pointed to the popular anger against bureaucrats that had been mounting over the first seventeen years of Communist rule. "Mao's call to 'smash the new ruling class' said exactly what a lot of people wanted to do," explained an editor from Shanghai. "And at the beginning, it was exactly those most downtrodden people who rose up." His colleague added, "Once the labels were available, once you could attack someone by calling him a 'revisionist' or a 'capitalist-roader,' the labels were used like cannon, just to attack anyone against whom you felt any grievance of any kind, whether public or private." But such explanations still, somehow, did not get to the bottom of things in a satisfying way. There was still something "in all of us" that had to be understood.

"The Cultural Revolution is still treated like an embarrassing secret," said one of China's best young writers. "In the publicly acknowledged version of what happened, *everybody* was a victim—intellectuals, workers, peasants, old revolutionaries, honest officials—everyone except for four. But this is an impossible version of history. It is more plausible to say, but difficult to admit, that almost everyone was at fault. We might better say we all turned abnormal for a while. But then, how do we explain *that*? We won't be done with the history of the Cultural Revolution until we can answer that question. The trouble is, few want to try. It requires self-dissection of a painful kind. Ba Jin has led the way, by honestly admitting his complicity in the Cultural Revolution mind-set.[29] Gao Xiaosheng was the first to point out publicly that it is absurd to say that four people manipulated eight hundred million.[30] Shi Tiesheng has a story

29. Ba Jin, *Random Thoughts,* trans. Geremie Barmé (Hong Kong: Joint Publishing Co., 1984), especially the essay "In Loving Memory of Xiao Shan," pp. 21–42.

30. Gao, a writer famed for his stories about peasants, made this comment at a conference in Nanjing on April 29, 1981. He made similar statements in print, although less directly. See, for example, his denunciation of the rise in "superstition, gambling, vulgarity . . . and even beatings" among peasants during the Cultural Revolution, in "Xiwang nuli wei nongmin xiezuo" (Hoping we will work hard at writing for the peasants) *Wenyibao* (Beijing), April 1980, p. 13.

in which he admits feelings of temptation to sell out a friend in order to save himself.[31] Qian Zhongshu has said that if all Chinese were to write frank reminiscences of the Cultural Revolution, we would all have to admit shame. We need more individual cases, more confessions, until everyone feels free to look honestly at himself. Then we need to ask, How did we all get sucked into such a situation? This historical question *has* to be thoroughly answered, because, so long as it is not, the problem will still lie there dormant, unexamined, unacknowledged, and ready to spring up and bite us again. We need to dig out this 'part of us' and face it squarely."

This young writer was more willing than most to explore the question of social responsibility for the Cultural Revolution. Most others seemed reluctant to push beyond the vague feeling that whatever caused the mass violence still lurks "in all of us." In 1986 Liu Zaifu publicly raised the issue at a conference in Beijing. In his presentation entitled "Literature and the Awareness of Repentance,"[32] he argued that the novels of Tolstoy and Dostoyevsky could achieve an elevated moral vision because of the religious concepts of sin and repentance in Russian culture. Chinese culture lacked such concepts, Liu said, but would do well to develop them when trying to come to grips morally with a catastrophe like the Cultural Revolution. Liu's paper, although never published, became famous in Beijing intellectual circles for its implicit call for more introspection and honesty. Nearly everyone seemed to share Liu's assumption that "lack of repentance" was a problem of Chinese culture—rather than of human nature more generally, or of Communist Chinese experience more narrowly. Indeed, the deep pride in Chinese culture felt by intellectuals was one reason they found it difficult to address the issue.

---

31. "Wenge jikui" (Notes on Cultural Revolution shame), *Dongfang jishi* (Eastern chronicle), no. 1 (1989): 41–43.

32. "Wenxue yu chanhui yishi" (unpublished paper, Institute of Literature, Chinese Academy of Social Sciences).

# The Reforms of the 1980s

During my year in China the reform decade of the 1980s was still too close at hand for intellectuals to raise many questions about reinterpreting its history. But one big historical question was already emerging. The reforms seemed to have made headway in the first half of the decade and then to have stalled in the second half. Why? Some pointed to the regime's Four Basic Principles (socialism; dictatorship of the proletariat; leadership of the party; Marxism-Leninism-Mao Zedong thought), which allowed economic reform before, but not a moment after, it began to entail political change; some pointed to the corruption and inflation that the two-price system (market price and state-fixed price) made possible; a few pointed to the disillusionment and pessimism in society.

But beyond this kind of immediate cause for the halt in reform efforts, Chinese intellectuals groped to identify a larger historical logic in the situation. Why is it that China seems trapped, unable to make significant progress toward a modern society and economy? During the 1980s two general answers to this question came into currency: (1) Chinese culture contains powerfully conservative elements that repeatedly pull China back into "feudal" patterns; and (2) the Marxist-Leninist system stifles development wherever it exists, including China. Although both explanations bear to some degree on China's predicament, intellectuals often discussed the two—perhaps for heuristic reasons—as if they were competing alternatives. The first explanation was dominant in the mid-1980s; by the end of the decade, and especially after the June 4 massacre, the second gained greater favor.

The appeal of the "cultural explanation" grew stronger as soon as the initial euphoria of the early Deng years had worn off. This euphoria had grown in the late 1970s, as the "smashing of the Gang of Four" had led to truth-telling "scar literature" and official slogans such as "Liberate Thought" and "Practice [that is, not dogma] Is the Sole Criterion for Testing Truth."

But these promising developments were quickly followed, during 1979–81, by the closing of Democracy Wall, in Beijing, where prodemocracy posters had flourished in 1978 and 1979; the curtailment of "scar literature"; criticism of the "sole criterion" theory; and a propaganda campaign against the writer Bai Hua for his filmscript "Unrequited Love" (which suggested that the party had exploited and abused the patriotism of intellectuals). By 1981 it seemed that the Deng Xiaoping regime had reverted to the authoritarian style of traditional "feudalism." China's intellectuals once again wondered what had happened: Why does such reversion happen so easily? What is it in Chinese culture that so resists change?

These questions gave rise to an intense exploration of certain aspects of China's cultural tradition. This trend, which began about 1983 and became most pronounced during 1985–86, was popularly called "culture fever" (or, in literary circles, "searching-for-roots fever"). As during May Fourth times, those drawn to the analysis assumed that the criticism of tradition could lead to a transcendence of its bonds and thus to the salvation of China.

"Culture fever" culminated in summer 1988 with the appearance of the six-part television series called "River Elegy."[33] (The connotations of the Chinese title amount almost to "mourning the nation.") "River Elegy" rather cavalierly traces most of China's contemporary problems to Chinese tradition. It presents a great parable on the past, present, and future of China, suggesting that China must emerge from the constrained, inward focus of "Yellow River civilization" and head out into the open "Azure Ocean civilization." In the process, the series clearly implies that China's "reformist" leaders, whom it praises personally, are on the right track. The conservative side of the party is associated with "feudal" tradition.

The audacity of "River Elegy," broadly exposed on national television, stimulated a tremendous popular response along with the determined opposition of conservative leaders. With Vice-

33. See chapter 1, note 22.

President Wang Zhen most prominent among them, these leaders criticized the work as "wholesale Westernization" (October
1988), then banned it (November 1988), and eventually rooted
out copies to crush beneath steamrollers (summer 1989). For
ordinary television viewers, unaccustomed to such frank debate
in the official media, "River Elegy" was like a great bolt of lightning that ignited numerous little blazes everywhere. The popular response was generally positive, despite some complaints
that the work "forgot the ancestors," meaning that it took
insufficient pride in Chinese tradition.

But if "River Elegy" was the culmination of the intellectuals'
"culture fever," the series may also have been its death knell.
Intellectuals generally praised the work for raising important
questions and bringing them to a mass audience for the first
time ever. But they also criticized the program for historical
inaccuracies and a sentimental, moralizing tone, which together
made its criticisms of Chinese tradition seem simplistic. Moreover, during the latter half of the 1980s, intellectuals were
beginning to consider their political system, rather than traditional culture, as the nub of China's contemporary problems.
Their growing awareness of the economic success of Taiwan
and Hong Kong, on the one hand, and the rumblings of discontent in Eastern Europe, on the other, was partly responsible for
this shift in view. A philosophy scholar, speaking in late 1988,
put it this way: "Taiwan has Chinese culture and a non-Com-
munist system; Eastern Europe has a Communist system and
non-Chinese culture. It seems pretty obvious that the problem
of stagnation lies in the system, not in the culture." In March
1989 Li Zehou, one of the original movers in the "culture fever"
discussions, sought to disassociate himself from the "radical
opposition" to tradition urged in the "River Elegy" series, and
to point to a different "root" of China's problems: "I believe
that the key problem, as of now, is not 'culture' or 'enlightenment' but reform of the political-economic system. Those who
oppose 'tradition' so vehemently have covered up precisely this
point. The implication of their excessive criticism of 'culture'
is to say that the fault lies equally with all of us. This, in turn,

tends to exonerate those who really should bear responsibility."[34] Although statements such as this seem to represent a rather sharp turn of mind, the shift was frequently less sharp than it appeared. Throughout the "culture fever" discussions of the 1980s, the word "culture" had, in fact, often been used as a code word for "politics"—allowing discussion of things one could not otherwise easily say in public. Similarly the term "feudalism" had sometimes been meant to stand for "communism," "emperor" for "Deng Xiaoping," and so on. When people began in the late 1980s to shift their indictment from "our tradition" to "our system," they were to a certain extent simply decoding earlier messages.

I noticed in a few cases that this shift toward explicit blame of the party seemed to be especially emotional—as if hard in coming but especially emphatic when it came. I am not sure how to interpret this response, but suspect it is related to the special anger that a true believer feels when jolted from the faith. The exalted expectations the revolution's ideals generated in Chinese intellectuals only seemed to increase their bitterness when the fall from faith finally came. A historian educated in the 1940s and 1950s recalled, "When the Communists came, they were 'our' party. We have never thought of the Nationalists that way. By now, of course, no one thinks of the Communists as 'ours' any more. We feel doubly bitter for having been rejected when we tried to help." A younger man, introspecting very conscientiously, said, "You grow up with beliefs that are supposed to be true, and that you would want to be true, but that gradually begin to feel like lies. You don't face the problem squarely, somehow don't *want* to face it. The thought is vaguely but deeply upsetting. When you finally do reach your new 'sudden enlightenment,' a rush of energy wells inside. You want to speak. You want to be sure that others are as enlightened as you are."

Yet I thought there was another reason for the sense of relief

34. Li Zehou and Sun Shangyang, "Wusi de shishifeifei" (May Fourth disputes), *Wenhuibao* (Shanghai), March 28, 1989, quoted from *Xinhua wenzhai* (New China digest) (Beijing: People's Publishing House, 1989), p. 29.

intellectuals felt when they began to argue that "the system" and not "traditional culture" was the primary cause of China's troubles. This had to do with the issue of identity. If China's problems were as basic and pervasive as its culture, where could reform begin? It was more pragmatic and comforting to associate China's problems with a foreign ideology that arrived in the twentieth century. This approach acknowledged, moreover, a continuing sense of pride in Chinese cultural tradition, even among radical "Westernizers." No matter how much in need of reform, China was still an ancient culture and the current generations its living inheritors. This problem of identity, which called for a discomfiting kind of self-examination, was seldom explicitly articulated. But it was visible, for example, in the impulse of student demonstrators at Tiananmen Square to call themselves "children of the dragon." The dragon was a symbol for traditional China that in the 1980s had often stood in antithesis to science, democracy, free speech, and the other "modern" ideals that the students were explicitly upholding. ("River Elegy" had only months before used the dragon as a symbol of all that was reactionary in Chinese tradition.) Yet the student rebels were proud to be the dragon's "children."[35] Indeed, their acceptance of this symbol occurred at so basic a level that I believe it went by largely unnoticed.

## The Course of Twentieth-Century Chinese History

Beneath their discussions of various events and periods in the twentieth century, Chinese intellectuals were concerned with the overall trajectory of their country's modern history. Their sense of this history was generally despairing, a feeling they

35. The phrase *long de chuanren* ("children of the dragon") came from a song by Hou Dejian that was popular with the student demonstrators. The word "children" in this standard translation is insufficiently strong. The sense of the whole phrase comes close to "those who inherit the spirit of the dragon." Later the phrase was also used by a group in New York called Human Rights in China as the title for its book chronicling the events of Tiananmen, in 1989. See Human Rights in China, *Children of the Dragon: The Story of Tiananmen Square* (New York: Collier Macmillan, 1990).

would emphasize when they wanted to accentuate the difference between their mood and the artificially rosy language of state policy—which for forty years had announced a brave new China with each policy reversal. But otherwise the intellectuals seldom spoke directly of their underlying conceptions of China's recent history, perhaps because of the distress explicit discussion would bring. To an auditor like myself, these underlying conceptions appeared as organizing principles holding other wide-ranging topics together.

One of these conceptions was of continuous decline in the quality of Chinese language and morality, including everything from daily courtesies to the pride of sharing a unique Chinese identity. The collapse of Confucianism as China's guiding ideology, followed by a briefly promising but ultimately disastrous attempt to replace it with Marxism-Leninism-Mao Zedong thought, left Chinese groping for a new alternative even as they were trying to rid themselves of remnants of the failed ones. "Marxism had its place in nineteenth-century Europe," said a well-known cultural critic, a man whose education in the 1950s had led him to a sincere belief in Marxism. "Marx's criticisms of European society made good sense. He called his theories 'science,' and they really were—at that time, anyway. But later, with Lenin, the theories were transformed into a tool (*gongjuhua*). They weren't quite science any more. With Mao, they were transformed into a religion (*zongjiaohua*)—even further from science. And that led to catastrophes. When a state ideology—*any* state ideology—is 'religionized,' disasters will follow. Look at the ayatollah in Iran."

Those who were more radically alienated from Marxism, including many of the young who had never really adopted it in the first place, were less interested in how Marxist theory had "decayed" than in the flaws in its basic constitution. Their common view—and it was common well before the collapse of Marxism in Eastern Europe—was that state socialism is simply a worldwide failure. In the words of the elder writer Wang Ruowang, a Communist for most of his life, "Wherever the socialist model of state ownership has been implemented, people have become destitute and the nation backward."[36] "The road we've been traveling leads nowhere," said a professor of aesthetics. "It seems only Albania and North Korea are still on it." A young poet expressed the view that the world owes China a debt for running the experiment of state socialism and demonstrating that it doesn't work.

The question of exactly why socialism doesn't work was approached by some as a topic for serious analysis. Differences between Leninist style and Maoist style, or between such disparate societies as those of Czechoslovakia and North Korea, became temporarily less interesting than the commonalities of socialist systems and their internal mechanics. I heard considerable talk (but saw almost nothing in writing) about *shegong wenhua* ("socialist-Communist culture"), examining such "properties" as the engineering of fear, manipulation of language, and obliteration of collective memory.[37] These discussions inevitably raised the question "How do you get out of the box?" and in this connection Mikhail Gorbachev in 1988–89 became a guide and even a hero. "He seems," said a young journalist, "to have recognized the failure of socialism. We in China especially admire him for allowing political reform as well as economic reform. He sees more deeply than China's leaders."

Although there was widespread agreement about China's general downward course during the twentieth century, there were differing views—held, it seemed, according to generation—on what the key turning points had been. The middle and older generations tended to see the 1950s as the century's crucial decade. "That is when the socialist system was set up," said one. "The Russians came, Marxist education was put in place, and big campaigns wiped out landlords, businessmen, and intellectuals as they had existed before. The 1950s marked

---

36. Quoted in Rubin, "A Chinese Half-Century of Satire and Dissent," p. 6.

37. After his exile from China in 1989, Su Wei, a writer and critic in his thirties, wrote a paper on *shegong wenhua* called "Zhongguo de 'dang wenhua' " ("The 'party culture' of the Chinese Communists"), *Minzhu Zhongguo* (Democratic China), no 1 (April 1990): 12–18.

China's major chance in the twentieth century to find a work-able new identity. And it was also the time when the seeds of the disaster were sewn." Younger intellectuals attributed less significance to the 1950s. A young writer from Sichuan dispar-aged the period as merely one of "dynastic change." "The Com-munists won, and then everyone adapted—of course! That happens when dynasties change. There was a lot of talk of a 'new' China, but so what? Where's the new China? I don't think the fifties were a turning point. I think the two turning points in the twentieth century are May Fourth and now."

Others doubted that there had been any real turning points at all. One of the commonest underlying conceptions of Chi-na's modern history viewed it as a series of fitful starts and stops aimed at restoring China's greatness, but amounting to noth-ing. "The crisis we face in China right now," said a young writer, "is really about the same old problem that China has faced throughout the twentieth century: how can China get big and strong? This was the fundamental question behind May Fourth. It was also the question that the 1949 revolution seemed to answer. Now everyone faces the fact that the 1949 answer failed. Meanwhile, the challenge from the West is even stronger, because the West seems to have barreled even further ahead than it was before. And so far the Chinese leadership has been able to come up with only one answer—'economic reform.' It's so narrow! It has been tried before and has left us where we started. The problem is broader, but since we all somehow wish it weren't, we don't look at broader solutions."

There was much regret over the waste that resulted from China's desperate trying first one thing and then another. "Our country does things in waves," said a professor of art in early 1989. "Now everybody is doing business—officials, professors, everybody. A few years ago doing business was heresy. We spent the 1950s learning Russian so that we could talk to Russian advisers, then spent the 1960s denouncing the Russians and forgetting their language. In the late 1970s almost everyone was studying English. Now they announce that 200,000 Russian tourists will be coming, so we all should learn Russian again."

Although Deng Xiaoping's "pragmatism" generally came as a relief after the terrible dogmatism of Mao Zedong, Deng's tendency to flip-flop also drew criticism. A popular ditty whose ironic first line is borrowed from the Cultural Revolution song "The East Is Red" went,

> Mao Zedong is like the sun: the land is bright where it shines its rays.
> Deng Xiaoping is like the moon: it changes every fourteen days.

"Why do you think China's direction zigs and zags so much?" one of China's leading sociologists asked me in late 1988. "Why are there so many policy reversals? Yes, of course, it is partly because the Communist leadership is continuously torn among factions. But fundamentally the phenomenon is much larger. The whole country is frantically searching for a way out, and has been for many decades, even before the Communists. We're like a big fish that has been pulled from the water and is flopping wildly to find its way back in. In such a condition the fish never asks where the next flip or flop will bring it. It senses only that its present position is intolerable and that *something* else must be tried. We intellectuals complain a lot about the influence of Soviet-style dictatorship in China. But originally, the 'Soviet path' was also just one of the flops of the fish, an effort to find a way to save China."

For a Chinese, it is understandably painful to think of China as inevitably in decline or to picture it as a helpless flopping fish. In the late 1980s some Chinese intellectuals derived a measure of comfort by examining historical parallels to their country's current predicament. At a minimum, this sort of analysis could suggest that China's plight was not unique.

## Historical Parallels

Although intellectuals drew some parallels to Western history, most were to earlier periods in Chinese history. The search for

Chinese precedents seemed to answer a need, perhaps especially strong in Chinese culture, for a way "to speak of" the
current historical period. Ancient conceptions of the moral
dimension of language still tended to require that the historical
record reflect not just what happened but "the proper view" of
what happened.[38] To look for ways to understand the current
predicament in earlier "proper views" was emotionally and
intellectually satisfying for many.

The most common comparisons were drawn to the late
Nationalist years. We have already seen the frequent complaint
that corruption in the late 1980s resembled a milder version
under the Nationalists in the late 1940s. Another oft-noted
similarity to this period lay in the decline in popular morale—
except, again, to say that the prevailing sense of frustration was
even stronger in the 1980s. "The Nationalists," as Liu Binyan
put it, "never claimed that they were the sole possessors of the
truth or that they represented the interests of the common people. And there was, after all, another political force—the Communists—upon whom one could pin hopes. For these reasons
the spirits of the Chinese people were considerably better then
than now." "Under the Nationalists," said an editor, "the government made it clear what you could not say—and everything
else was all right to say. In the case of the Communists, there
were certain things you *had* to say, and beyond that . . . well,
it wasn't clear, you never knew, except to know that almost
anything could be dangerous."

Parallels were drawn as well to the late-Qing period (1900–
1911), when a moribund regime attempted a "reform program"
that ground to a halt in midcourse. The likeness was frequently
noted, and only partly in jest, between Deng Xiaoping and the
empress dowager Cixi—two aged, "muddleheaded" autocrats
who put others in the front positions of government but held
firm control behind the scenes. "Cixi was actually more flexi-
ble," commented a young computer scientist. "She could see

38. Contemporary China also inherits the Stalinist tradition of falsifying the past
to serve the present. The Chinese tradition I am speaking of is more deeply embedded
and subtle than this, but has combined with it in the Communist period.

that the Eight-Legged Essay [required in the imperial civil service examinations] was only the shell of a dead ideology, and she finally discarded it; Deng Xiaoping informally advises African leaders 'not to take the socialist road,' but he still won't throw off the dead shell of Marxist ideology."

"Both in late-Qing times and now," said a graduate student in political science, "the government decided to strengthen China by 'reforming' education, by encouraging foreign investment, by borrowing as much Western technology as possible, and by sending students abroad. But—and this is the most interesting similarity—in both cases they insisted that China's cultural and ethical 'core' *(ti)* remain the same. Just as students in late Qing were given copies of the Confucian classics as they were shipped off to the West, so now they're supposed to bring the Four Basic Principles with them. China in both cases is like a big, dilapidated house. The leader knows the house is rotten and sends out for emergency repair, saying, 'Go ahead and rebuild any part, but *don't touch the foundation.*' Actually, however, the foundation is as rotten as the rest, and the more rebuilding that goes on in the superstructure, the more likely it becomes that the whole thing will topple."[39]

Some pushed the analogy between late Qing and the late 1980s back a few decades, pointing out likenesses between two devastating preceding events, the Taiping Rebellion (1850–64) and the Cultural Revolution. "In each case," said a young businessman, "there was a tremendous upheaval inspired by an egomaniac autocrat [Hong Xiuquan, the visionary leader of the vast Taiping movement, and Mao Zedong]. Each concocted an ideology that was half his own and half that of a foreigner-savior [Jesus Christ and Karl Marx]. Each whipped up religious fervor, preaching egalitarianism, built communes, and declared that the end of selfishness was at hand. In each case the pretty

---

39. For a fuller version of this argument see Feng Shengping, "The 100-Day Reform of 1898 and the Democracy Movement of 1989," in *China: The Crisis of 1989, Origins and Implications*, ed. Roger DesForges, Luo Ning, and Wu Yen-bo, vol. 1 (Buffalo: Council on International Studies and Programs, State University of New York at Buffalo, 1990), pp. 55–58.

dream exploded, millions perished, and China was left considerably worse off than it had been before. The empress dowager and Deng Xiaoping were in somewhat analogous positions even before they got started."

Some even pointed to parallels between the late 1980s and the late-Ming period (the early to mid-1600s), specifically to the practice of "moral remonstration" by intellectuals in both eras. In spring 1989 over a hundred intellectuals petitioned China's rulers for democracy and the release of political prisoners. They did so fully aware that their message would not be welcome and that they were incurring personal risk. Some of them pointed to their predecessors in late-Ming times, the "Donglin party" of Confucian scholars, who felt that the decline of the dynasty was the result of incorrect philosophical views and an unconscionable decay in morality at court. In the 1620s their challenges grew sharper and eventually triggered a brutal crackdown—which nevertheless did not prevent the demise of the Ming some twenty years later. The "proper view" of the Donglin scholars came to portray them as upright men who sacrificed themselves for principle and the good of China.[40] I heard the Donglin analogy several times in early 1989, before that year's harsh crackdown was in sight. Whether the analogy was meant as a prediction of the crackdown, I cannot say.

Nearly all the analogies to earlier times in China that I heard were to the *ends* of eras, perhaps an indirect expression of the hope that the current regime would soon pass from the scene. But these parallels also reflected a fearful uncertainty about the immediate future, in which it seemed almost *anything* could happen. "Something is in gestation now," said an elderly literary scholar in January 1989. "It could be very good, and it could be horrible—we just don't know what it is." This apprehensiveness was heightened by the lack of direction in the leadership itself. A power struggle was clearly going on, and even the paramount leader, Deng Xiaoping, had to characterize his reform

40. For more on the Donglin party, see Charles O. Hucker, "The Tung-lin Movement of the Late Ming Period," in John K. Fairbank, ed., *Chinese Thought and Institutions* (Chicago: University of Chicago Press, 1957), pp. 132–62.

program as "fording the river by feeling the way from rock to rock."

## The Problem of Pessimism

The burning interest of Chinese intellectuals in historical reevaluations sprang almost entirely from their concern for China's future. There seemed a frightening potential in the late 1980s for China, as it had several times in earlier decades, to lurch one way or another. Rumors that the moderate leader Zhao Ziyang was being jockeyed out of position struck fear in Chinese intellectuals as early as summer 1988, well before Zhao's eventual fall in May 1989. Would Zhao's disgrace open the way for a resurgence of Maoism at the top? But even as the party leadership inspired fear and uncertainty, the possibility that the party might lose power also provoked apprehension. In late April 1989, when it appeared briefly that the Communist party might actually lose control of the streets of Beijing, worry overshadowed joy for one of China's senior historians. "If the students rule the streets, who rules Beijing? Who rules China? We might see nationwide chaos. There are about a million 'hooligans' in Beijing alone; they could run wild. The Communist party and its bureaucracy, odious though they may be, are *all that we have.* You Americans perhaps cannot understand this fear. You don't have to worry that your local police department will dissolve if there is a transfer of power in the White House." A young filmmaker captured the same point in a metaphor: "Fifteen years ago Mao Zedong thought was like a giant magnet that ordered the pattern of all the individual iron filings. With the big magnet gone, one solid jolt could scatter the filings everywhere."

Some considered the party too far gone to hold things together for long. Mao Zedong's "series of perverse acts and policies," said the writer Wang Ruowang, "paved the way for the death of the Chinese Communist Party."[41] "The real tragedy," said a senior editor, "is that they did not *have to* destroy themselves.

41. Quoted in Rubin, "A Chinese Half-Century of Satire and Dissent," p. 6.

The party was strong in the 1950s and basically popular. No foreign force, or domestic group, could have destroyed its prestige then. The leaders destroyed it themselves." The repugnant massacre of June 4, 1989, greatly spread and strengthened the view that "the party has destroyed itself." Many concluded that rulers who could turn tanks and machine guns on their own citizens now could represent only tanks and machine guns.

Beneath the nerve-racking uncertainty about the immediate future lay a vague gloom about longer-range prospects. An important cause of this pessimism was the sense that the foundation of the future—education of the young—was being badly neglected. This problem was more basic than flips or flops in the political line. "It seems to me that pressure is building for another policy shift in China," commented a linguist. "Within ten years things will be different, I think. But I worry: will it be a change for the better? There are so many illiterates in China. There is a social base for ignorant, emotional reaction. Something like the Cultural Revolution could very easily happen again." A professor of fine arts, noting the decline in contemporary public morals, blamed Maoist education. "Children were taught to imitate Lei Feng.[42] He was their model of Communist virtues. When the Lei Feng idol collapsed, should we be surprised that morality collapsed as well? Young people had such a narrow education that they had nothing else to go on." "The harm of Maoist education," said a scholar of philosophy, "cannot be ended simply by changing education. Even if we completely changed Chinese education overnight, we would still face a tremendous problem: What do you do with all the *products* of this system? They're still here."

The senior economist Qian Jiaju wrote that education during the reformist 1980s, although certainly an improvement over practices during the Cultural Revolution, still boded ill for the future of China. Teachers were sorely underpaid, and curricula emphasized narrow technical skills at the expense of broadly humane values. Of the future, Qian wrote, "If we do not really

42. See chapter 1, note 20.

set our minds to it, do not genuinely *work on* education rather than just sloganeer about it, do not double or triple the pay of primary school teachers instead of talking about 10 or 20 percent increases, do not regard education as the nation's 'basic construction,' indeed the most basic of basic construction, then, I ask, *when will the bill come due?* It will be due in the twenty-first century, and our children and grandchildren will have to pay it."[43] Qian capped his argument with a shocking question: "Will China in the next century be able to stand within the community of civilized countries of the world? We must draw a big question mark here."

Qian's question mark had rhetorical parallels in the extreme pessimism expressed by other intellectuals: hopeless as these assessments seemed, they were almost always grounded in the conviction that things need not—and must not—be allowed to deteriorate so. In effect, extremist statements like Qian's were arguments by moral reductio ad absurdum whose concluding line, unspoken but powerfully implied, was "That *can't* be our future; it *just can't.*" In one such exchange a bright sociologist in his thirties, who had a wife and an infant daughter, ended a series of gloomy predictions for China with the thought "It's all over for my generation; I only hope my daughter's generation can have a better chance." "But you're still young," I commented. "How can you say it's over?" "You don't understand our system here," he answered. "It doesn't move easily. The top leaders can change national policies overnight, but the basic system, for the average person, moves very slowly, if at all. If you push it, it snaps at you. Our optimistic thinkers, like Liu Binyan, talk about 'reforming the system.' I can't agree. Our system is good at only one thing, and that's preserving itself. For example . . ."

He then launched into a critique of Chinese society that was detailed, carefully considered, and morally acute at nearly every turn. Would he bother with all this analysis if he *really* thought his life was over? I wondered. Why wasn't he lying in bed

43. "Qian Jiaju tan wujia, jiaoyu he shehui fengqi" (Qian Jiaju talks about prices, education, and the public ethic), *Wenhuibao* (Hong Kong), April 4, 1988, p. 6.

depressed? Or, like others in his environment, devoting his full attention to climbing the bureaucracy, making money, or emigrating to the West? I concluded that his excessively negative statements must have been another example of the "shock treatment" that young Chinese sometimes used in their efforts to jolt their listeners—and themselves—into new mind-sets, free from the controlling power of accustomed views. In any case his ideals, however deeply packed within his rhetoric, were clearly still alive. They set him off, in the last analysis, from the cynicism that permeated his environment, where the constant struggle over small advantages and disadvantages so dominated daily life. In this context the willingness of intellectuals like him to step back and worry about the good of the whole society seemed endearingly naive, indeed almost blockheaded.

Some were willing to set out their hopes more plainly. Liu Zaifu, while fully acknowledging the frustratingly slow pace of change in China, still cited three grounds for patience or, as he put it, "defenses against total despair": "First, China is big. Therefore reform has to be slow. How could it be otherwise? . . . Second, part of China's problem is its system of state socialism, the choking knots of which are being untied elsewhere in the world. The lessons of how to untie them may help us before long. . . . Third, we should measure our progress not just in material terms [as too many young people do] but in nonmaterial things as well—such as our freedom to think, read, and do scholarship. However angry we may be, what we can say and do now [January 1989] is much more than we could fifteen years ago. This is valuable progress we should not overlook."

A young writer of literary reportage saw hope in the fact that the current senior leadership was elderly and would soon die. "I do not mean," he explained, "that the next generation of leaders will be better, or more moral. No one can say that. What I mean is that the prestige, and hence the power, of the Communist leaders inevitably declines with each passing generation. When our current group of old men die, the next generation won't have their prestige. There is only a certain amount of power in the country. Mao Zedong, with his tremendous prestige, could have *all* of it. Deng Xiaoping had to parcel some of it out to others in order to stay stable at the center. The next generation will have to parcel even more out. If Li Peng were to try to be an autocrat in the manner of Deng, others in Li Peng's generation would look at him and say, 'You didn't create this state; why should I listen to *you?*' So, whether anyone likes it or not, China is going to have to become less autocratic."

Most expressions of optimism were not accompanied by this sort of concrete argument. Most were vague—and animated less by historical judgment than by an emotional need to cling to hope. China would "certainly get better," many said, usually adding one or more caveats: there would be setbacks along the way; progress would be difficult; it would take a long time; it would depend on a whole generation rather than just a few heroes; it might involve bloodshed. But in the long run the future would have to be bright.

What nurtures this perduring optimism of the intellectuals, as stubborn as it is vague? Although they seldom spoke directly to the point, I felt that their pride in China's rich and distinctive history infused the attitudes of even some of the most modern-minded ones. The dust in which Confucius and Mencius trod—and Qu Yuan, and the first emperor of Qin, and Liu Bang, and Zhuge Liang, and Tao Qian, and Wang Wei, and Zhu Xi, and countless other unique philosophers, poets, statesmen, courtesans, and warriors—is, whatever else happens, *this* dust which therefore is not the same as any other.

I had for a decade known a young writer and literary scholar named Su Wei. I first met him in 1980 when he was a senior at Zhongshan University, in Guangzhou, where I was doing research. I was quite taken by his infectious enthusiasm and broad-ranging interests, and later helped him come to UCLA for a master's degree. As he finished his work and prepared to return to China in 1986, he was made the object of friendly teasing by other Chinese students at UCLA. His visa status would have allowed him to apply for permanent residence in the United States, which was an opportunity that the other students intensely coveted and sometimes went to great lengths to secure. To them Su Wei seemed daft for throwing away that opportunity. But Su Wei said China was the place to be if you wanted to do something in contemporary Chinese literature, and he left for Beijing to accept a position that Liu Zaifu had offered him at the Literature Research Institute of the Chinese Academy of Social Sciences. As fate would have it, he arrived in China in January 1987, in the teeth of a crackdown on "bourgeois liberalization." The campaign put Liu Zaifu under considerable pressure, and the result for Su Wei was a postponement of work, salary, and housing for many months. He began to write me letters about "reverse culture shock," but remained determined to work in Beijing.

Su Wei comes from a large Cantonese family most of whose members live in Hong Kong, where his sister runs a thriving textile trade and lives very comfortably. On a trip to Beijing in winter 1988, the sister invited Su Wei to come see her in her room at the luxurious Shangri-la Hotel. When he showed up in his old padded coat and cloth shoes, wet from his bicycle ride through the snow, the sister began to ask about his living conditions and salary. The sister well knew why Su Wei had chosen to work in Beijing, but in the end she could not resist urging him, "Come live with us in Hong Kong. You can stay at my house. Living like this is bad for your health."

But her brother answered, "No, I'm still interested in Chinese literature. This is where I need to be. Hong Kong is too far away. I think I can do something here. I can't help very much from Hong Kong." After lunch the sister watched helplessly as he remounted his bicycle and headed back through the snow.

# Four

# IDENTITY: LANGUAGE AND IDEOLOGY

The intellectuals' sense of pride and responsibility at living inside Chinese history was based on a particular conception of knowledge and its moral power. *The Great Learning*, a seminal Confucian classic, explains that the success of ancient rulers originated in their "investigation of things," which led them successively to a "thoroughness of understanding," a "sincerity of will," and a "personal cultivation" that in turn carried the power to "regulate the family," then "properly govern the state," and finally "bring peace under heaven." This theory—which implicitly held for all human beings, not just ancient rulers—found institutional expression in imperial China's civil service examination system, which tested scholars' mastery of classic texts and literary skills as a measure of whether their cultivation warranted appointment to office. Formal language, literary education, morality, politics, and public service formed a continuum in the Confucian tradition; public office was the crowning achievement of the successful scholar.

Over the last 150 years the situation of Chinese intellectuals, physical as well as broadly cultural, has changed greatly. Traditionally a dispersed and largely rural landowning gentry guided by Confucianism, they have become a bureaucratically organized population inhabiting large urban universities and research institutes in a Marxist-Leninist state. These changes have posed strong challenges to their self-conceptions—challenges by no means resolved as the end of the twentieth century approaches. Modern Chinese intellectuals are still struggling to adjust to two traumatic uprootings: from their local communities, and from their Confucian ideology. Although most who are alive today were born after both these uprootings had taken place, the problem of adjusting their inherited culture to the new conditions is still very much their problem.

The uprooting from communities in which literati had enjoyed positions of respect and had borne responsibilities for local governance and welfare reverberates today in the desire of Chinese intellectuals for their traditional standing. They still want—so fundamentally that it usually goes without saying—a world in which they enjoy respect from the populace and have the ear of the governing authorities. Yet over the course of the twentieth century, the state's attitude toward them has turned from indifference (in the early decades) to active hostility (in the Communist period). Popular respect for learning, although still alive, has eroded as well. When modern intellectuals have tried to "serve the country" in the traditional manner, they have appeared futile and sometimes even pitiful—like "inverted tortoises flailing their legs in the air," as one put it.

The uprooting from Confucian ideology has created an even bigger problem, which affects not only the intellectuals' social relations but their sense of inner solidity and confidence. In teaching "cultivation" and "proper behavior," Confucianism had served as a compass for a person's internal bearings; with the inner life in order, proper behavior would follow. Confucianism has now lost its official status, but the cultural habit of seeking an inner guide persists in Chinese intellectuals. They seem to long for a codified, morally unassailable set of ideas by which to orient themselves and gain confidence to face the world. For a time, in the late 1940s and 1950s, Marxism-Maoism seemed to fill this need. Despite the great differences in content between Confucianism and Marxism-Maoism, they performed comparable ideological functions: both could be studied in texts, served as guides to behavior, stressed "morality," provided an avenue to public service, and connected one to the highest political authority. But after the 1950s, as intellectuals became increasingly disillusioned with Marxism-Maoism, they had no other public ideology to turn to. Their problem of finding a place in modern China was compounded by the lack of a guiding internal compass.

Chinese intellectuals do not commonly use the word *rentong* ("identity"), and when they do, it has the modern-sounding ring of a translation from Western usage. But their predicament does raise questions that Westerners would understand as matters of identity, and even identity crisis. For present purposes I use the term "identity" to mean "a sense of being the same with something larger," those larger things being (a) ideologies and (b) various groups. This use of the concept will help return the discussion to Chinese terms of discourse because, although "identity" is not familiar in Chinese, the term "alienation" has been widely used in the 1980s to describe basically the opposite idea—namely, a sense of difference between oneself and an ideology or a group.[1] We will consider ideology and the problem of identity in the present chapter; in the next we will turn to identity with groups.

## Living with the Official Language

The disillusionment of Chinese intellectuals with Marxism-Maoism went hand in hand with a growing alienation from its language. As the status of the Communist official fell further and further from that of moral exemplar, there developed an ever-larger gap between Communist ideology and life. The continuing decline in the moral prestige of the party made its official language, which continued to claim moral superiority, increasingly hypocritical. A professor of music, who in the 1940s

---

1. Here "alienation" refers not to the specifically Marxist definition of the term but to the broader sense in which it is used in the West and—informally—in China as well. (see chapter 2, note 13).

had strongly sympathized with the revolution, mused in early 1989, "A few days ago Deng Xiaoping announced that he personally had nothing to do with his son's Kanghua Company [widely accused of profiteering through personal connections]. How can he just say that and expect us to accept it? How can we feel good, feel confident, as we did forty years ago? How can the 'spirit' today compare with that of the Long March? No one believes the words any more. But Deng still expects us to believe—or at least pretends to expect us to believe."

By the late 1980s the language of Marxism-Maoism would have been wholly irrelevant if not for its continuing role, circumscribed but important, as a means of mediating political power. In this sense, Chinese Communist ideology has become, as we've already observed, a language game that forms the medium of China's official realm. The distinction between official and unofficial language has become widespread and unmistakably clear. The official language is used in exercising bureaucratic functions or holding formal meetings, as well as in newspaper and radio reports. It consists of standard phrases, slogans, and ideas that one uses not to express one's own thoughts or intentions (at least not directly) but through judicious manipulation to advance one's interests or to defend oneself. Ideological terms that still bear the face values of altruism are used as pawns in moves whose real aim is personal advantage. The instrumental meaning of official language is plain to everyone—whether one is in the senior leadership (as analysis of *People's Daily* editorials will show) or the most powerless citizen, who may be manipulating the language only to minimize his suffering in a prison or labor camp. Even if people find this reduction of language distasteful, they must resort to it in official contexts in order to cope with life—and we must remember that nearly all aspects of daily living, including work assignment, salary, housing, education, medical care, access to rationed goods, permission to travel, and even political status and therefore social respectability, are within the control of the party bureaucrats and thus bound up in the language game. Ground down by these daily necessities, any general sense of indignation at the cynical use of language has long since eroded away. Chinese society as a whole has come to accept the language game for what it is and to recognize that no individual can be blamed for playing it. But the widespread use of official language, coupled with the continuing assumption that it *ought* to relate to a vital ideology even though it does not, raises important problems of Chinese "identity."

The principles that underlie the language game are basically the same for all who play it.[2] But the texture and tactics of the game can be best appreciated if we look first at how the regime plays its side and then at some of the ways in which ordinary citizens respond. From the regime's point of view, one of the most useful features of the game is its vagueness. In 1987, for example, the party mounted a society-wide campaign against "bourgeois liberalization," and millions of Chinese suddenly had to ask themselves, "What exactly is it?" Wearing bell-bottom trousers? Reading foreign novels? Having a boyfriend before the age of twenty-one? Having long hair? (How long?) Wanting to eat a bit better? Conceived broadly, such a vague offense could apply to anyone. Enforcement was equally vague: In what circumstances are charges brought? What is the punishment for one judged guilty? Why is one person found guilty while others who have done the same thing, or worse, are not? It is well known that who one is, whom one knows, where one works, and so on are crucial in determining answers to these questions; and it is equally well known that from time to time the leadership singles out "negative examples" for especially heavy punishments in order to warn others. One effect of this overall

2. A full study of the official language game in China would necessarily be complex, nuanced, and lengthy and would have to account for the viewpoints of both regime and populace, as well as historical development over several decades. No such study exists in any language, although Michael Schoenhals has opened the field, at least on the topic of the regime's manipulation of language. See "Selections from *Propaganda Trends*, Organ of the CCP Central Propaganda Department," a special issue of *Chinese Law and Government: A Journal of Translations* 24, no. 4 (winter 1991–92), guest editor Michael Schoenhals. For an analysis of the use of official language in literary censorship, see Perry Link, "On the Mechanics of the Control of Literature in China," in *Stubborn Weeds: Popular and Controversial Chinese Literature after the Cultural Revolution* (Bloomington: Indiana University Press, 1983), pp. 1–28.

vagueness in the definition of misbehavior and in the punishments for it is to induce a powerful self-censorship. If most Chinese can't know where the border lies between safety and punishment, at least they know that the farther they are from it, the safer they will be.

A related technique, which has been used by the party for decades, is to state that only "a tiny minority" (or handful, or clique) of people are the troublemakers. With such language the regime implies that it represents the majority—ironically a claim that it makes all the more fervently as its popularity diminishes. The government's use of the term *renmin* ("the people") to label its various organs and functions—the people's bank, the people's post office, the people's airline, the people's currency, the *People's Daily,* the People's Republic, and many others—also reinforces the notion that the regime is in the mainstream and that anyone who feels otherwise is, automatically, both wrong and in the minority. As it operates on individuals, the "tiny minority" message is a dual one. It not only carries a threat against deviation but offers comfort as a reward for docility: those who are obedient can join the "mainstream." The effect is to strengthen the impulse toward self-censorship. People are made to feel that if they join the majority in denouncing "bourgeois liberalism" (or whatever the error of the moment may be), they can sink into an anonymity that, however boring, at least will be safe.

In the crackdown after the June 4, 1989, massacre, the regime's "linguistic engineering" became more forcible and less subtle. The official press warned, for example, against "love-capitalism disease," a term that combined a surface vagueness with a devastatingly negative connotation. For the ordinary citizen the surface meaning of "love-capitalism disease" was, like that of "bourgeois liberalism," impossible to pin down and thus frighteningly expandable. Did the scope of the term include the "one-person enterprises" found in countless trades in the free markets of the cities? Did it include a student's wishes to study in a capitalist country? Or—as some dared to hope—did it also include the massive corruption that had appeared in China's officially connected new companies? There were no answers to such questions, and the party meant it so. But there was an answer, an extremely powerful one, to the question of whether "love-capitalism disease" should be avoided. Apart from its negative political connotations, the term in Chinese, *aizibing*, was a homonym of the word for AIDS. No citizen could miss the cruel associations of "catching the disease." A similar method was used in 1983 during the "campaign against spiritual pollution," when politically threatening Western ideas were defined vaguely as "pollution" and then concretely exemplified by cases of pornography. In this technique the two components of meaning—vague denotation and strong negative connotation—combine in powerful fashion. One element tells the citizen that the referent of a term, whatever it is, must be avoided at all costs, and the other tells her that, to be on the safe side, she should interpret the scope of the term as broadly as possible.

By disguising broad political controls in the garb of relatively unquestioned evils like pollution and pornography, the regime also makes it harder for others—who are obliged to play the language game in terms of the surface meanings of words—to argue back. Who could possible argue in *favor* of "AIDS," even if it is a pun? However unsubtle the language game may become during times of stress in China, the regime does not abandon the game's basic rule: that the surface meanings of words should make sense at a level of pretense whereas actual meanings lie deeper. So in the days following the June 4 massacre, people were required to pretend that "rioters" had taken over at Tiananmen; to pretend that the government had had no choice but to use force; to pretend that more soldiers than citizens had died; and to pretend that no pretending was going on.

Even when it becomes desperate, the regime does not want to admit to itself or to others that it is forcing its view on people, since this would be to admit failure in two ways: it would allow that "the people" began without a natural consensus and that the regime must resort to coercion to change the situation. The Chinese regime is not unique in facing these quandaries—the exercise of political power in other Marxist-Leninist systems has also relied on fictions and official language games.[3] But in China, with its heritage of Confucian assumptions that the official language should have moral power and that this power should attract the people's emulation rather than force their obedience, to admit that life is not proceeding in this way is especially costly to a ruler's "face" and, therefore, power.

The leadership's need to maintain face and prestige also explains its tendency to use red herring issues in attacking its critics. By distracting attention from the real point, the regime avoids embarrassment over it. In 1979, when Wei Jingsheng was sentenced to fifteen years in prison for advocating democracy too strongly and too publicly, the official charge against him was that he "divulged military secrets"—which turned out to mean he had repeated a flimsy rumor about China's border war with Vietnam to a foreigner. Wei Jingsheng's trial was conducted in euphemisms; but there was no confusion, among either officials or the populace, about what the real issue was. Similarly, in 1983, the leadership launched the national campaign against "spiritual pollution" (meaning Western cultural influences) with a call to "wipe out pornography."

These are obvious examples, but the technique has long been used in subtler ways, such as in the criticism of literature. In 1979 a play called *What If I Really Were?* attracted great popular attention in China.[4] It presents a young man who is turned away from the door of a theater because the performance is "sold out." Noting that late-arriving officials are still permitted to enter, the young man decides to pass himself off as the son of a high official and try again. His clever impersonation deceives the theater manager, and he gets a ticket. But word of the arrival in town of this "high official's son" spreads quickly, and other

3. See Czeslaw Milosz, *The Captive Mind*, trans. Jane Zielonko (New York: Octagon Books, 1981), chap. 3, especially pp. 55–56 and 79; Václav Havel, "The Power of the Powerless," trans. P. Wilson, in *Václav Havel; or, Living in Truth*, ed. Jan Vladislav (London: Faber and Faber, 1987), pp. 95–99 and passim; and Vladimir Shlapentokh, *Soviet Intellectuals and Political Power: The Post-Stalin Era* (Princeton: Princeton University Press, 1990), pp. 80–91

4. *Jiaru wo shi zhende*, by Sha Yexin, Li Shoucheng, and Yao Mingde, translated by Edward M. Gunn in Link, ed., *Stubborn Weeds*, pp. 200–250.

fawning officials, all the way to the municipal party secretary, shower him with gifts and favors, together with their own requests for illicit assistance in return. Sucked against his will into a whirlpool of corruption—whose lively description fills most of the play and sparked its tremendous popularity—the young man is eventually discovered and brought to trial.

In early 1980 the Deng Xiaoping government criticized the play. It had obviously gone too far in exposing corruption. But to criticize the playwrights for too much truthfulness would not do, and to charge them with exaggeration would be unappealing to the broad populace and would only further undermine the regime's position. The official criticism finally charged that the young protagonist "had used a bourgeois method in order to handle a problem in socialist society."[5] On the strength of this judgment the play was banned. The pronouncement was a brilliant move, from the regime's point of view. It was formally correct—indeed, irrefutable—on the narrow issue it raised, and thus allowed the regime to maintain the upper hand morally while sidestepping the main issue. Most readers saw through this tactic, but that did not change the regime's success in the formal terms of the official language game.

The ways in which the Chinese people respond to the official language game are as complex and varied as the regime's arsenal of methods. Some of China's more daring intellectuals have actually adapted the game to the purposes of resistance. In early 1989, for instance, when the Chinese regime suddenly announced that mainland intellectuals could apply to visit Taiwan, they apparently were "playing a card" in a delicate game of words and face with the Taiwan authorities. Pretending to take the official announcement literally, Fang Lizhi applied to visit Taiwan. Both Fang and the regime well knew that they were playing a symbolic game. The regime would never let Fang actually

5. See Chen Yong, "Cong liangge juben kan wenyi de zhenshixing he qingxiang-xing" (Realism and political trends in literature as seen in two plays), *People's Daily*, March 19, 1980, p. 5; and Li Geng, "Dui juben 'jiaru wo shi zhen de' de yijian" (My opinions of "What If I Really Were?"), *Renmin xiju* (People's drama), no. 3 (1980): 7–11.

go, and Fang knew this; moreover, the regime must have known that he knew it. What was the point, then, of Fang's entering into the game in the first place? It was precisely to expose the hypocrisy of official language, and thereby to challenge the power that depends upon the pretense that the language is not hypocritical.

In spring 1989, students at Tiananmen were doing a similar thing when they held up banners quoting the Chinese constitution on the right of free speech. They knew that as Chinese citizens they did not enjoy this right; and they certainly did not imagine that they would gain it simply by holding up signs. Their point was not to claim a right but to expose a lie. By picking such a key example, they were challenging the language game at its fundaments. The strange vulnerability of official power to seemingly quixotic appeals to law, even if the law is empty, has been noticed by critics of other Marxist-Leninist regimes. In 1978 Václav Havel wrote of the Czech system, "Because the system . . . is hopelessly tied down by the necessity of pretending the laws are observed, it is compelled to react in some way to such appeals. Demanding that the laws be upheld is thus an act of living within the truth that threatens the whole mendacious structure at its point of maximum mendacity."[6] Those who play the official language game in reverse do so to invert the meaning of official terms and to create two opposed senses— the inverted sense that expresses what they want to say, and the original face value of the term, which by remaining in place acts as a shield from criticism. For example, during the final, grim days of the Tiananmen uprising, the students were fond of singing China's national anthem, which begins,

> Rise up, you who would not be slaves,
> Let us build our flesh and blood into a new great wall.
> The Chinese people have reached their most dangerous hour;
> The very last scream has been forced from each of us.
> Rise up! Rise up! Rise up! . . .

6. Havel, "The Power of the Powerless," p. 98.

Seditious? Quite. Representatives of the regime could not possibly have been unaware of the students' intended meaning. It was too obvious.[7] Why didn't the leadership stop them? First because the song was, after all, the national anthem. To ban it would require a very fancy navigation of the official language game. But more profoundly, the regime left the students alone because the subversive level of their meaning was, in the last analysis, less important than the preservation of the fiction—even though everyone knew it was a fiction—that they were supporting the People's Republic and, thus, the Communist party.

Following the massacre, however, the regime's tolerance of such blatant irony from students reached a limit. In July 1989, students at Beijing University, showing remarkable courage, met by candlelight to sing "Without the Communist Party, There Would Be No New China." This song, which had in the 1950s been a genuinely popular expression of credit to the party for saving China, had in 1989 come to mean the opposite: without the Communist party, there would be no (such disaster as) "new China." This time the party issued an order forbidding the students from singing the song again. In Guangzhou, during the crackdown after June 4, Deng Xiaoping's lengthy report on the "necessary military action" was read aloud at a required meeting of all staff at a large publishing house. After the reading, the party secretary rose to initiate the required "discussion." "Well," he asked the assemblage, "what do you think of Chairman Deng's report? Was it good?" For a long time there was dead silence. Finally a single voice called out, "Good!" *(hao!)*, then repeated the word several times, extending it into an anguished *h-h-h-a-a-a-o-o-o!* so that no one could mistake its ironic intent. In this case the irony went unremarked, and the party secretary simply declared the discussion over. This may have been an instance in which the party secretary himself was as disgusted with the

7. Up close, anyway. From across the Pacific, some commentators interviewed in the American media during the Tiananmen events cited the singing of China's national anthem—and of the "Internationale," another song popular with the students because of its two-leveled possibilities—as evidence that the students were still committed socialists. Commentary such as this, when it filters back to China, reinforces Chinese stereotypes of American naïveté.

official language as were others and, as the Chinese saying goes, "opened one eye and closed the other."

In early 1991 one of the "model revolutionary operas" from the Cultural Revolution, *The Red Lantern,* was revived on the Beijing stage. One might expect this ultraleftist handiwork of Jiang Qing and the Gang of Four to have drawn only derision from the Beijing populace. But performances quickly sold out. Part of the attraction may have been a purely aesthetic nostalgia for the famous arias, which the Beijing youth of twenty years earlier had memorized virtually to a person, and still occasionally sang with ironic pleasure at parties. But a more immediate cause for the enjoyment of the opera in 1991 was evident in the patterns of the audience's applause. When an actress read the lines "In 1923, railroad workers organized a general trade union," the audience applauded. When she continued by saying, "All the workers went on strike . . . tens of thousands marched in demonstration . . . ," the audience broke into wild cheering. When a grandmother sang the line "a debt of blood musts be paid in blood," the audience hooted again, as it did when another character sang, "What a dreadful thing is the Communist party!" None of these lines had drawn applause twenty years earlier; the "inappropriate" cheering was censored when a videotape of the 1991 performance was prepared for television broadcast.[8]

In a story published in 1990, the young writer Wang Shuo, who has a reputation as the "hooligan" voice of supercynical youth, imagines the citizens of a back alley in Beijing kneeling down before a great leader and thanking him for deigning to visit them. Wang strings together official clichés (and a peppering of unofficial expletives) to achieve an absurdist effect: "Beloved, wise, dear teacher leader helmsman guide pioneer developer architect beacon torch dog-cudgel father mother grandpa grandma old ancestor old ape overlord sovereign Great Jade Emperor *Guan Yin* bodhisattva commander-in-chief: occupied as you are with a myriad of state affairs, burdened with ten

8. Ya Lan, "Cong yan 'Hongdengji' chuxian qiyi xiaoguo" (Strange effects as "The Red Lantern" returns to stage), *The Nineties* (Hong Kong), April 1991, pp. 96–97.

thousand hardships, struggling to change old patterns, straining under a constant overload of work, addicted to your own habits, shouldering heavy burdens, speeding across the sky like a heavenly steed soaring aloft, supporting the weak and aiding the poor, upholding righteousness, destroying vice and dispelling evil, driving off rheumatism and frailty, strengthening the *yang* [male] element, feeding kidney and brain, nourishing the liver, settling the stomach, stopping pain, suppressing cough, moving bowels—ever so busy and yet: you your very person very self very presence arriving presence descending presence luminous presence have come to inspect, observe, regulate, examine, patrol, investigate, espy, probe, visit, interrogate, and console our humble alley. You bring to our alley immense concern, immense inspiration, immense arousal, immence comfort, immense confidence, immense consideration, immense glory, and immense favor. We little people, rustic people, common people, lowly people, children, grandchildren, little sprouts, little dogs, little cats, vulgar herd, ignorant masses, broad masses, and ordinary folk feel entirely blessed, entirely excited, entirely unworthy . . . (and so on) . . ."[9] It may seem strange that sarcasm as blatant as this could be published after the 1989 crackdown. Superficially it could have passed official muster as an attack on the Gang of Four, still a legitimate target after fourteen years. But the absurdist flavor of Wang Shuo's language is much more typical of the late 1980s than of the late 1970s, when "smashing the Gang of Four" was in vogue. Moreover, there are signs that clearly place Wang Shuo's luminous leader within the Deng Xiaoping era. He is credited with "bringing order out of chaos" (*boluan fanzheng*), which was the Deng regime's own description of its reversal of Cultural Revolution policies. He is also credited as a "single-handed smasher," where "smashing" (*fensui*) is the verb for what was done to the Gang of Four. No editor contemplating the publication of a Wang Shuo story could have overlooked these implications. But many editors could have winked at them.

9. Wang Shuo,"Qianwan bie ba wo dang ren" (Whatever you do, don't view me as human), in *Zhongshan* (Bell mountain) (Nanjing), no. 6 (December 1989): 41.

These various examples of ironic deflection and counterattack do not, however, describe the most typical patterns of popular response to the official language. Those who invert its meanings as a form of protest are comparatively few. The majority are more timid and self-protective; they assume a passive stance in the hope that anonymity will assure them that the blow, if it falls, will not fall on them. (Most people in the Communist bloc nations of Eastern Europe behaved similarly until 1989, and so, I believe, would the majority of any national group under similar conditions. Mass conformity in a repressive system is not a "flaw in Chinese character," as some Chinese intellectuals fear.)

For ordinary people, the first rule about official language is to use it only when you must and to avoid it otherwise. A senior historian who had returned from a visit to the countryside commented on political slogans he had seen pasted prominently on walls in a village. One said, "Without the People's Army, the People Have Nothing"; another said, "To Carry Out the Population Policy Is Glorious; to Violate the Population Policy Is Shameful." The historian commented, "People seldom read the slogans. The local officials who put them up don't expect others to read them. They just go through the motions, and then their job is done. That's what everyone expects." Just as intellectuals study *People's Daily* "upside down" for signs of the leadership's "wind direction," when common folk take notice of a slogan painted on a wall, according to this historian, it is not to take its message to heart so much as to discern what the leadership wants. "If there is any mention of those slogans again," he continued, "it would be, for example, for use by the local officials in blaming someone for an unauthorized pregnancy—one that fell outside the quotas handed down from above." For the ordinary citizen the question of whether or not it really is "shameful" to have another child does not arise; the point of knowing the slogans is to know whether one's next pregnancy, if it comes, should be hidden from officials.

In situations that require direct use of the official language, most people approach it cautiously and instrumentally: how can

I get what I need, and then be gone? I frequently observed this attitude in the course of my work arranging "official" scholarly exchange in China. One group of rural county officials, for example, were hosting some Americans on the CSCPRC scholarly exchange program, for which I was working. As part of their compensation, the officials wanted my assistance in purchasing an American Jeep. In order to get a loan from Chinese banking authorities, they needed a formal statement from my office that the Jeep would be for use by the American scholars in the rural county. When I pointed out that this was not strictly true, they explained that the statement was only a "formality," and made it clear that it would be quite unfriendly of me not to write the statement. So I did. Then a few weeks later, with their loan secured, the same county officials came back asking for another formal statement, this one certifying that the Jeep *would not* be used by Americans. If the Jeep were for Americans, they explained, regulations required that it be bought in foreign exchange currency rather than Chinese currency. I decided to call the Bank of China to point out the directly contradictory regulations and to ask for guidance. This decision perplexed the rural officials. "Why do *that?*" they asked indignantly. "Just write another statement. It doesn't matter." To them, contradictory statements were a mere nuisance that should not impede the task of acquiring a Jeep. They said—correctly, I have no doubt—that theirs was "the Chinese way" of viewing such things.[10]

But the tasks that minor officials such as these must perform in matching their words to the requirements of higher-ups represent only half of their overall problem with the official language. The other half comes in mediating the official language with the people below them. This role involves a constant dilemma: the small official has to say something, yet lacks the

---

10. The county officials did eventually obtain their Jeep. Before I got around either to calling the Bank of China or to writing a statement that I could live with, they made a separate appeal to my Chinese office assistant, who, acting on the principle that I was a generally well-intentioned person who of course would want to help, wrote a statement for me and affixed the official CSCPRC chop to it.

authority to give specific directives. The only clear guideline is to avoid "mistakes." Those who survive in the system become expert at guarding "personal histories" that are "pure" (*qingbai*). Mastery of the verbal gymnastics necessary in handling questions from below while never transgressing a twisting, turning—sometimes lurching—political line from above becomes for many the work of a lifetime. Here we can consider only a few basic principles. One is that, in response to any request or proposal from below, "no" is a safer answer than "yes" if there is any doubt. So long as nothing happens, it is hard to be accused of doing something wrong; errors of omission are less dangerous, and less attributable, than errors of commission. (In cases where a "yes" answer is clearly available, the small official does best not to say "yes" on his or her own authority but to quote from a policy and let the listener take responsibility for inferring the application.)

Answers of "yes," "no," or "maybe" are usually delivered in standard codes that leave a margin of ambiguity through which the official can escape if the answer turns out to be wrong. "Yes," for example, can be expressed as *wenti buda* ("no big problem"). This phrase is enough of a "yes" to make a petitioner temporarily go away; there is no point pushing for a more positive response until authoritative word can come down from a higher level. But if that word eventually is "no," *wenti buda* did not entrap the small official; his or her "history" can still be "pure." Similarly a "no" answer will often be "not too convenient" (*butai fangbian*) or "there are some difficulties" (*you xie kunnan*). These phrases not only protect the small official from the descent of a "yes" from above but soften the problem of face in having to say "no" to a person who will continue to live in one's environment. The most famous of the standard answers are the "maybes": *yanjiu yanjiu* ("we'll study the matter") or *kaolü kaolü* ("we'll think it over"). These normally mean that the small official will refer the matter to higher-ups. Difficult requests, whose adjudication in either direction is risky, are sent to successively higher levels until someone feels confident enough to decide, or until the request gets lost. (This is one important reason why the slowness of Chinese bureaucracy generates so many popular complaints; requests referred to higher levels converge on the desks of people who are simply too busy to attend to them one by one.) To the ordinary citizen, an answer of *yanjiu yanjiu* or *kaolü kaolü* also means "you will have to come back and press the matter again at a later time." Without such pressure, the phrases amount to a "no."

As we noted above, ordinary citizens generally avoid the official language when they can, especially when it raises politically sensitive topics. In recent years, however, there has been evidence of widespread observance of a moral dictate to protect others when possible. This impulse of mutual protection has been especially strong since the crackdown after June 4, 1989. When people are called to account for having said something politically "incorrect," a common defense is to say one "heard it somewhere." But this invites the demand to know from whom it was heard, and it is a well-established principle of the control system that a person can win reprieve by implicating others. In recent years it has become a standing joke that "incorrect" thoughts always seem to be overheard in public toilets, and always by a person of the opposite sex. After all, if one is squatting in the men's toilet and hears something over the wall from the women's side, one can hardly be expected to describe the offending source further. A student from Zhongshan University, in Guangzhou, told me that once he and a group of friends— ten in all—had been apprehended for saying something improper, and all had been interrogated, separately, as to where they had heard it. Fully six of the ten used the standard answer of the public toilet. The confluence of their fibs lent their story a credibility that was both undeserved and unintended.[11]

---

11. Another joke, which I take as an apocryphal story but a bona fide joke, tells of a dialogue between an interrogator (I) and a citizen (C):

I: What did the person look like?

C: Don't know.

I: How can you not know? What clothes was he wearing?

C: No clothes.

I: Hunh?

C: We were in a public bath. [*continued*]

Beyond the temptation to protect oneself by implicating others, the most damaging consequence of the majority's passive acceptance of the official language is that its ways can seep into ordinary life and affect personal relations of many kinds.

A well-known contemporary writer had this to say: "The official language leaves ordinary people no choice but to speak falsely. Situations that require its use are common enough that lying gradually becomes 'acceptable.' When that happens, people begin to use it in ordinary situations, even when they would not have to. This transference of lying to the government into the daily life sphere of lying to one another is strengthened by the fact that no one really knows where to draw the line between 'them' and 'us.' People in one's own work unit and neighborhood might be informers. During the Cultural Revolution children were encouraged to report on their own parents. Any person can choose to become an informer for a day if he has a grievance against you. You can never be sure whom to suspect and therefore never know whom to trust, either. The result is that you suspect and fear almost everyone. Then, to protect yourself, you might increase your use of the official language, or at least remain icily withdrawn in public. But when everyone does that, the appearance that 'they' are everywhere gains strength. People forget that others are caught in the same trap; they don't realize that 'I' am in 'them' and 'they' are in 'me.' The whole environment seems hostile, and insincere manipulation of language seems the safest response to it."

I asked this writer what he thought of the sharply ironic use of language by university students. "The students invert the meaning of official language so clearly that the result is, actually, one of the more pellucid uses of language anywhere. When the students are ironic they mean *exactly* the opposite of what they say, and what they express are their sincere views on what is best for all of China. Where else does the official language stand

I: I see. Well then, how tall was he?
C: Don't know. . . . We were sitting down in the water.
I: What did his face look like?
C: Hard to say. There was steam rising from the water.

in such a clear relationship to anyone's ideals? Normally the official language, whether used by officials or common people, is simply a means to an end—how to get something, control someone, or defend oneself. It would be strange to ask what ideals it expresses." A young man who had returned from several years as a student in Canada said, regarding his stay overseas, "I tried, for a time, to speak only English, even with Chinese people, in order to try to get entirely free from habits that seemed built into Chinese: always analyzing who a person is, what I can get from him, how to play a role, what words to speak, flattering the powerful, backbiting, and so on. But I had to give it up. People thought that by refusing to use Chinese I was 'worshiping the West' and looking down on China. That was not my point."

For Chinese intellectuals, with their well-rooted cultural assumptions of the unity of language, morality, and public service, such radical and complicated alienation from official language amounts to a fairly profound "identity" problem. If Marxism-Maoism has become so debilitated, where do we now turn? What is our ideology? Or do we need one? If not, what will hold China together? And who do we, who are in the habit of defining ourselves with reference to a morally confident ideology, say we are? What can we point to, other than our past, that makes us proud to be Chinese? It is not easy for Chinese intellectuals to discuss these questions—partly from fear of repression, but also, I believe, because such discussion entails the acknowledgment that they have lost much of their inner confidence and self-respect. As a result, these important questions have become some of the most private and poorly articulated of their worries.

## The Search for an Ideology

On the few occasions when friends dared to share their more private worries on the matter of ideology, I was surprised at how *personal* these worries seemed to be. I had assumed that the question of embracing an ideology would fall into the impersonal category of "affairs of the nation." But a young historian told me, "I need something to hold on to, a 'point of purchase' (*zhichidian*); I think many of us feel this way; it may be the special weakness of Chinese intellectuals, but we need this." A young writer said, "It doesn't need to be a whole ideology—just something to believe in. In the past we could believe in moral perfection, in imitating [the model hero] Lei Feng; or we could try to be 'both Red and expert,'[12] or aim to join the party. But now even these smaller ideals are gone; we have no ideal to give us direction."

A middle-aged poet, speaking in fall 1988 when political pressure on Chinese intellectuals was unusually low, said, "The problem isn't *them* any more; we can say just about what we like these days. The problem is bigger and scarier than that. It's the emptiness inside. We peer inside, where there should be something solid, something that is 'us'—and there's nothing there. This is frightening, and people don't want to keep looking. So they turn where everyone else does—toward money. Even the intellectuals have lost all values except for money. Even the good ones, the ones who still cling to some ideals, are on the general downward curve. People's internal characters have changed—that's our most frightening problem."

There was discussion of alternatives to China's ruling ideology, including foreign ideologies that might be adapted to Chinese conditions, and various eclectic combinations. But except for the brief period of the democracy movement in spring 1989, all such discussion, however exciting, remained highly theoretical, since it was punishable to make any public suggestion of departing from Marxism.

A measured renewal of interest in Confucianism was fed by the writing of scholars such as Li Zehou, Tang Yijie, and Pang Pu, as well as by the overseas Chinese scholars Yu Ying-shih, Tu Wei-ming, and Lin Yü-sheng.[13] Recalling the moral quali-

---

12. That is, both devoted to the Communist party and proficient in some technical skill. The phrase was widely used during the Cultural Revolution.

13. The major influence of these overseas scholars is remarkable, given that none

ties of the Confucian scholar-official seemed to be a way to fill the inner emptiness that many Chinese intellectuals felt. Moreover, the economic successes of Japan, South Korea, Taiwan, and Singapore suggested that some aspects of Confucianism were advantageous in modern society: benevolent authoritarianism, a high value on education, loyalty to one's group, a nonconfrontational approach to conflict resolution, and so on. But the interest in Confucianism was always selective; no one, in my experience, advocated a comprehensive return to Confucianism.

I heard one young poet argue that China should return to a figurehead emperor who could serve as a unifying symbol for the nation. The poet had been reading the early-twentieth-century reformer Liang Qichao,[14] and felt that Liang's idea of a constitutional monarchy might be just right for China. "China has to have a symbolic center," he said, "and as a nation we're still feudal minded enough that the symbol really has to be a person. So perhaps we need a monarch, but beneath the monarch we could set up a modern constitution that would guarantee basic rights and eventually lead toward democracy. The monarch could be like the queen of England." But another young writer objected to this idea, even as she acknowledged its logic. "No formula that goes back to the beginning of the century can ever become the state ideology," she said. "The sense of retrogression, of 'turning the wheels of history backward' would

of them has lived in mainland China since the 1940s and that they have traveled there only briefly since then. In the late 1980s Yu Ying-shih's book *Shi yu Zhongguo wenhua* (The scholar and Chinese culture) (Shanghai: Shanghai People's Publishing House, 1987) was almost a handbook on how the integrity of the traditional scholar could be relevant in China's modern situation. Many were attracted to Tu Wei-ming's idea that the contemporary period could become the "third period of development of Confucianism" (the first being original Confucianism in the third to fifth centuries B.C. and the second being the "Neo-Confucianism" of the ninth to twelfth centuries A.D.). Lin Yü-sheng was known through the Chinese translation of his book *The Crisis of Chinese Consciousness: Radical Antitraditionalism in the May Fourth Era* (Madison: University of Wisconsin Press, 1979).

14. Liang Qichao (1873–1929), thinker, writer, and editor, was China's most prolific and influential "reformist" intellectual during the last fifteen years of the Qing empire (1896–1911). See Hao Chang, *Liang Ch'i-ch'ao and Intellectual Transition in China, 1890–1907* (Cambridge: Harvard University Press, 1971).

be just too strong. And there is a more practical problem: where, in today's China, would we find the monarch—a person who could be universally accepted as an appropriate symbol?" Others considered the young poet's idea too close to the "New Authoritarianism" then being pushed by the Zhao Ziyang faction of the Chinese leadership. This theory, which promised that China could be saved by an autocratic modernizer, created much apprehension among China's intellectuals.[15]

The idea of moving directly to democracy has been under lively consideration by Chinese students, as the world learned in the spring of 1989. But the conceptions of "democracy" that informed the student movement were fairly superficial. As the students seemed to understand it, the term essentially meant liberation—a thoroughgoing exercise of *fang* ("relaxation" of state controls). Some students advocated more nuanced ideas, to be sure, but the shared ideology of the movement was not much more complex than the notion "get off our backs." Simple as it was, this powerful wish infused immediate life into ideas such as "freedom of speech, assembly, and the press" and to phrases such as "pursuit of happiness." But the goal of liberation did not lead very far into democratic theory or practice, about which most students had only an idealized understanding. Seldom did they show any awareness of the agreed-upon limits binding the actors in a democracy: that a minority must yield to a majority vote and that the majority, after winning, must respect the rights of the minority; or that democratic governments operate on the basis of a separation of powers with each branch checking the others to assure that no single branch can control everything. One student marcher, upon learning that I was American, said that George Washington was truly a remarkable man, a moral exemplar. "He could have been king," the young man said. "But he chose to step down for someone else. He set an example that others have followed ever since. That's really great."

Beneath the democratic veneer of the student protest move-

---

15. See below, pp. 283–90, for more on New Authoritarianism.

ment, the abiding political assumptions were much more Chinese than Western. [16] For example, the strongest issue animating the democracy movement—as measured both by breadth and intensity of popular support—was undoubtedly the criticism of official corruption. Banners read, "Official Profiteering [guandao] is Treason," and "Liberate [the high officials' resort at] Beidaihe." Hundreds of bitter jokes circulated about the details of profiteering in the reform economy by the families of high officials. This kind of criticism is continuous with a strong Chinese popular tradition of recent centuries. The eighteenth-century novel The Scholars (Rulin waishi) satirizes imperial scholar-officials for embezzlement, profligacy, and other violations of the moral trust entailed in their official roles. In the early twentieth century there appeared a spate of "castigatory novels" as the moribund Qing government collapsed and early attempts to establish a republic foundered in warlordism. And in the late 1970s the post-Mao "scar literature" owed much of its feverish popularity to the exposure of official wrongdoing during the Cultural Revolution.

The Chinese tradition that officials should be morally impeccable, and that they deserve sharp popular criticism if they betray their trust, had much more to do with the democracy movement of 1989 than did Western democratic theory. In marching down to Tiananmen Square, Beijing students were not only expressing popular dissatisfaction with officials but also implicitly offering themselves as a reminder of a better moral alternative. The Beijing populace in general viewed the students in fairly traditional terms: they were the cream of China's young scholars, acting out of sincere concern for the condition of their country. Westerners may have found the student demand for "dialogue" with the state authorities somewhat strange; student protests in the West normally proclaim more concrete demands, such as "U.S. out of Vietnam" or "Divest from South Africa now." But for the Chinese students, and the urban citizenry

16. In saying that the underlying assumptions were not "Western," I mean to include Marxism and Leninism. The claims of some Western observers that Marxist ideals underlay the activities and slogans of the Chinese student movement are not correct.

that supported them, the issue of dialogue had great symbolic significance. Would the state authorities formally recognize these students, these "sprouts of scholarship" with a "responsibility" to advise the leaders? Or would they reject the protesters, as the ruler of Chu had rejected the heroic poet Qu Yuan in the third and fourth centuries B.C.? To reject the students would put the regime in a bad light by traditional standards; but to sit down with non-state-appointed student leaders would be to break the Communist state's monopoly on legitimate organization. The difficulty of this dilemma reflected the shrewdness of the students' demand.

The drama at Tiananmen Square was highly charged symbolically. Indeed, the symbolic roles that the students were playing, and that all Chinese parties to the drama were playing, lay at the heart of the matter from a Chinese point of view. When the students chose to send representatives to kneel on the steps of the Great Hall of the People, entreating a hearing from the prime minister, they were enacting a powerful drama whose intended audience was the Beijing populace as much as the prime minister himself.[17] Li Peng's decision to spurn that entreaty also was a clear symbolic statement that surely raised his standing among hard-line leaders even as it lowered his prestige among the Beijing populace. From mid-April to early June of 1989, Tiananmen Square—the symbolic center of China's polity—could be viewed without too much exaggeration as a huge Chinese opera stage. Simply to enter the square was to make a statement, and important groups announced their arrival by holding up banners declaring their work units: the physics department at Qinghua University, the office staff of the Cen-

17. Some Western observers have held that the 1989 protests at Tiananmen were being played out primarily for observation by the Western press. Although student leaders were certainly aware of the Western press, were thankful for it, and cooperated with it, to imagine that the events at Tiananmen would have been significantly different in the absence of world attention is a misunderstanding that reflects the self-importance of the West while it underestimates the self-obsession of the Chinese. The Western press did, however, make an important difference in spreading the news of the Beijing movement by radio to other Chinese cities, where sympathetic movements quickly arose.

tral Party School, the workers of Capital Iron and Steel, and so on. As one group after another arrived, the Beijing populace spoke of who "had come out" (chulai le), with the phrase "come out" carrying a dual significance: first, literally coming out, on the streets, under a banner; and second, "coming out" with one's view, letting it be known where one stood.

While most of the students and supporting populace were fully absorbed in this drama, democracy remained an idealized, almost millenarian vision, too distant for careful examination and too clearly an ideal to call for such examination in any case. To be sure, leading scholars such as the political scientist Yan Jiaqi[18] were well versed in democratic theory and also quite aware of the distance between it and the popular ideas of their countrymen. One of the questions that worried these scholars most was how to introduce democracy into China, assuming that one could define an appropriately Chinese version of it and build a consensus favoring the transition. Fang Lizhi's view that the first step would be a recognition of basic human rights, followed by a gradual movement toward a full democratic system, seemed too slow to some, especially among the young, who felt that no real political change would come until there was some kind of electoral competition. But the idea of elections in Chinese villages often elicited skepticism. "The villagers don't read," said a journalist. "And they don't have anything worth reading anyway. They would vote for their own clan. How can elections be the first step?" Others, however, such as Liu Binyan, have consistently held that intellectuals underestimate peasants. "In my experience Chinese peasants are pretty good at understanding their interests and making choices," Liu has said. "I'm not sure elections would not work."

One day, in the course of my work in China, I found myself with nothing to do for an hour in a small Chinese village. I was squatting next to a mud wall in the company of a thirty-five-year-old farmer with whom I had a limited acquaintance. I decided, as an experiment, to ask him what he thought of

18. See David Bachman and Yang Dali, trans. and eds., Yan Jiaqi and China's Struggle for Democracy (Armonk, N.Y.: M. E. Sharpe, 1991).

democracy, and to do so in writing, since I could barely understand the local dialect. The following is a translation of our
written conversation:

Link:    What do you think of democracy?

Zhang: It's good. Very good.

Link:    What is it?

Zhang: When you choose a village leader, you can freely
decide by yourself on an able man.

Link:    And above the village level?

Zhang: The village level chooses the next-highest level. It's
democratic centralism. We go from centralism to
democracy.

Link:    What is centralism?

Zhang: Centralism means a few people are named.

Link:    By whom?

Zhang: By a few other people.

Link:    Whom would you vote for at the highest level?

Zhang: I have never thought about that. They never ask us
peasants about it.

Link:    But whom do you *like* at the highest levels? Deng
Xiaoping? Li Peng?

Zhang: I don't know. I'm not acquainted with any of them.

Link:    Whom would you vote for in your village?

Zhang: Someone named Zhang.

The last statement is not as narrow-minded as it may seem. We
were in a single-surname village, where nearly everyone was
named Zhang. Later I shared my transcript with a number of
intellectuals in Beijing. "I like Zhang's peasant honesty," commented a historian, reflecting an affectionate condescension
toward peasants that I often found among intellectuals. "He
says 'I'm not acquainted' with the top leaders, so would not
know how to vote. His comment has *glasnost*." The historian
then went on to point out the obvious difficulties of importing
democracy to Zhang's village. "How can there be an election,
if he has no opinions on the highest leaders and would vote for
his own clan in the village?" But the man's college-age son,
who was present, demurred. "The peasant's definition of

democracy isn't bad: 'You can freely decide by yourself on an able man.' He might do pretty well with that idea, if given a chance."

The questions of what kind of democracy might suit China and of how to introduce it are the fundamental, long-term questions that Chinese advocates of democracy must address. But these questions are almost always overshadowed, indeed often made impossible to discuss, because of another great barrier to democratic change in China—the resolute opposition of the Communist party. The problem of battling government repression understandably preoccupies Chinese advocates of democracy. It draws their attention away from the complexities of the issue itself and at the same time provides them with a solidarity that they otherwise would lack. During periods of high political pressure, intellectuals dare to speak of democracy only in securely private contexts. But even when the pressure from above lessened, such as in fall 1988 and winter 1989, the discussion of democracy remained artificially simple because resistance to the regime continued to be the overriding issue. The very opportunity to come together at a dinner party or a seminar and talk about democracy was so exciting to intellectuals that the job seemed done before it really got started. People were satisfied, indeed exuberant, simply to show that they were in league with one another. Differences over what "democracy" meant seemed minor problems by comparison.

After many of China's leading advocates of democracy fled to the West in 1989, the fissures in their understanding of democracy became increasingly apparent. Suddenly out from under state repression (although never entirely free of it, because of family and friends remaining in China), they had less incentive to maintain solidarity with one another. As their underlying ideas emerged, many found stronger differences than they had imagined over important questions such as whether a "new authoritarian" regime could be trusted as part of a transition to democracy or how the constricting effects of China's official language could be purged.

Despite the problems of conceiving and discussing democracy, it has been the favorite alternative in intellectuals' search for a new ideology for China. The interest in reviving elements of Chinese tradition antedating the Communists was much less intense and was often checked by the worry that "feudal" habits were inextricably tied to traditional culture. As another possibility some proposed, in an echo of the May Fourth movement of the late 1910s and early 1920s, that science could be a guide in organizing society. They pointed out that science is not just a way to solve technical problems but also a spirit of inquiry and an outlook on life that naturally disrupts dogmatism, favors freedom, independence, and equality, and produces progress. But the advocates of science as ideology were few—mainly scientists—and they did not have much luck spreading their viewpoint to nonscientists. Fang Lizhi, who with his wife, Li Shuxian, expounded this view as clearly as anyone, wistfully observed, "Our common people—and actually our political leaders, too—don't realize that science is a kind of culture. They think of it as just something that . . . well, something that lets you repair electric lights. They don't understand the system of thought that lies behind." A younger scientist, after pondering this observation for a moment, expressed himself in deadpan humor: "It seems to me that if we Chinese really want an ideology that works for us, something that we do naturally and that will really give us distinctive status in the world, because nobody else can do it as well as we can, then we shouldn't pretend to do (gao) socialism, or democracy, or capitalism. We should do feudalism. That's what we're good at! Nobody can beat us at that!"

Some felt that it might be better to reject the perennial thirst for an ideology. "To insist that we need an ideology is dangerous, especially when we feel the pressure of a crisis," observed a journalist. "When China was in crisis during the May Fourth years, we desperately sought a new ideology, and we seized upon one—Marxism-Leninism—that eventually brought us great trouble. We would have done better to go slower on ideology. Now we're in crisis again, and I don't think we should be eager for another ideology. All we really need is a basis upon which to share ideas freely. Then we can watch for areas of consensus to emerge." Fang Lizhi, although expecting that China, like human society generally, would evolve increasingly toward democracy, also espoused a kind of practical eclecticism in regard to China's immediate ideological alternatives. "Imagine a dilapidated old building, about to collapse of its own weight," he said. "It won't do to insist [as did Deng Xiaoping with his Four Basic Principles] that the structure of this building remain the same while you import new bricks. Precisely the opposite is needed: the overall structure is what needs changing, but some of the existing bricks could be rebuilt into the new building. Confucianism, for example, stresses education, and China desperately needs better education. So this is a good Confucian 'brick' to build into the new structure. Socialism asks that no one should starve to death and that the gap between rich and poor should not be allowed to grow too large. These 'bricks' from socialism could be kept. There's nothing wrong with this approach. This is the way scientific ideas change. Einsteinian physics undermined Newtonian physics and defined a new basic framework for the science. Today it still has a lot of Newtonian 'bricks'; but the structure is Einsteinian."

## Patriotism

The collapse of the Communist creed in China, combined with the continuing cultural predisposition toward ideology, caused many intellectuals to fall back on a fairly simple but deeply rooted patriotism as an interim stand-in. Beneath all the tumult over China's situation, intellectuals retained a rather firm sense of Chinese identity, as well as the conviction that if they cannot be proud of that identity, it is only because something is temporarily wrong.[19]

19. By "Chinese" here I mean Han people and their civilization, not the more modern (but less successful) definitions of "China" as comprising several ethnicities. The efforts of the Communist government, and the Nationalist government before it, to define "China" to include Manchus, Mongolians, Tibetans, Uzbeks, Uighurs, and others coequally with the Han make sense in theory but have failed to gain acceptance

The remarkable power of this idea, especially among the middle and older generations, can be illustrated in a story that one of China's eminent historians recalled, in winter 1989, about his parents. In 1937, when Japan invaded north China, the family was living comfortably, indeed luxuriously by the standards of the time, in a traditional-style Beijing courtyard. When the father was summoned by the Japanese police to a meeting, the real purpose of which was to force him into collaboration, the parents decided to flee, keeping only what they could carry with them. They made their way a thousand miles overland to Chongqing, in Sichuan province, the Nationalist government's wartime capital, where they lived in poverty for several years. They could not afford shoes or proper medicine for their children.

"But I never heard my parents complain," said the historian. "They were doing it for China. Once, in fall of 1944, the Japanese approached to within a two days' march of Chongqing. I asked my parents what they would do if the Japanese actually arrived. My father just looked out the window at the Yangzi River and said, 'We Chinese have an old method: the river.' I panicked when I realized what he meant. 'But what about *me?*' I asked. I was in high school then. My father answered, 'If such a day really comes, can we still care for you?' "

Chinese patriotism as intense as this is rare today, especially among young people. Years of insistence by the Communist party that "love of country" mean "love of party" has complicated the issue of patriotism and caused many intellectuals to feel ambivalent about it. Yet the idea has great staying power and is visible in various altered forms. At bottom the assumption that China's history is special, and that all Chinese are responsible for the maintenance of Chinese pride, remains a

---

in daily usage. For example, the term "Chinese language" (*Zhongwen*) still is automatically assumed to mean the Han language. Except among anthropologists, or in stiffly formal official contexts, people in China would be quite puzzled to hear the Mongolian or Manchu language referred to as "Chinese." Similarly, a Han person is a "Chinese," and a Han living outside China is a *huaqiao* "Chinese residing aboard"; no one would think of calling a Chinese Uzbek who had moved to Samarkand a "Chinese residing abroad."

cultural axiom even among many of the disillusioned young. A few days after I heard the historian's story, I repeated it to one of China's outstanding young humanists, a man in his early thirties.

"I find that father's answer to his son strange," he said. "I would even call it abnormal. I have a son and *can't conceive* saying such a thing to him." He went on to explain the "independence" of his generation of intellectuals, attributing it to their stronger identification with world culture as well as to their utter contempt for China's current government. Later in the interview I pressed him a bit further about his sense of identification with China as a country. "If you were on an academic delegation going overseas," I asked, "would you speak just for yourself, or feel you had to represent China?"

He thought for a moment and said, "I would definitely feel I had to represent China. I would be concerned with two things: not to offend the foreign hosts and not to lose face for China. Others on the delegation would be watching me and could report my 'mistakes' back home. But that's not what I mean. I'm talking about something that's deeper inside. I mean that as a Chinese I would feel a duty to represent China's dignity."

This embedded sense of the primacy and dignity of China is something that the regime and the intellectuals, despite their antagonism on most other issues, have in common. They share it so fundamentally that neither side thinks to acknowledge it as an area of agreement. It is simply assumed. It could be seen, among the intellectuals, in their overwhelming propensity to worry about China and to speak of little else.[20] This strong identification was also evident in the protests of spring 1989,

20. Even at academic conferences whose formal topics lay elsewhere, talk about contemporary China seemed to dominate. At a December 1988 conference on Sino-American relations sponsored by the Chinese Academy of Social Sciences (CASS), about 90 percent of the actual discussion, as I heard it, was about problems in contemporary China. The same was true at a May 1989 conference on the May Fourth movement sponsored by the Academy of Chinese Culture. A March 1989 conference at CASS on the theme "Images of Women in Modern Foreign Literature" was so dominated by discussion of images of Chinese women in Chinese literature that the organizers eventually acknowledged the change formally.

when students who had seemed to be thoroughly cynical suddenly marched toward Tiananmen Square proclaiming their readiness to "lay down [their] lives" in order to "rid [their] country of tyranny."

Many Chinese, including intellectuals, assume there is something irreducibly unique about China. This sense of China's special status came forward whenever comparisons arose with the "Four Little Dragons" of South Korea, Taiwan, Hong Kong, and Singapore. Chinese intellectuals often pointed to the Four Dragons as evidence that something was wrong with China's system: after all, look how well people from similar ethnic stock and cultural background have done elsewhere. But simultaneously, at the deeper level where the Chinese nurtured their sense of the primacy and dignity of their heritage, the success of the Four Dragons could also be unsettling. The Four Dragons were fringe societies from the Chinese point of view. They could experiment with modernization, and even amass great wealth, but they could never be, in some ultimate sense, superior or more important. At bottom it was absurd to compare China to a place like Singapore. Comparisons with larger countries, including Western countries, seemed superficially more legitimate but ultimately provoked the same twinge of absurdity.

To some, this China-centeredness seemed a burden. Fang Lizhi, in an effort to remove the issue from its strongly sentimental context, compared China to France. "Just as France has felt itself the center of Europe and has never fully adjusted to the rise of the English, so China, as the center of East Asia, finds it hard to abandon its sense of centrality." Others, although acknowledging China fixation to be a burden, chose to bear it nonetheless, as a sort of moral imperative. A senior historian who had lived in the West illustrated his feelings by comparing himself to a young couple, a Chinese man and his American wife, who lived in New York: "They spent several years writing about China, worrying constantly about China, and spending every ounce of energy on China. Finally the wife, who after all was American, had to stop. 'I've had enough,' she said. 'It's fine to be concerned about China, but I can't let it consume my whole life. I have to cut off.' But that," said the historian, "makes the crucial point perfectly clear. She could cut off. She is American. I also feel exhausted. I also feel my life is being consumed. But I *cannot* cut off. I simply do not feel that I have that option."[21]

But this historian, even while feeling inextricably bound to his Chineseness, wanted to distance himself from what he regarded as the vanity in Chinese pride. "There is a problem," he said, "with maintaining Chinese pride at a point in Chinese history when there is very little to be proud of. The demand for pride, on the one side, and the emptiness that answers it, on the other, flatten Chinese pride into a thin thing we call face. Lu Xun pointed out this problem brilliantly in the 1920s with his 'True Story of Ah Q.'[22] The problem is still with us, and you will find many Chinese intellectuals like me who are proud of China but embarrassed at China's 'Ah Q–ism.' "

For many the divide between justifiable pride and fatuous face-saving could be difficult to negotiate. In the fall of 1988 the historian Pang Pu published an interview in a newspaper for intellectuals in which he defended the uniqueness of Chinese cultural tradition.[23] This theme could easily have been well

21. I found a very few intellectuals, among the young and modern minded, who seemed able to transcend the preoccupation with China by identifying with the world as a whole. They express concerns about worldwide pollution, the greenhouse effect, nuclear arms, earthquake prediction, and so on. Yet, in nearly every one of the contexts in which I observed someone raising such issues, a special air of unreality seemed to undermine the speaker. The global perspective seemed, first of all, borrowed from the West; therefore the speaker was viewed as avant-garde or even ostentatious. His or her pose itself seemed to be more interesting than the issue he or she was raising. More important, the global concerns always seemed to pale next to the excruciating immediacy of everyone else's worries about China. (I exclude from this generalization the serious professional meetings of scholars from the Chinese Academy of Sciences discussing problems of the greenhouse effect and desertification. There was no air of unreality at such meetings. But they still were quite removed from the mainstream of informal opinion.)

22. Lu Xun's Ah Q is a fictional character famous for symbolizing the "flaws of Chinese national character," such as saving face by the "technique of moral victory," for example, slapping one's own face in order to identify with the slapper. The story is translated as "Ah Q—The Real Story" in Lu Xun, *Diary of a Madman and other Stories*, trans. William A. Lyell (Honolulu: University of Hawaii Press, 1990), pp. 101–72.

23. Gang Jian, "Wenhua de minzuxing yu shidaixing: Fang Pang Pu" (The national

received, but Pang pushed it to a point that irritated some of his readers. He began by arguing that just because the West has certain things China does not, Chinese need not regard themselves as inferior, for they also have things that Westerners do not. He went on to contend that because a country's strengths and weaknesses are intricately entwined in a cultural whole, it is impossible to make comparative evaluations of entire cultures. One can only point out similarities and differences, without evaluation. It is possible to speak of "backward" and "advanced" developmental stages within a single tradition, but if one is comparing traditions grounded in fundamentally different assumptions, then one has no way to make evaluations. For example, it is not legitimate to compare Chinese and Western medicine, since they are grounded in different assumptions and theories.

"Pang Pu wants to be proud of China, and so do I," commented a young reader, a physicist. "But it seems to me he's just setting up two kinds of truth, one that can be universally tested and one that can't, because it's 'cultural' truth. But what determines when to use one test and when the other? I'm afraid it's just when national pride comes along, and we want to protect ourselves from rejection or defeat, that we suddenly decide to use the 'cultural' test. This is also what lets so many of us cling to the idea that there is magical power in Chinese *qigong* ('breath exercise'). I'm afraid Pang Pu's conclusion is nothing but 'Ah Q–ism' in intellectual wrapping."

The great popularity of *qigong* in the late 1980s surprised me, because the practice had been much less evident when I had last lived in China, a decade earlier. An ancient art in whose name *qi* stands not only for "breath" but also for a mystical thing that is both force and substance, *qigong* spread widely in the later 1980s as a health-sustaining exercise. As a physical regimen there is no reason to doubt it; but the widespread stories about *qigong* "masters" who could cause tables to levitate, see through walls, cure cancer, and so on only made me think of similar charlatans in the West. *Qigong* itself was less intrigu-

character and time character of culture: An interview with Pang Pu), *Guangming Daily*, November 24, 1988, p. 2.

ing to me than the attitudes of Chinese intellectuals toward it. I was frequently surprised to hear intellectuals who were otherwise modern minded express their belief in the supernatural aspects of *qigong*. A Beijing literary critic famous for his style of cutting through pretensions, both intellectual and political, told me that he was utterly skeptical of *qigong* until, one night on a lawn at a conference site outside Beijing, a *qigong* master emitted invisible rays that caused his head and shoulders to lurch involuntarily to one side and the other. I did not know what to make of this story, and still do not. He is a man of great intellect, and I am quite sure he was not kidding me. His view, moreover, was not unusual. Among Chinese intellectuals, I observed more believers in *qigong* than doubters.

What I found most interesting about the doubters, like the young physicist who commented on Pang Pu, is the angle from which they questioned *qigong*. They argued that because *qigong* is Chinese in origin, it is useful in bolstering Chinese pride. But it achieves this through a deception, by defining a special area in which Chinese ways can have validity beyond the reach of "Western criteria." "*Qigong* answers a need," said a young engineer. "It is the need for a fortress around our Chinese self-respect, a place that will always be safely Chinese, whatever else happens. Personally, I think we Chinese deserve our national pride. But I think it's silly to do it this way. Those *qigong* masters can't do anything a good magician can't do." Fang Lizhi offered the sardonic comment that "the way to stop the spread of *qigong* in China is to put out the story that foreigners had it a long time ago."

The borderline between legitimate cultural pride and self-deceiving Ah Q–ism was much harder for Chinese intellectuals to pin down in themselves than it was to notice and criticize in others. The top leadership, in whom the problem of national pride was said to merge with personal vanity, were favorite targets. Big, highly publicized projects such as the Asian Games, the Beijing proton accelerator, and the Yangzi Gorges Dam were cited as the pet projects of one or another leader whose real aim was to reap glory, not to serve China's needs.

In early 1989 the writer Dai Qing decided to go public with

intellectuals' criticisms of the Yangzi Gorges Dam project, and within only two weeks edited a volume detailing widespread doubts and worries.[24] The dam, planned for construction at the famous scenic gorges between Sichuan and Hubei provinces, was to be about two hundred meters high, impound a reservoir of nearly forty billion cubic meters, and facilitate navigation and control of floods and silt. It would also generate nearly seventeen million kilowatts of electricity, more than twice as much as its nearest rival in the world.[25]

But intellectuals objected that the project would flood 2,850 square kilometers of prime agricultural land and displace 1.3 million people. The only land in the area to survive the inundation was mountainous and agriculturally useless. Where would the people go? What would it cost to move them? The whole project was supposed to take twenty years and cost 36 billion yuan. But counting interest and inflation, one eminent academic estimated the total price at 100 to 120 billion yuan.[26] What were the alternative uses of such a large sum? Granted that China needs better flood control and badly needs more electricity, would it not be wiser to build several smaller dams that could be finished sooner, cost less, displace fewer people, and destroy less land? Decentralization would also make distribution of the electricity easier and reduce the proportions of a catastrophe should a dam fail.

Some also raised environmental and cultural questions: Does it make sense to engineer out of existence some of the world's most dramatic natural scenery? Inundate historical relics? Destroy

24. Dai Qing, ed., *Changjiang, changjiang* (Yangzi, Yangzi) (Guiyang: Guizhou People's Publishing House, 1989). For more comments on both the Beijing proton accelerator and the Yangzi Gorges Dam, see above, pp. 67, 75–76. For more on Dai Qing, see above, pp. 144–49.

25. The statistics in this and the following paragraph are taken from Lu Qinkan, "Sanxia gongcheng shidazhengyi gaishu" (A summary of ten major controversies surrounding the Yangzi Gorges project), in Dai Qing, ed., *Changjiang, changjiang*, pp. 21–29.

26. Zhou Peiyuan, "Guanyu sanxia gongcheng de yixie wenti he jianyi" (Some questions and suggestions concerning the Yangzi Gorges project), in Dai Qing, ed., *Changjiang, changjiang*, p. 10.

sites that inspired some of China's best classical poetry? Sacrifice a lucrative tourist attraction?

That no one had adequately thought through all these issues raised a second order of questions that were basically political: Why aren't China's trained experts—the scientists and economists—more involved in these decisions? Why should they be left to the private fancy, or serve the personal glory, of one or two powerful people?

On the latter question, Dai Qing was more frank and specific in an interview than in writing. "The leaders who have supported this dam project don't know the difference between a country and a family," she said. "To them, the dam is fun, like their big toy. It gives them great face. They want what Mao got when he built the great bridge at Nanjing. Hosting the Asian Games [in fall 1990] excites them for the same reason. They hope China can be a 'major sporting power.'[27] And it's not just the leadership that has this problem. When Chinese volleyball teams beat teams from other countries, the students at Beijing University rampage. To me all this 'national prestige' business, at the Olympics or anywhere, is shallow, worthless stuff. It reminds me of the story about [the late-Qing empress dowager] Cixi in the early 1900s. A foreigner gave her an automobile, but she refused to use it because the driver *sat* in front of her, instead of kneeling as he ought. She wanted him to kneel and use his hands to operate the pedals. So the car was useless. What good is pride, I ask you?"

Reflections such as these pushed some even to question the value of patriotism. It was a difficult step to take. Through more than a century of wars, rebellions, humiliations, invasions, and

27. In 1988 Zhao Yu, a writer of literary reportage, published a widely discussed piece called "The Dream of Being a Strong Country" (*Qiangguo meng*), in which he criticized China's pursuit of prowess in international sporting events. Zhao held that China's national obsession with winning came from a need to compensate for a century of humiliation at the hands of foreigners, but that mere national pride must not take precedence over, or divert resources from, much more urgent needs. See Liu Yangdong and Meng Chao, eds., *Zhongguo chongjibo: Dangdai shehui wenti baogao wenxue xuan* (Chinese shock waves: A selection of literary reportage on contemporary social problems) (Beijing: People's Publishing House, 1988), pp. 145–242.

mass political campaigns, the single value that seemed beyond reproach, and that stood throughout as a reason for struggling on, was patriotism. But by late 1988 Fang Lizhi was quietly asserting, "Patriotism should not be our highest priority."[28]

"Since Newton," argued Fang. "Western science and technology have been ahead of China's. This made Western influence on China inevitable. Problems arose because the West brought its influence in the form of guns and colonialism. This stimulated a concept of 'patriotism' in China that was resistant toward others and protective of Chinese pride. . . . Modern Chinese xenophobia remains a powerful force beneath the surface of our society. A country, just like an animal, will lash out and kill if it feels trapped in a corner. A Boxer-like response is still quite possible."[29]

Fang further argued that China's Communist rulers have tried to attach the people's patriotism to themselves. The word "patriotism" in Chinese, *aiguo* (literally "love of *guo*"), begs the question of whether to understand *guo* as "country," "state," "ethnicity," or, as the Communist leadership has always maintained, also "party." Fang recalled the hostile interrogation of a Chinese intellectual in 1955: "Which *guo* is it that you love?" demanded the interrogator, "the Nationalist party's *guo* or the Communist party's *guo*?" In this use of the word, Fang pointed out, we see the meaning of *guo* narrowed down to "party" and even "party leadership." Not content to rely on the idea of "love" to attract people willingly, the party threatens, "If you disagree with us, you are not patriotic." If *guo* means "state," Fang continued, then consider: Lenin defined "state" as the "apparatus of state" and specified these as the police, army, courts, and

28. See "Aiguozhuyi buying fang zai diyi wei" (Patriotism should not be put first), *The Nineties* (Hong Kong), January 1989, pp. 96–98; see also "On Patriotism and Global Citizenship," in George Hicks, ed., *The Broken Mirror: China after Tiananmen* (London: Longmans, 1990), pp. xxi–xxv.

29. In the late nineteenth century Shandong peasants formed a secret-society group called the "righteous and harmonious fists," and rose in rebellion against foreign encroachment in China and the weak Qing dynasty that tolerated it. They were called Boxers in English because of their use of martial arts techniques, which they believed could withstand even the bullets of the foreigners. See Joseph Esherick, *The Origins of the Boxer Uprising* (Berkeley and Los Angeles: University of California Press, 1987).

jails. Does that mean that patriots should "love" the police, army, courts, and jails?

Fang further argued that the Communist party has had to draw more and more on patriotism to shore up its position. During the 1980s neither Marxism nor Maoism could inspire any popular enthusiasm, and even the underlying moral authority of Confucian ethics had been severely weakened by the widespread perception that the leadership was corrupt. Patriotism was the last source of moral authority that the rulers could tap. This explains, in part, why the party mounted campaigns in the 1980s against Western "bourgeois liberalism," as well as against "spiritual pollution," with its metaphor of "infection" from the West and its lumping together of such disparate threats as democracy, long hair, and AIDS. The party continues to allow conspicuous privileges to foreigners, Fang argued, in full knowledge that these privileges sow deep resentment among ordinary Chinese.

But Fang's reasons for questioning "patriotism" went beyond the problems of narrow-minded chauvinism and its exploitation by political authority. He argued that all countries will find patriotism less and less useful as the interdependence of modern societies proceeds. He cited with approval some of the predictions of Albert Einstein (a hero of Fang's, as both physicist and social thinker): that nationalism around the globe would wither in the next century and that the concept of "citizen of the world" would begin to evolve. "Fifty years ago people thought Einstein's social views were only the quaint imaginings of a genius," said Fang. "But we can see already that he had remarkable foresight. Humankind in recent centuries has more and more been discovering things that are basic and universal." Among these things are scientific truths; gradually, Fang maintained, human rights will become so as well. Basic freedoms will increasingly be regarded as the rights of all, and the argument that such matters are the "internal affairs" of sovereign states will gradually lose credibility. Even if some wish to resist this growing worldwide interdependence, Fang held, we are all impelled in its direction, whether we like it or not, because of the many complex problems—energy, the environment, population, the international economy, and national security—whose only real solutions will have to be global. Eventually patriotism will come to seem, as Einstein called it, an "infantile disease."

Most Chinese who have tried to compare Chinese and Western culture seem to agree with Pang Pu that the two are fundamentally different. Many others, without thinking too deeply about it, simply assume this to be true. But Fang Lizhi's conclusion challenged this way of looking at the world. "I like to avoid terms like 'East' and 'West,' " he said. "Such terms tend to stimulate chauvinistic responses that only make progress more difficult. We can use terms like 'progressive' and 'backward,' or 'correct' and 'incorrect,' and apply them around the world uniformly."

So far, however, patriotism has seemed to survive Fang's carefully reasoned argument as well as many blunter ones. Some of the intellectuals who attack the idea most sharply nevertheless continue to act upon it as a value in their lives. One literary critic who was well known for his view that scholars should remain strictly above political involvement was at Tiananmen Square organizing petitions in May 1989. In a broad perspective the views of Fang Lizhi, Dai Qing, and other critics of Chinese patriotism ironically can be seen as sincere suggestions for how to help China. Some of China's intellectuals preferred to cling to patriotism, in both theory and practice, whatever the pitfalls. "It's all we have," argued Liu Binyan.[30] "By now our other moral resources have been largely devastated. Patriotism is the one value that can still hold us together."

For many Chinese intellectuals, the inner search for a guiding ideology is an exalted quest with both moral and spiritual dimensions. It can even become a preoccupying worry on a daily basis. But at the same time the more mundane aspects of life require individuals to maintain a number of identifications that rarely fit easily together. These practical associations determine the contours of everyday Chinese living.

---

30. At a conference of Chinese intellectual leaders called "China Symposium, '89" (Bolinas, California, in April 1989). See also Liu Binyan's autobiography, *A Higher Kind of Loyalty*, trans. Zhu Hong (New York: Pantheon, 1990).

# Five

# IDENTITY
# WITHIN GROUPS

In 1980 the Chinese writer Wang Meng (who later, from 1986 to 1989, served as China's minister of culture) published a story called "The Butterfly."[1] The title refers to a famous vignette about the ancient Daoist philosopher Zhuangzi (flourished fourth century B.C.), who awakens from dreaming that he was a butterfly—but then wonders whether he is a man who dreamed he was a butterfly or a butterfly now dreaming that he is a man.

The protagonist of Wang Meng's story has similar identity problems. A Red Army soldier in the 1940s, he becomes a high municipal official in the 1950s, a stinking "enemy of the people" in the 1960s, and a rehabilitated official in the late 1970s. A workaholic at mental labor in the 1950s, he suddenly shifts to hard physical labor in the 1960s and then back to desk work in the 1970s. In the 1950s he has a doting young wife, half his age, who later divorces him and commits suicide because of her own political taint. She is briefly replaced in his affections by a manipulative urban sophisticate and, later, after his banishment to rural labor, by a good-hearted nurse. When he regains his official post in the late 1970s, he asks the nurse to marry

1. "Hudie" (The butterfly), *Shiyue* (October), April 1980, 4–37, translated by Gladys Yang in Wang Meng, *The Butterfly and Other Stories* (Beijing: Panda Books, 1983), pp. 35–101.

him, but she flatly refuses. He also asks his son by his first marriage to come back to the city with him, but the son, originally
sent to the countryside as punishment, has learned to appreciate the peasant values of diligence and honesty. In declining to
go to the city, both the son and the nurse also express misgiv-
ings about becoming "high official family members." Thus for
the protagonist, the bobbing in and out of several identities is
made doubly confusing by inversions in the valuation of his
roles.

The shifts, ambiguities, and difficulties that Wang Meng writes
about have affected many Chinese people, especially the intellectuals, in nearly all their social roles—from those that define
official relations with the state to those involving private relations with family and friends.[2]

## Identity with the State

In what sense can Chinese intellectuals, who are so thoroughly
disillusioned with their state, its representatives, and its ideology, nevertheless share an identity with it? This paradoxical
question goes to the heart of explaining the public behavior—
meaning the large part of life that is subject to state supervision
and control—not only of intellectuals but of all citizens of the
People's Republic. It also helps explain how Communist Chinese
society can hold together in spite of the mutual antagonism and
suspicion among citizens that the state-imposed unit system
generates in daily life. Chinese citizens are simultaneously pulled
and repelled by their state, and each person must struggle to
find habitable ground between the push and the pull. This habitable ground itself is forever subject to change, varying not
only with the "wind direction" of national politics but with
countless ad hoc circumstances in a person's situation and web
of personal relations. The struggle can be especially difficult for

2. This is not to suggest that Wang Meng is responsible in any way for the other
views and analysis in this chapter.

intellectuals because of the political sensitivity of their social roles.

In the last chapter, we defined "identity" in terms of a sense of sameness. But the identity that links Chinese and their state is not a willing or congenial sense of sameness of the sort one normally feels as part of a family, religious group, or social club. It is a sense of being bound in an unequal relationship to something quite "other" than oneself, something like the identity shared by vassal and lord or, in the metaphor of a young Chinese physicist, ox and plowman. We have already noted how Chinese, speaking informally, refer to the authorities at any level simply as "they." The little pronoun neatly captures both sides of the paradoxical "identity" that ordinary citizens feel with their state: "otherness" and close familiarity.

We have already seen some of the forces binding citizens to the state in China. One source of cohesion is the cultural tradition that calls for the proper playing of public roles, and thus at least the ritual appearance of identification with the groups to which one belongs, including the state. Another is the regime's claim that "party" and "nation" are synonymous. This claim has had considerable success ever since the 1940s in drawing popular patriotism toward the Communist party, which has further buttressed the tendency with its sophisticated techniques of propaganda and implied threats warning citizens to shun dissent. Citizens have learned that there is real comfort to be gained from acquiescing in the mainstream the state claims to represent, even if they know that the state's claims are false. In exchange for a sense of security, people become willing to proffer their "guilt," and the state reinforces this psychology by demanding confessions and promising leniency to those who confess well. In all its manipulations of language and circumstances, the state insists that it be recognized as occupying the moral high ground.

The most important elements binding citizens to the state lie within the dynamics of the work-unit system. The work units mediate all applications of state power to citizens, excepting the few dissidents famous enough to get attention directly from central leaders. Since the vagueness of official language leaves much room for arbitrary interpretation, unit leaders can use official authority in the pursuit of local or even personal goals. In determining, for instance, who will be offered up as a unit's "bourgeois liberal," the unit leader has considerable latitude. And he can bring to bear some significant controls, ranging from social stigma to job and housing assignments, to permissions to travel or have a child.

There is little recourse for those abused by the unit system. No one even thinks of a legal appeal, because the courts are known to be organs of political control, not justice. Personal appeals to outside authorities are possible—but fraught with difficulty. One must first get through the smoke screen of false language that surrounds any case of persecution within a unit. The unit leader will have his "way of putting it" that can make the most petty-minded abuse seem reasonable. The burden of proof then falls back on the petitioner, whose task is now doubled: he must convince the outside authority that the unit leader is not only a bully but a liar as well. He is building up a considerable debt of bad blood, which will merely worsen his situation if the whole effort fails. Moreover, no outside authority is fully independent: he operates within a web of power relationships that connect his own interests with those of many others in the ruling elite, perhaps including the person he is being called upon to criticize. When battles between officials do occur, they lead to complex alliances, and the spending of political capital, on both sides. It takes a powerful case—or, more likely, a powerful personal connection—to induce one authority to attack another.

The little people subject to the unit system know that it is foolish to get entangled in the web of authority. But sometimes it is unavoidable. Two teenage girls ran the elevators at an apartment building that I visited from time to time. One was fourteen years old and small for her age—not much more than four feet tall. The other was larger and older but mildly retarded. Both were friendly and always cheerful. In spring 1989 the younger one disappeared. I asked the older one what had happened. "One day an old woman was moving things at one of the other elevators. XXX [the girl's name] went to help her. Our leader happened to come along, and he asked where she was. He blamed her for 'leaving her post.' But she argued back. She said she was helping a woman at the other elevator, so it could not be said that she had 'left her post.' When she argued back, the leader became very angry. He said she was not fit to work here any more."

"Where is she?" I asked.

"At home. She has no work now."

"Can she get new work?"

"I don't know. I think she must do something for her leader."

The only bright spot in this dismal story was the loyal friendship between the two girls. It was especially noticeable because, as a general rule, friendship among co-workers does not easily survive the pressures of the unit system. Competition for limited goods and privileges, control of which is concentrated in a few hands, normally breeds jealousy and suspicion among co-workers, causing them to scheme for advantage by "hooking hearts and locking horns" (gouxin doujiao), in the Chinese cliché. A contemporary proverb says, "In making friends, look outside your unit."[3]

3. Václav Havel in 1985 described the situation of the ordinary Czech citizen in a way that strongly resembles the Chinese case. The similarities should, in a peculiar way, cheer those Chinese intellectuals who see their country's work units as microcosms of a distinctly Chinese "feudalism." Havel wrote, "[The] citizen knows 'they' can do anything they want—take away his passport, have him fired from his job, order him to move, . . . bar him from higher education, . . . build a factory producing mostly acid fumes right under his windows, . . . arrest him simply because he attended a rock concert, raise prices arbitrarily, any time and for any reason, turn down all his humble petitions without cause, prescribe what he must read before all else, what he must demonstrate for, what he must sign, how many square feet his apartment may have, whom he may meet and whom he must avoid. The citizen picks his way through life in constant fear of 'them,' knowing full well that even an opportunity to work for the public good is a privilege 'they' have bestowed upon him, conditionally. . . . The average citizen living in this stifling atmosphere of universal irritability, servility, perpetual defensiveness, backbiting, nervousness, and an ever smouldering compensatory contentiousness, knows perfectly well, without having to read any 'dissident' literature, that 'they' can do anything and he can do nothing." See "An Anatomy of Reticence," trans. E. Kohák, in Václav Havel; or, Living in Truth, ed. Jan Vladislav (London: Faber and Faber, 1987), p. 171.

Chinese intellectuals enjoy analyzing and exposing the techniques of manipulation employed by officials at every level, from central progaganda to work-unit bullying. Although they make no secret of their distaste for these methods, they seldom act in overt defiance of them, and the reasons for this "timidity" are more complex than Westerners usually appreciate. Westerners often conceive the matter of defiance—as it appears, for example, in the cases of famous "dissidents"[4]—as the simple presence or absence of courage. Certainly courage is involved in any decision to defy the authorities, but so are many other elements.

There is, first of all, the question of whether it is effective to answer oppression with an act of raw courage. In a rational accounting, what does one achieve, and how does that weigh against the likely punishment? Many intellectuals conclude that more is lost than gained and regard those who engage in overt defiance with a certain puzzlement. Why expose oneself and one's family to suffering? Does the imprisonment or internal exile that may follow really promote progress in China? Isn't it better to be patient and inch forward? A distinguished archaeologist, who was as bitterly alienated as anyone I met in China, said, "We have to go slow in China. I wish this were not true. But the trap we are in makes it true. To try to go fast means to risk going backward."

A second factor that weighs heavily against overt dissent is less a matter of calculation and more strongly rooted in the emotional terrain of identification with the state. It is the range of impulsive responses that are naturally elicited by the state's use of language. Before a person even reaches the point of considering whether to think or act in opposition to the state, the fear of stigmatization as a "small minority," which can turn "everyone" into enemies, can generate a fear not subject to

4. "Dissidents" is put in quotation marks here to signal that the normal understanding of this term in the West (that is, "disagreeing with the majority opinion"—*The Random House College Dictionary*, 1975) does not fit Chinese realities. "Dissidents" like Liu Binyan or Fang Lizhi stand out in China because they dare to say publicly what many others say only in private. They do not stand out because their message falls outside the mainstream. Indeed, they are popular precisely because their words do represent a repressed mainstream.

rational control. Such fear can spring suddenly from the unconscious in what is described as *houpa*—"delayed fear"—an emotional surge that surfaces in one's consciousness days or weeks after an intimidating experience. A Chinese friend, upon hearing that my eight-year-old daughter was awakening with recurrent nightmares in the weeks after the June 4 massacre, commented, "This is *houpa*. I'm sorry it happened to your daughter. It happens to us a lot. We can analyze it; but that does not stop it."

Yet the role that fear of state power plays in daily life goes further than this. Although fear undergirds all contact with the state, dealings with local officials are so common that standard modes of operation develop. The approaches that work become conventional and normally are free of the immediate sting of fear—although everyone is at least vaguely aware that the conventions originated in fear and that the reason for following them is to minimize exposure to fear. The ways in which ordinary people use the official language provide good examples of this. When everyday citizens fashion their language to fit official views, they do so not because they are "caving in" to intimidation, as a Westerner might imagine. They are "playing" words in a game that, although defensive in its essence, can be played aggressively. The abandonment of truth and sincerity as standards for evaluating statements is generally accepted as morally neutral on the grounds that people have no choice about whether to play the game. The sense of whether or not a statement is "a good move" replaces these standard criteria. On this basis the official language game, although born out of fear, can proceed smoothly without fear's constant presence.

If, as occasionally happens, someone with "raw courage" decides to state a truth in defiance of the rules of the game, this person not only asserts a particular truth but, much more radically, challenges the game itself. Such an action can have the disturbing consequence of bringing to the surface the fear that undergirds the language game but that, in daily life, is deadened by the force of convention. It is this willingness to confront fear that makes ordinary citizens sometimes judge truth tellers to be slightly obtuse or even annoying. To people who are observing the conventions of the official language, the sudden introduction of a blunt truth can seem simply a "bad move." "Why do *that?*" they want to ask. But a more common response, at least among people who understand the larger implications of what the truth teller is doing, is to admire him or her while maintaining a safe distance. This kind of admiration of others for saying what one wishes one could say oneself explains the tremendous popularity stirred by truth-telling writers like Liu Binyan in the early 1980s; it also explains, from the other side, what such writers mean by "speaking for the people."

Most of the pressures inducing Chinese citizens, both intellectuals and others, into a certain "identification" with the state are generated by the techniques of the Marxist-Leninist system, and have their parallels in other such states.[5] But for Chinese intellectuals there are additional inducements, inherited from Chinese tradition, for maintaining at least a tenuous "identity" with the state. The traditional ideal of state service called for offering one's advice to the ruling authority even if it meant "speaking for the people" in opposition to current policy. If one's proposals were rejected, there was no alternative way for pressing one's views upon the state; in that event, one could retire from public affairs to read, write, and cultivate oneself morally until the opportunity to offer one's services arose again. The wisdom of Mencius remains alive and often quoted among contemporary Chinese intellectuals: "When in power, seek to benefit the world as well; when out of power, work to cultivate your own self (*Mencius* 13:9)." In extreme cases it was better even to die than to abandon the ideal of serving the world via the ruling authority, as the persisting glory of the ancient poet Qu Yuan makes clear.[6]

These underlying conceptions of the intellectual's role have persisted well into the twentieth century, despite Western

5. See Václav Havel's analysis of the "reticence" of Czech intellectuals in "An Anatomy of Reticence," pp. 164–95. See also Czeslaw Milosz, *The Captive Mind,* trans. Jane Zielonko (New York: Octagon Books, 1981), pp. 205, 239, and passim.

6. See above, p. 12.

influences on intellectuals and the "antifeudal" campaigns of the Chinese state. In spring 1988 Li Tuo, a literary critic and editor of *Beijing Literature,* published an article called "The Invisible Hand," which aimed to uncover some of these cultural assumptions among intellectuals.[7] The article was typical of Li Tuo—dense, hard to read, but penetrating. Li Tuo himself was one of the most distinctive characters on the Beijing intellectual scene. A member of the tiny Daghur national minority from China's northeast, Li Tuo wore long sideburns and scruffy sneakers and flouted convention with his utter frankness. In discussions he would zero in, not fluently but stubbornly, on the most profound thought he could uncover, apparently without regard for anything else—least of all the face of others present. I once saw him at a seminar sitting across from the filmmaker Huang Jianxin, whose new work *Samsara (lunhui)* had just opened. "If one of our best filmmaker's can do something as bad as this, how can there be any hope for Chinese film?" asked a frowning Li Tuo, seemingly to himself as much as to anyone else in the room. Without even pausing over this rather "minor" point, he went straight to his specific analyses of the film's use of clichés and lack of artistic unity.

Li Tuo intended his title, "The Invisible Hand," to suggest that, like the invisible hand Adam Smith argued was at work in free markets, an invisible hand of deeply embedded cultural tradition governed the behavior of contemporary Chinese intellectuals. Li Tuo contended that intellectuals have inherited two basic modes of responding to the political world: the Confucian mode of offering service to the state, and the Daoist mode of withdrawing into oneself. These two positions thrived together for many centuries because they complemented each other; the intellectual could pivot into one stance or the other according to political conditions. Eventually this habit of pivoting became deep-seated, and intellectuals took it for granted that there were always two "faces" they could alternately employ.

7. Li Tuo, "Kanbujian de shou: Tan dianying pipan yu shenceng wenhua xinli" (The invisible hand: A discussion of film criticism and the deeper levels of cultural psychology), in *Dangdai dianying* (Contemporary film), no. 4 (1988): 30–40.

It follows, according to the argument, that no matter how disillusioned with the state and how deep their withdrawal from it, Chinese intellectuals have always sought to preserve the *possibility* of a return to state service. This, in turn, has made many intellectuals reluctant to do anything that would mean a final break with the state. In spring of 1989 a prominent historian, after expressing his great admiration for the outspoken Fang Lizhi, added, "Fang has, however, been 'booted outside'; whatever he says, the state will never listen; I don't want to take that step. They still have to—or at least might—listen to me."

A professor of international relations, who shared Li Tuo's theory that Chinese intellectuals pivot between activism and withdrawal, used it to explain their great dependence on state authority. "Chinese intellectuals are strong on analysis of problems, but weak on finding solutions. This comes in part from our traditional roles and self-conceptions. But it means we don't carry through with our ideas. We expect someone else, someone in the government, to do that. Hence even our own ideals pull us toward 'identifying' somewhat with the state." An art professor concurred and went one step further: "We feel dependent on the state not only to correct the wrongs that we find but, even more deeply, to hold society together. We're very afraid of chaos. During the Cultural Revolution we came close several times to outright civil war. In Guangxi [the local strongman] Wei Guoqing was just slaughtering people. The prospect of a return to chaos is terrifying. Much as we dislike the party today, we sometimes panic to realize there is nothing to replace it if it goes. The fear of chaos is something we share with the regime, even if we disagree on everything else."

Another bond between contemporary intellectuals and the state is the sense of personal glory that still attaches, despite the dismal reputation of the state, to being officially "put in an important position" (*zhongyong*). This enduring sense of honor among intellectuals results partly from the psychological techniques of the Communist party. But it derives also from deep cultural assumptions about the relation of scholars to the state. A respected senior writer explained, "The traditional notions that the successful scholar, having become an official, 'returns home in silken robes' to 'cast brilliance upon the family lintel' and 'bring honor to the ancestors' involve a kind of vanity that is still very much at work. In the early years of the People's Republic, when the prestige of the Communist party was high, intellectuals naturally felt it a great honor to be employed or trusted by the state, and correspondingly felt intense shame and dishonor when criticized. The Communist party reinforced this thinking by always claiming the superior moral position. As a result, even now, even among people who feel thoroughly disgusted with the party, there is often a strange uneasiness about making a final break. There is still a residual sense of shame about being fired from one's post or being expelled from the party, even among people who are quite clear and deliberate and are acting on high moral principle when they choose to risk punishment by speaking out."

For all these reasons, the desire to stay "inside" and avoid a final break with the state can be surprisingly tenacious. One might think that the refugee intellectuals who fled China after the June 4 massacre would all, for the act of fleeing alone, be indisputably "outside." But many, whether out of deeply engrained habit or because they despair at the dwindling influence they can have on Chinese affairs from their positions in exile, still observe distinctions between those who are and those who are not "completely" outside. In summer 1990, I encountered a writer who had fled China illegally, had renounced Chinese citizenship in favor of U.S. permanent residence as a refugee, and was working on a full-length novel on the roots of evil in the Deng Xiaoping regime; he still did not rule himself completely outside. He drew a line between himself and a good friend he had known for decades, and who had fled China in similar fashion, on the grounds that his friend had, as he had not, formally joined the Front for a Democratic China, which is dedicated to replacing China's Communist regime with a democracy.

This tension between enmity toward the state and the tenuous possibility of reconnection also influences the state's behavior. Zhao Fusan, who had been vice-president of the Chinese Academy of Social Sciences, head of its foreign affairs department, and, according to many intellectuals in the academy, an officer of the state's secret police as well, after June 4 became the highest-ranking official in intellectual circles "not to return" to China from a trip abroad. Zhao made his displeasure at the massacre known, but also has remained careful to say nothing to force a final break with the Chinese government; the regime, for its part, has seen fit to refrain from denouncing Zhao as it has others and to extend some ambiguous "leaves of absence" to him. Even people living in the West who are on the regime's "most wanted" list have been indirectly contacted by the highest levels of the Chinese bureaucracy in order to negotiate deals that entail "toning down their rhetoric" in return for an exit visa for a spouse or child.

The degree of an intellectual's identification with the state can vary from issue to issue, depending on the level of personal interest involved. People feel the least identification with the state on issues that do not touch their daily lives; the pull of the state increases when everyday concerns are at stake. When intellectuals trade stories of the tremendous embezzlement that allegedly goes on in the remote levels inhabited by state leaders, their alienation seems total; but when the same scholars receive instructions from state leaders that the Writers' Association should hold such and such a meeting, each one begins to calculate whether and how much he or she should cooperate.

Attitudes toward the state's foreign policies offer another illustration of this phenomenon. Deng Xiaoping's policy of opening China to the West has attracted wide interest and support among intellectuals because of its liberalizing effects and because it has enabled some to go to the West, whether temporarily or permanently. But intellectuals show much less interest in other areas of foreign policy. Although Mikhail Gorbachev's *glasnost* policy was often mentioned in discussions of what China needs, I could find almost no interest in China's policy toward the Soviet Union. China's border conflict with Vietnam in the late 1970s attracted some notice—mainly in protest of the loss of Chinese life rather than interest in the state's policy. On most questions of third-world foreign policy, I detected only boredom. A young reporter at *People's Daily* explained, "Ordinary Chinese people don't care *at all* what the state leaders think about Cambodia, or Prince Sihanouk, or relations with Africa. Articles on such topics appear in our press every day, but most people don't even consider reading them. If they have a view on Sino-African relations, it is based on the conflicts between Chinese and African students on Chinese campuses—which are not reported in our press. The 'Chinese-African Friendship' proclaimed by Zhongnanhai [that is, the top leadership] doesn't mean a thing. No one even takes it seriously enough to have an opinion on it."[8]

Even the issue of Tibet generates surprisingly little interest among China's intellectuals. Although they, like the leadership, consider Tibet to be a part of China and thus, one might imagine, "closer to home," they barely notice events in Tibet. The military repression of peaceful demonstrators in Lhasa in March 1989, which in many ways foreshadowed events in Beijing that June,[9] was widely known to Beijing intellectuals. Yet during all of the free speaking in spring 1989, they scarcely remarked upon the government crackdown in Tibet, and when they did their main interest was focused on its possible repercussions in China proper. Intellectuals noted that the brutality of the government action showed what "they" are like—and thus are capable of doing to the Han Chinese as well.

State-convened writers' meetings offer a good example of the

8. The gulf between the Chinese people and their government's foreign policies is a fact that Western experts in international relations, including U.S. government officials, either overlook or frequently forget. Even the China experts in foreign policy discussions habitually speak of "the Chinese" as holding particular views, when actually they are speaking of the views of a very small, unrepresentative group of state leaders. In the case of the China experts, it is fair to hope that they know about the gulf and are simply using "the Chinese" as shorthand for "the leaders of the Chinese state." But the linguistic shortcut can mislead their superiors—as is obvious, for example, when Henry Kissinger refers to Beijing as a city of "eight million Marxists" or when George Bush stresses the need to stand by Deng Xiaoping, lest we "ignore one quarter of humanity."

9. In that repression an estimated 400 were killed, 1,000 wounded, and 3,000 imprisoned. See Tang Daxian, "Cidao zhizhi Lasa" (The bayonet pointed at Lhasa), in *Minzhu Zhongguo* (Democratic China), no. 3 (August 1990): 33–50.

2 2 6    EVENING CHATS IN BEIJING

pull of the state on matters touching daily life. In 1979 and
again in 1988, the authorities announced national conventions, held in Beijing, of the All-China Federation of Literature
and Art Workers. Attendance at these huge meetings carried
both the prestige and the complications of association with state
power—as well as privileges of travel, hotel residence, and banqueting. Participants in the 1979 meeting were strongly attracted
by the theme of the convention, "Liberation of Thought," upon
which former "rightists"[10] such as Liu Binyan and Bai Hua spoke
with great eloquence and upon which the state leader Deng
Xiaoping conferred his blessings. With alienation from the state
at a relative lowpoint, several thousand people attended the
convention and many others were turned away. By 1988, however, the mood had drastically changed to one of widespread
alienation. Invitations to the convention were ignored, and
attendance fell below 1,200. There was considerable discussion
among literary scholars over the proper stance to assume: Was
it best to boycott? To attend and try to protest? To join "them"
and try to "work from within"? These questions generated, in
turn, others about personal motive: Is so-and-so really going to
"work from within" or just to climb the official ladder? Is so-
and-so boycotting out of principle or trying to look noble?

State authorities, aware in advance of the "irresolute" responses
among their "literature and art workers," sought to forestall
trouble at the 1988 meetings by announcing "three forbiddens":
(1) no big meetings (other than the official ones); (2) no "net-
working"; and (3) no elections. These "three forbiddens" stood
in poignant contrast to the "three forbiddens" of the 1979 conference, which were directed at party officials who had mis-
treated writers in the past and now were forbidden from (1)
clubbing (bullying), (2) affixing caps (stigmatizing with political labels), and (3) pulling pigtails (seizing upon flaws and refusing
to relent). In 1988 the leadership announced that officeholders
would be nominated in advance and "elected" by general
applause, not vote—a move that frustrated a number of writers

---

10. That is, recently exonerated victims of the Antirightist Campaign of 1957.

who were planning to offer "abstentions" as de facto negative votes.

After the 1988 meetings, the writers who had agreed to be "elected" to office became the subjects of animated discussion among their colleagues. Many felt that their decisions to compromise with authority had been opportunist and disgusting, while others defended them, claiming their hearts were in the right place. The debate was not just about intentions; it also concerned the nature of the system into which the newly elected writers were stepping. "Feng Jicai [a writer in his forties who had agreed to be elected vice-chair of the federation] is clear about what he wants to do," said one young writer. "He knows what's happened and wants to have a good influence. But he doesn't realize that, as soon as he steps onto the official ladder, it will start to change him. From now on, his talk will have to be 'appropriate.' But as he repeats more and more of this 'appropriate' talk, his thought will begin to follow. After a while it becomes very hard to break out of the mind-set of official talk. When you're always talking about 'correctness,' you start to believe you are actually correct. This tendency is reinforced by the perquisites that attach to every little step on the official ladder and that come to dominate the jealous calculations of the small official. So I don't think Feng Jicai's sincerity has much chance of survival, if he stays in very long." Another young writer recalled Liu Binyan's paradoxical comment that he felt "lucky" in retrospect to have been labeled a rightist in 1957 and sent for labor reform. "In 1957 Liu Binyan was already high enough in the official system that, if he had coasted peacefully into the 1960s, he would almost certainly have been caught up in the vested interests that permeate the system. This probably would not have completely killed his integrity, but at least it would have clouded his vision. He could not possibly have achieved the same trenchant views that he got by living among China's poorest people in the late 1950s."

Some were even less charitable in analyzing the motives of the officials to be, viewing the claim of intending to "work from within" as insincere—as a cover for official ambition or, at least, for the pursuit of personal security.[11] An elderly historian felt that "the main attraction of becoming a petty official is not the material advantages, which after all are very small. The main benefit is the sense of *security* it can offer." He went on to explain how becoming an official can reduce the vulnerability and powerlessness one always feels in daily life, provide a sense of belonging to a specially protected group, and also "make it a little easier to get your personal errands done."

Those who defended the new officials pointed out that in the past, especially during the Cultural Revolution, sympathetic leaders had occasionally protected intellectuals targeted for political attack. "We may still need such officials in the future," argued one young scholar in fall 1988, not suspecting that his prediction would come true within less than a year. The mollifying effect of "protective" local officials became especially apparent during the crackdown that followed the June 4 massacre. By November 1989 it was abundantly clear that the central directives ordering that supporters of the "counterrevolutionary riot" be rooted out at every level were not, in fact, having much effect at the grass roots. Local officials found ways to protect people in their own work units, for example, by declaring suspects "innocent" after investigation or "reformed" after pro forma confession. The central authorities became sufficiently frustrated that Li Peng issued an urgent order to redo the whole investigation, this time "thoroughly." But still the center failed to break many of the supporting webs. The strands of these webs, which cross the official / unofficial boundary in countless ways, form another connection between ordinary citizens and the state. Insofar as these "good" local officials are, at least formally, representatives of the state, they still tenuously support a sense of identity with it. But other, smaller groups also offer Chinese intellectuals bases for an identity.

11. See below, pp. 262–66, for more on the dilemmas of "working from within" as an official.

## Identity with Other Groups

THE "TRUE" PARTY. For some middle-aged and older intellectuals, the Chinese Communist party—or at least its idealistic remnants—stood apart from the rest of the bureaucratic state as a body still worth identifying with. In the early years of the Deng Xiaoping regime (1978–81), the party drew this sort of respect from a fair number of China's intellectuals. During those years the Deng regime was urging Chinese to repudiate the excesses of the Cultural Revolution (1966–76), purge its influences, and return to the "true path of socialism" that had been followed during 1949–66, a period nostalgically referred to as "the seventeen years." In fact, those seventeen years had been fraught with purges and famines, and most intellectuals did not remember them nearly as fondly as did the leadership, especially the elderly leadership. Still, to most Chinese in the late 1970s, "the seventeen years," during which the young Communist regime had unified the country under a basically rational bureaucracy and promised progress toward an ideal society, did seem clearly better than the time of chaos China had just been through. From a practical point of view, moreover, the model of "the seventeen years" seemed the best that one could hope for from the Communist party. Alternatives farther afield would not be tolerated.

For some, die-hard identification with the "true party" seemed to express an emotional need as much as a rational choice. This kind of attachment was most powerfully symbolized for me in the case of one elderly editor. During the Cultural Revolution he had spent years in prison, written many "self-criticisms," and seen his only son driven to suicide. In the late 1970s he was returned to his post and allowed to go home, where he drank himself into a stupor nearly every night. Yet he applied to join the Communist party and worked relentlessly until he achieved this goal.[12] "You don't understand," he explained to me, his

12. He succeeded in the mid-1980s, only to resign in disgust after the June 4, 1989, massacre.

voice quavering from a mixture of emotion and scotch. "The party is still China's only hope. The point is to get good people into it. That's what we need." The old man's determination reminded me in certain ways of American families who supported the Vietnam War after they had lost sons in it. In both cases, the cause *had* to be good, because if it were not, the sacrifices would be a waste and all the more unbearable.

There were, I felt, some other sources for the emotional need to maintain faith in the "true party." One such source was the thirst, discussed in the last chapter, for an ideological core—a set of beliefs that could guide one's actions, establish the moral realm, and help define a modern Chinese identity. In its battered condition, the Communist party may not have been an ideal answer to this deep need; but what else was there, especially for older people reluctant to withdraw a faith once so wholeheartedly invested? Within this group, which was small but still significant in the late 1980s, the Communist party's identification of itself with the fate of the Chinese nation retained a basic credibility. A middle-aged historian illustrated this point by referring to what a senior intellectual, a logician who had died in 1983, wrote in his will. "His first sentence said, 'I am deeply grateful to the party . . . because the threat of national dismemberment has been ended once and for all.' You Americans," continued the middle-aged historian, "probably cannot understand, just as our young people cannot, the awful, haunting fear that comes when your country is invaded. In the 1930s and 1940s we were reading about places like Poland, Vietnam, and India and were deeply frightened. Would we lose our country, too? Would it be torn apart? When our younger generation wonders why the older is so strangely tolerant of the Communist party, so slow to reject it, that is the part they don't understand."

AN "OPPOSITION." Had it been permitted, some kind of organized political opposition would have appeared long ago in the People's Republic of China—probably as early as the middle or late 1950s. By the late 1980s there certainly would have been an alternative to the party for people seeking identity with a national-level organization. But there was nothing in China resembling Solidarity or the Catholic church in Poland, or even a banned group like the African National Congress in South Africa. The closest things to independent organizations in China were a few outspoken publications, which nevertheless always remained at the mercy of the state control system. In the late 1970s, literary magazines such as *Anhui Literature* in Hefei and *Literary Works* in Guangzhou pressed the borderlines of permissible expression and attracted millions of readers, but never exceeded the scope allowed them by their protectors in the "reformist" wing of the ruling elite. In the mid-1980s, when their official support declined, these magazines became far less outspoken, and their popularity fell off sharply.

In the late 1980s another group of marginally "oppositionist" publications began to appear—the newspaper *World Economic Herald* (Shanghai) and the magazines *Eastern Chronicle* (Beijing and Nanjing), *Research on the State of the Nation* (Beijing and Changsha), *The Thinker* (Shanghai), and *The New Enlightenment* (Shanghai). In varying degrees these journals maintained tentative ties with reformist elements in the leadership; more important, they represented, for the first time in the People's Republic, attempts by intellectuals to establish their own public voices, however cautiously. While generally eschewing direct political comment,[13] the magazines raised serious intellectual issues upon which political opinions could rest. All five were ordered to close down in 1989. The only significant publication for intellectuals to survive that year was the Beijing monthly called *Reading,* which used indirection to express views beyond the tight limits imposed from above.

Independent groups with more structure and scope than this have been quickly repressed and have either ceased their opposition or gone underground. Group identities that have survived a clandestine existence range from Christian churches to semicriminal brotherhoods like the Triad Society, but any expression of opposition is strictly forbidden and rarely occurs

13. *World Economic Herald* and *Research on the State of the Nation* were politically somewhat more direct than the others.

in public. Work units have occasionally asserted quasi-independence—for example, at the University of Science and Technology, in Hefei, Anhui province, where in the mid-1980s President Guan Weiyuan and Vice-President Fang Lizhi encouraged independence among faculty and students. In spring 1989 the leadership faced the specter of a broader assertion of independence when groups marched into Tiananmen Square under banners proclaiming the names, and implicitly the rebellious viewpoints, of people in their work units. During the demonstrations students formed the Union of Autonomous Student Associations at Beijing Universities in explicit competition with the officially sponsored and party-controlled student associations at the various campuses. State leaders promptly denied the legitimacy of the students' autonomous union, even though—indeed, because—it was the overwhelming favorite of students. After the June 4 massacre even its unofficial existence became impossible.

In sum, efforts to form an opposition—whether through publications, established work units, or separate associations—have fallen far short of what the Chinese public would support if allowed to. The contrast between the vast discontent in China and its tiny and ephemeral outlets can strike a Westerner as strange, as does the ironic fact that intellectuals are almost completely dependent upon government repression to produce any broad-based solidarity. They become most involved and unified when their government begins leveling charges about "spiritual pollution" or the like; they trust one another most when drawn together in moral support of a colleague who has been targeted in a campaign. But when the government eases or halts its attacks, content to stifle any organized initiatives, intellectuals develop a dispirited sense of aimlessness. This was their predominant mood during much of 1988, when with no government belligerence to which to respond they could find no way to frame an overall issue despite the problems all around them. The result was a frustrating sense of "listlessness" (mei jin).[14] Although the crackdown in 1989 was a major blow to

14. See above, p. 122.

intellectuals, it did help temporarily to refocus their opinion. In the weeks and months following the massacre, listlessness returned, but there have also been lasting gains in the strength of the opposition identity.

FAMILY AND FRIENDS. Loyalty to family and friends—strong values throughout Chinese history—have been under attack by the state from the start of the People's Republic in an effort to replace them with loyalty to the party and state. This protracted conflict has forced the traditional loyalties to retreat into the private spheres of life, where they have thrived in spite of state-sponsored values and, indeed, have sometimes been honed to greater strength by the battle itself.

A professor of music who thoroughly admired the Communist party in the 1940s experienced his first inkling of disaffection in 1958, when he saw party values contradict the traditional loyalty to friends. In that year the literary commissar Zhou Yang wrote a long article arguing that recent purges of "rightist" intellectuals had been "entirely correct," citing the two examples of the writers Hu Feng and Feng Xuefeng.[15] But it was the nature of Zhou Yang's evidence against the two that caught the attention of the young music scholar. Hu Feng was judged guilty because of things he had written to a friend in a private letter, which the police had confiscated and Zhou Yang had published. Feng Xuefeng was charged as a rightist because, when he noticed a friend making a political mistake, he went to the friend with a well-intentioned warning. He should, argued the commissar Zhou Yang, have gone straight to the police, behind his friend's back. "I had trouble accepting these ways of thinking about friends," recalled the professor. "I thought Feng Xuefeng was right to go to his friend with advice. And I thought that if you really do go to the police in such circumstances, you should go *first* to your friend and explain what you're doing. As I look back on it now, I realized how naive I was then. I didn't realize that Communist morality was going to demand that all of us bare ourselves to the state and completely accept the state as if it were our family."

15. Zhou Yang, *Wenyi zhanxianshang de yichang da bianlun* (A great debate on the literary battlefront) (Beijing: Writers' Publishing House, 1958), pp. 1–49.

The mass campaigns of the Communist period, in addition to all their other purposes, can be seen as attempts to destroy family and friendship loyalties in order to clear the ground for direct state power. During the Antirightist Campaign of 1957, many couples were forced into divorce by the threat that a "tainted" spouse would ruin the lives of the untainted spouse and the children. During the Cultural Revolution, Red Guards encouraged children to denounce their parents and provide information on them that could lead to their arrest and even execution. The children were then urged to "draw a clear line" between themselves and their "black" families, and start anew by "offering up their Red hearts to Chairman Mao."

In the short run, the mass campaigns produced political enthusiasm and, for the young, even a sense of euphoria at liberation from a "backward" social world into a heady new order directly connected to a great leader and a shining ideal. But simultaneously, and less noticed at the time, the campaigns prepared the ground for long-term alienation from the state. No campaign succeeded in truly destroying the values of family and friendship so much as it drove them from public view. The demand to "surrender one's heart to Chairman Mao," to open the private realm entirely and let it merge with an all-knowing state, shrunk the private realm but did not eliminate it, and ironically increased the importance of the private space that survived. A veteran of a Cultural Revolution labor camp wryly observed that the only location at his camp where natural human warmth could be expressed was the latrine. There, as two men faced forward, alone, urinating against a wall, one could whisper to the other, "Take care." Although pressed into a tiny corner of daily life, those two words, in that context, could help to sustain morale for many days.

Under more ordinary circumstances, the unofficial connections of family and friendship remain prominent and, indeed, form the mainstream of daily life. The ubiquitous offices of the state, which work slowly and awkwardly if at all, are surrounded everywhere by more effective informal networks built from private connections—including not only family ties and genuine friendships but also "friendships of convenience" based on the mutual trading of favors. These unofficial networks, although humorously acknowledged by participants as improper "back-door connections" or "unhealthy tendencies," are widely taken for granted as the only way to get things done. And so, in the end, the effort to break family and friendship ties and replace them with state allegiance ironically has stimulated a cancer-like growth of unofficial ties, swelling and distorting the same traditional loyalties that were to have been replaced. Although citizens are obliged in several ways to identify with the state and its work units, the identity they feel with their networks of family, friends, and personal connections is more intimate and true.

## Individualism

In asking Chinese intellectuals which groups they identify with, I often heard answers such as "None; I want to identify only with myself." This was, to be sure, always a wish more than a reality. Even those who pursued individuality seemed to do so, paradoxically, because their peers were doing it. But their aims were sincere, and the wish for individuality inspired another sort of Chinese identity.

"We are called *Zhongguoren* [literally, 'China people'],"  observed a young writer. "But this has always meant two things: (1) that we are Chinese people, and (2) that we are people 'of' China—that is, who 'belong' to China. For years our leadership has emphasized loyalty to 'country,' 'party,' and 'state.' Gradually it seems that all Chinese 'belong' to this party-country-state. After a while the notion sinks into us and remains lodged inside even when we want to get away from it. Recently XXX [a famous contemporary writer] admitted that he has acted like a 'dumb bird' for years, always wanting to 'help' the party, and feeling somehow satisfied and 'properly in place' when he does help—instead of listening to his own values. The state's 'own-ership' of us is carried out in part through the 'pan-moralism' (*fandaodezhuyi*) of the official language. The 'glorious party' is the same as 'our ancestral land,' and it's 'always correct' . . . and it's all so great that you wouldn't dream of questioning it."

May Fourth intellectuals sometimes stood as exemplars of individuality.[16] Dai Qing said that she wanted in the future to write about Chen Duxiu (a founder of the Communist party in 1921, purged as a Trotskyite in 1928)—not to cast him as either hero or villain, but because he was one of the last Chinese intellectuals to display "personal character," a trait she considered lost for several decades but now, happily, making a return. A young writer attributed the attraction of Dai Qing's work to her consistent emphasis on the individual: "Sometimes the biggest questions of our time, or of human life generally, are revealed by a close look into one person—and not measured, as we have been taught to think, by numbers of people."

Liu Zaifu, through his famous article entitled "On the Subjectivity of Literature,"[17] became closely associated with the ideal of the intellectual's independence and the values of freedom, responsibility, and integrity that underlay it. Liu argued that the annihilation of individual nature by group nature was a fact of twentieth-century Chinese history that most had overlooked. "We fought the Opium War for national face," he said. "On that issue, the problem of losing one's individuality did not arise, because individual wills and collective will naturally coincided. But in the middle decades of the twentieth century, collective will took over and pushed individuality out. Consciousness was 'nationalized' and also 'idealized.' In literature, for example, the images of 'noble' prostitutes came to be very different from the realities of prostitutes' lives. Later we got 'revolutionary romanticism,' which described wars in an even more idealized way. All I'm saying now is that we need to restore

16. On the importance of May Fourth, see above, pp. 128–34. Although May Fourth intellectuals were not revolting against the imposed conformity of a Marxist-Leninist system, their revolt against "feudal" social conventions raised a problem of individual liberation that current intellectuals considered similar in kind, if not degree, to their situation. In addition to taking May Fourth intellectuals as models, younger intellectuals often harbored an idealized concept of "the Western intellectual."

17. See chapter 3, note 13.

the place of the individual's judgment, in addition to having national policies." Liu's argument was a challenge to party authorities because it seemed to undermine the iron discipline referred to as "party nature." But Liu denied that his point was primarily political. "Moreover," he explained, "I have never been opposed to supporting the party *if one wishes*. I'm just saying that the individual's own judgment should be the basis for the decision."

Liu's case for individual integrity has appealed especially to the younger generation. This points up another sort of group identity available to Chinese intellectuals: the generations defined by landmark events in recent Chinese history.

## Four Generations

Their collective sense of victimization by the state has given Chinese intellectuals in the post-Mao period a much stronger solidarity than they experienced during the Maoist years or than intellectuals in Western societies normally feel. When they differentiate groups within their community, they still conceive of such groups as parts of the larger whole. The fissures that separate the parts are of several kinds. For example, in the late 1980s some natural scientists felt they could understand China more "objectively" than their social science colleagues, whom they considered to be entangled in culture-bound assumptions. Intellectuals in commercial cities such as Shanghai and Guangzhou sometimes found their colleagues in Beijing too idealistic, carried away by the self-importance of the capital city instead of being appropriately practical. Beijing intellectuals, in turn, criticized their Shanghai and Guangzhou counterparts as excessively mercenary.

But the most common way in which intellectuals subdivided their community was by generation, and they usually distinguished three or four. The older generation comprises those whose formative years preceded the 1949 revolution. They had relatively Westernized educations, and their initial impressions of the Communist movement included heroic episodes in the Long March and the Anti-Japanese War. Those in the middle generation were educated in the 1950s when China was heavily under Soviet influence and before the problems of the revolution were sufficiently apparent to create much disaffection. The younger generation comprises those whose education was interrupted by the Cultural Revolution. Although they have felt embittered ever since, they have often replaced their broken schooling with a tough independence of mind won from the harshness of their lives. Some Chinese intellectuals also distinguish a fourth generation, the youngest, those who were educated during the moneymaking decade of the 1980s and who find the various tribulations of their elders to be, on the whole, irrelevant.

THE OLDER GENERATION. The educational opportunities available to the older generation were often the envy of the younger, who pointed to "free" or "Western-style" education as the source of the broad vision and powerful integrity that they admired in the best of their elders. "How can we ever compare to Ba Jin [the famous writer who studied in France] or Qian Zhongshu [the renowned literary scholar trained in England]?" asked a young writer in Beijing, who had spent ten of his formative years in a Central Asian desert. "Back in those days, even the ones who didn't go abroad could get a good education in China. There were good schools in China then, ones that provided *real* education. The older generation has always had this basic resource to draw upon; it has had fundamental standards by which to interpret all the chaos that's followed. No other generation in China has that."[18]

18. This comment fits with my impressions of Qian Zhongshu during the first and only time I met the eminent man. It was in fall 1979 at a reception for American scholars newly arrived to do research in China. Such research had just become possible for the first time in thirty years, and the atmosphere was still somewhat tense and awkward. I was accompanied to the reception by two official "companions," ostensibly literary scholars but actually party functionaries assigned to supervise and report. After shaking hands with me and them, Qian Zhongshu looked at me and asked, with a self-assured calmness that only made his challenge to the face of my "companions" more astonishing, "Have you met any scholars yet?"

But if the prerevolutionary grounding of the older generation seemed to give it a moral gyroscope of its own, the steady view that resulted also sometimes included a sympathy for the origins of the revolution that younger generations had trouble accepting. The experience of the Japanese invasion and the resulting sense of high-minded patriotism remained deeply embedded in the older generation's worldview. The Communist party's credit with the older generation for helping to rid China of imperialism had been fatally undermined by the late 1980s, but that generation's residual sense of a duty to be self-sacrificing and group minded remained strong. Older intellectuals generally looked with disfavor upon the "selfish" tendencies of youth.

THE MIDDLE GENERATION. I often heard the view that the middle generation was the "weakest" and "most useless" of those currently on the scene. The young said this most often, but even some of the middle generation's own prominent members expressed this opinion. "My generation," according to a famous middle-generation literary scholar, "was not really 'educated,' strictly speaking. We were *trained* in the 'new classics' of Marxism-Leninism and then directed into special fields according to the needs of the party. We became the happy tools of the party." The younger generation often referred to "the 1950s crowd" as a sort of deadweight barrier that lay between it and the intellectual tradition that had been cut off in the 1940s. "Somehow," said Su Wei, the young writer and critic who preferred to ride a bicycle through the Beijing snow than live in Hong Kong, "some of the fifties crowd are also the ones who offer up the most crotchety opinions, like charging young people with various kinds of 'un-Chinese' behavior." With his characteristic frankness, the middle-aged Li Tuo said, "My generation has been good-for-nothing. We're hopeless if we can't start by admitting at least that much."

The question of whether the middle generation could indeed admit this became a subject of debate. One young writer felt that those who had made their names in the 1950s could never—despite twenty or more years of persecution—be fully free from "the fifties mind-set" and its faith in "the true party" and "true socialism." "They can't deny the 1950s without denying themselves," she said. "There are certain questions they just can't ask." An editor who had been educated in the 1950s and was a lifetime party member allowed, "We in the middle generation can easily see that the party is corrupt now. What many still cannot see is that it was founded in 'peasant consciousness' *from the beginning* and has been anti-intellectual all along. During the Cultural Revolution, the party hacks were *delighted* with the slogan 'Intellectuals Are Ignorant'; for them it was a call to arms. Even now the party opposes investment in education. All along the party has been like a great cat, crouching to spring onto intellectuals. The middle generation has been blind to this fact."

But however severe the criticisms of the middle generation, they were conceived at bottom as differences "among us" about how to handle "them." For example in 1988 some young scholars criticized Liu Zaifu's advocacy of "humanism" and "individualism" on the grounds that these were "eighteenth-century" Western values and now "out of date"; but as soon as Liu was attacked from the *other* side, by party ideologues who castigated his ideas as "bourgeois deviation," the same young people immediately closed ranks in defense of Liu. There was, moreover, a forgiving tendency to view people harboring "the 1950s mind-set" as its victims rather than its perpetrators. "Objectively speaking," said a young historian, "the 1950s generation has been our weakest. But you have to blame the situation; you can't blame individuals." Dai Qing put the point more pungently, describing her own "crippled" generation in an astonishing image. "At the old entertainment fairs in China, they used to display children who had been raised inside a basket so as to grow up deformed, in the shape of the basket. When this happens, do we blame the child, or the one who caged it?"

THE YOUNGER GENERATION. A logician in his early thirties—a rising star academically—described his generation as "not having the historical burden of the older generations." He went on, "We were not defined by the 1940s or the 1950s. To me, talk of 'liberation,' the 'golden age,' and the Antirightist Campaign seems almost like talk about a mythical past. My identity is not there. My generation feels basically cold to politics of any kind." His friend, a literary scholar, said, "We don't have heroes, either Chinese or Western, as our elders had. Forty years ago, in literature, there were Lu Xun, Ba Jin, Mao Dun, Lao She, and so many others; and overseas there were Darwin, and Goethe, and Ibsen, and Tagore. But now there are no heroes, no models for us. Heroism is gone. That's partly good, I guess, because that old-style 'heroic patriotism' is also gone. Our generation has a more worldwide perspective; we measure things by world standards, not 'Chinese' standards. In our work we seek truth for its own sake more than our elders, who still are beholden to the idea of 'knowledge in service of the state.' "

A young writer explained the difference between her generation's view of the party-state and that of older generations. "They think in terms of the party's 'mistakes'—its deviations from its original and proper course. You can try to convince them that the problem was more fundamental—that the revolution was misguided from the start—and if you give them enough evidence, you might convince them. But right here is the difference between their generation and mine. We don't need to search for evidence; for us it is not a question that needs investigation. When we grew up, during the Cultural Revolution, the sky was blue and the government bad. No need to analyze it. Our sense of these things is *intuitive*. What those of the middle generation see as the need for evidence, we see as their struggle to purge themselves of their own myths."

But the middle generation had criticisms of the younger as well. A computer scientist who was also an administrator of a research institute observed, "There is a lot of carping—especially among the young—that is made possible only by the progress we have made in the 1980s. Compared with the 1970s, we have higher living standards today and more freedom of expression. The expectations of the young have risen far too fast; actual progress can't keep up. And so they complain. They feel aggrieved and become more and more selfish. I can see it very clearly in my research institute. The people in their forties and older will still do a good job because their conscience, their sense of personal responsibility, tells them to. Unfortunately, in China, we often can't reward our people adequately, and the difference between doing a good job or not is left to people's consciences. The middle and older generations still seem to have their own standards, but the young don't." Liu Zaifu found a certain contagious quality in the cynicism of youth. "There is a devil-may-care disease adrift in the land," he said. "It's one thing to be utterly disillusioned, but quite another to respond by acting irresponsibly."

THE YOUNGEST GENERATION. This generation (aged roughly 16 to 24 in the late 1980s) resembles the "young generation" (aged 25 to 35) in many ways. Older generations often do not distinguish the two. Indeed, it is the 25-to-35 generation that most feels the need to distinguish itself from a younger group. The two diverge most clearly in their experience of the Cultural Revolution. Those in the 25-to-35 group have painful memories of the period. Some saw their childhood families torn apart, and many feel aggrieved—at least in retrospect—that their schooling was interrupted. Their anger at the party-state still strongly colors their worldview; yet this same obsessive bitterness keeps Chinese politics and society at the center of their concerns. Members of the 16-to-24 group, by contrast, being only toddlers during the Cultural Revolution, absorbed most of their social influences from the "make money, study abroad" ethos of the 1980s. Their attitude toward the party-state has in a sense moved beyond cynicism to a kind of postcynical nihilism that finds official presentations not even worthy of rejection, but simply irrelevant.

An investigative reporter in her early thirties, a member of the "disgusted but still concerned" group, disapproved of the nihilism of the very young, but also managed to find a positive side to it. Her description of this constructive side is a measure, however, of how deeply alienated both the younger generations were. "The youngest," she said, "think Chinese society and politics are all absurd. Their attitude is that if you can get a bit of material advantage, then do it—that's all that matters. I don't agree with this attitude, but I don't spend time trying to change their minds, either. I think it's probably good for China to have people like this around. They are an antidote to the old style of politics—a style so stubbornly entrenched that you might say it *needs* an antidote of this strength. Of all the people in China, these youngest ones are alone in breaking out of the networks of state-authority-plus-personal-connections. They sometimes act without considering all the ramifications. Their 'random behavior' eats away at the networks, and that's good for China. They also are eager to go abroad, to leave China. But that's good, too. For them, it's a kind of personal liberation; and if they come back to China, the influence they bring back will be good for China, too."

The wish among elite university students to leave China, which became almost universal after the June 4 massacre, had been growing ever stronger since the crackdown on the 1986 student movement. Students' preoccupation with the TOEFL test, and the shrewdness of their personal strategies for obtaining visas, foreign currency, and admission to Western universities, were all rapidly intensifying through the late 1980s. Some older intellectuals, while understanding the motivation of the students—and supporting it in their own children—also felt regretful that the young were so determined to leave China. "The Beijing University students are in sullen withdrawal," a physicist observed in fall 1988. "Their attitude is: if I try to do something for China, I simply waste my time. Therefore I work for myself. But I can't work for myself very well in this country. Therefore I leave. This year? Fine. Next year? Okay. The year after next? Also okay. *But I leave.*"

One may wonder what course the radical alienation of China's youngest intellectuals will eventually take. Will they carry their complete disaffection through the later stages of their lives, or will they eventually inherit the intellectuals' traditional sense of responsibility for China? Much depends, of course, on events that are hard to predict. If the political situation were to improve, their alienation would begin to melt. But even assuming little change on the political scene, there is evidence that the embers of their Chinese pride will still smolder and that their sense of Chinese "identity" will persist. Their participation in the patriotic demonstrations of spring 1989 is one indication of this. So too have been the unusual but significant cases of Chinese students who have studied in the West and voluntarily returned to China, eager to help.

## The Returned Student

Western university officials generally do not appreciate that the overwhelming goals of Chinese students who come to the West are (1) to stay and (2) to make money. (Officials at China's State Education Commission have a much more realistic understanding of these facts and do their best to cover them up.)[19] These goals of the students arise within their campus cultures inside China and are already well formed before they leave for the West. Among those headed to America, strategies for getting the coveted "green card" that certifies permanent residence and can eventually lead to citizenship are well known and sometimes carefully considered in advance. They include such methods as marrying an American citizen or "buying" a card illegally—in addition to the standard route of finding a job that qualifies. Students who participate in this culture of the would-be émigré are clearly marked by it even before they leave China. If they actually are accepted at a Western university, their special identity becomes immediately more distinct. The exercise of having to apply for a passport and get other bureaucratic permissions—which, like so much else in China, can require the use of personal connections, gift giving, and other "back

19. During the 1980s China's State Education Commission periodically published statistics showing that "the majority" of Chinese students and scholars have returned or intend to return. But they could produce these statistics only by including in the aggregate, without pointing out the relevant distinctions, cases such as the following: middle-aged and elderly visiting scholars; short-term visitors and delegation members; students on state scholarships whose families back in China would be subject to punishment if they failed to return; and students who, although they have no intention of returning, are understandably reluctant to report this fact to consular officials.

door" influence—adds a sharp impatience to the distaste students normally feel toward state offices. In 1988, students in Beijing referred to the period between their acceptance by a foreign university and the date of their departure from China as "the period of cultivation of loathing." Nearly all who make it to the West aim to stay if they can.[20]

There are, however, an admirable few who return to China voluntarily, and their cases help illuminate the problem of group identity for Chinese intellectuals. Those who return to China reenter an environment in which they continue to be considered special cases, now even more so because of their peculiar decision to leave the place to which everyone else is trying to go. In the late 1980s there was a curious two-sidedness in their immediate colleagues' attitudes toward returned students. On the one hand, they admired the returnees, as if pilgrims back from Shangri-la who still carried some of its dust in their pores; returnees in Beijing referred to this perception as "the halo effect." But they were also regarded with envy, jealousy, and a fear born of insecurity over whether these anointed ones would outshine and upstage those who had never left China.

Some of the returnees had come back to China relying on their government's promises of good treatment, especially in housing and employment, and were bitter that the promises seemed to turn empty as soon as they were back. "If I had known how hard it would be, I would not have come back," said an idealistic young man with a Ph.D. in chemistry from an American university. "I knew it was true that China 'needed' me, and I believed that the government was sincere in promising to put my skills to use. But I arrived back in the middle of the [1987] drive against 'bourgeois liberalization.' The officials in my institute wouldn't come out and say so, but they were afraid to assign an apartment to me, because they were afraid others could accuse them of helping a 'bourgeois' type. They just said they were 'working on it,' and told me to wait. But where was

20. Chinese who come to the West, become citizens, and return to visit China on Western passports are given much more respect by the Chinese government than they received as Chinese citizens.

I supposed to live? I went back to Chengdu to live with my parents, and then the leaders said I had 'left work' and that they would stop my salary until I returned to Beijing. Nearly a year later, after the political campaign subsided, they finally found me a one-room apartment with its own small toilet and kitchen, so I moved back and went to work. The laboratory conditions in China are not very good, so my work went slowly—but that's all right. I expected that. What I didn't expect were the jealousies among my colleagues. They always asked my help in setting up experiments, but constantly talked behind my back. I found it very hard to make friends. I understood their viewpoint better after one of them, one day, lashed out about my housing assignment: 'Your apartment is bigger than any of ours. And you're not married, but we have families. If you had stayed in America, one of us could have had your apartment. And you, in America, would have had something bigger, too. Wouldn't we all have been better off?'

"From that day, I never could feel at home in my work unit. It's strange, but I didn't even feel entirely Chinese. They regarded me as part American, and I started to feel that way myself. That's funny, because when I was in America, I always felt very Chinese; now back in China, I feel part American. I started to feel suspended between the two places, as if I would always be half-and-half . . . or no, actually, not just a half-and-half mixture but what we in chemistry call a compound—something whose properties are different from those of any of its constituents. I am a compound. I felt less strange, though, when I began to talk to a few other returned students. I learned that others had the same problems of 'the halo effect,' the jealousies, and the sense of being a misfit. One of these people told me he had declined to be considered for a promotion in his department. He insisted that others deserved it more, and his gesture helped his relations with his colleagues somewhat. Another told me that the 'compound' problem would never go away, but that she likes to go back to the United States for short-term visits to escape the frustrations of work in China. She called this 'recharging her battery,' with the double meaning of 'catch up in her field' and 'recover her energies.' "

Another returnee had been trained in Chomskyan linguistics. "When I work with my colleagues," he said, "I have to be extra careful about how I mix professional comments with considerations of their face. This can be frustrating. I see a lot of wasted effort that is simply based on ignorance. But if I point it out, they react defensively." I asked for an example, and the young man answered with an analogy.

"Imagine two engineers pedaling their bicycles along a Beijing street," he said. "They are arguing with each other about who will be first to get to the moon. They have read that people have got to the moon before, but don't know that you need a rocket in order to do it. They naturally assume that a bicycle is the way to go, and each has put meticulous thought into improving his bicycle in marginal ways, aiming to be the first Chinese scientist to get to the moon. Now I come along, and I have been trained—one, two, three—in how to build the kind of rocket that can reach the moon. I offer to teach them about it, and a part of them wants to learn, but the other part reacts defensively. They say, 'You don't understand Chinese realities. You come back with your fancy foreign theories and think you're better than us.' Beneath this reaction lurks the innuendo that I am an 'imitation foreigner'[21] or even, if someone wants to say so during a political campaign, a 'bourgeois liberal.'

"So," he continued, "after a while I just decided not to interrupt them any more. They work on their angle, and I work on mine. I don't go to their seminars any more. It only bores me, and it threatens them. I work at home. I feel lonely and depressed most of the time. To whom can I talk? The colleagues my own age are too envious to be friendly. The older generation feel secure in their positions, but in China the traditional relations between 'teacher generation' and 'student generation' make it impossible really to be *friends* with an older scholar."

This young man did have one friend, a returnee whom he had met in the United States and who worked in an entirely different field. I asked the friend about the loneliness problem.

21. "Imitation foreigner," another phrase made famous by Lu Xun's *The True Story of Ah Q* (see chapter 4, note 22), refers to a Chinese who puts on Western airs in an attempt to raise his status among Chinese.

"He works very late every night," was the answer. "Then he sits alone and drinks until he falls asleep. He likes me to come to his room late at night and drink with him. We have some good heart-to-heart talks. But even if we don't talk, he likes me to sit with him and share the silence."

In sum, contemporary Chinese intellectuals must be chameleons in their ability to shift among identities. Seldom is it possible to identify fully and comfortably with any one ideology or social group. The individual must find a balance among several identities and—even more important—adjust them to suit the demands of the situation. A person might wear some identity with the state in official contexts and then shift to a wholly antistate identity when commiserating with a friend; or take on the identity of a "foreign-influenced type" in order to get assigned to a delegation going abroad, but then want to "represent China" while overseas. Such flexibility of identity may be common to members of all complex societies; but it is especially pronounced, and sometimes painfully awkward, for Chinese intellectuals.

It is, moreover, not what they want. Their ideal, which emerges from the tradition of Chinese literati, is to know exactly who they are, to be proud of it, to be respected for it by society, and to feel that this identity will not change. Rather than having to shift identities from context to context, they would like to peer inside themselves and sense a solid core—a set of values or a moral ideology that would provide a reliable guide to behavior. There has been a good deal of self-scrutiny in China recently, but the core is not there.

# Six

# RESPONSIBILITY

As the months of my posting in Beijing passed and I began to assimilate the discovery of extensive gloom and bitterness among China's intellectuals, a second kind of surprise, more enigmatic and less depressing, began to take shape in my perceptions of their mental world. They called this attitude their *youhuan yishi*, or "worrying mentality." At a conference on Sino-American relations in late 1988, one Chinese scholar sighed regretfully as she said, "Americans can never, never really appreciate what we mean by this term." She may be right, and yet the purpose of this chapter is to come as close as we can.

## The Worrying Mentality

*Youhuan yishi* is, first of all, related to patriotism in the sense that China, one way or another, is always the main object of worry. The entire mentality is couched in the big question "What can we *do* about China?"—a question that often takes on a despairing tone. In its pessimism and self-doubt, *youhuan yishi* stands apart from the chauvinistic or jingoistic varieties of patriotism. In fall 1988 an investigative reporter published a review of the large body of "literary reportage" that had recently appeared on problems such as inflation, overpopulation, the housing shortage, the brain drain, low educational standards, and even the "unmentionable" ones—prostitution, abortion, and begging. Yet his overall point was to praise the *youhuan yishi* and "the sense of mission and responsibility" of the authors of the reviewed works.[1] Never celebratory in its mood, *youhuan yishi* dwells on "the dark side" of society, on the very facts that undermine chauvinistic claims.

Yet the intensity with which Chinese intellectuals undertake this self-examination rests upon their fierce conviction that China can and should be an exemplary culture and society. This pride undergirds the whole spectrum of complaints about the dark side of society, creates an especially sharp contrast between social ideals and reality, and impels the demand that China, certainly *China*, must do better. But even this underlying pride—an essential component of *youhuan yishi*—is not exactly the same as ordinary patriotism, because in the end it aims at a morality that is fundamentally human, not just Chinese. It holds that in a proper world, China should exemplify the best way to conduct human affairs. Other societies should—and would, in a proper world—emulate China.[2]

*Youhuan yishi* is, in one form or another, pervasive among Chinese intellectuals in all fields, localities, and even generations. The young, to be sure, exhibit it less, although it remains to be seen whether they will articulate it more as they mature. Intellectuals in Beijing, close to the political and intellectual centers, seem somewhat more smitten than their colleagues elsewhere. Natural scientists are usually as deeply affected as humanists and social scientists, differing only in that they can generally maintain a clearer borderline between *youhuan yishi* and their professional work.

In winter of 1989 a professor of Chinese at Beijing Univer-

1. Zhang Shengyou, "Baogaowenxue de juewu" (The awakening of literary reportage), *Wenyibao* (Beijing), October 8, 1988, p. 1.

2. There is, of course, an arrogance to this view, even after allowing for its pan-humanist assumption that others can learn. But we should recall that confidence in the civilizing value of one's own culture is not unique to the Chinese; among nineteenth-century Westerners it contributed to the impulse to colonize Asia and Africa.

sity published an interview on the roles of contemporary intellectuals, distinguishing three main types: first, those who "taint" themselves by engaging in commercial activity or compromising with the state by accepting official posts; second, those who bury their heads in their own scholarly work, usually living in poverty and virtual anonymity; and third, those who dedicate their work to improving society. All three types, the professor argued, exhibit *youhuan yishi* and deserve sympathy and respect. Those who fall into the first category do not really want to taint themselves; they are driven to do so and feel guilty about it. Those who bury their heads still hope that their scholarly results will be broadly useful in the end. Yet they often find that their labors of love are ignored and that they have become "separated from the times." Those who work to improve society, whether they succeed or not, represent the courageous ideal of the Chinese intellectual in its fullest form.[3] A literary scholar commented that events such as the Tiananmen demonstrations in spring 1989 show that *youhuan yishi* is latent in the first two categories of intellectuals and emerges in times of crisis: many scholars apparently wedded to their desks began to march and sign petitions in spring 1989; others tainted by moonlighting jobs donated both time and money to the demonstrators.

Most Chinese I spoke with attributed the origins of *youhuan yishi* to traditional conceptions of the intellectual's moral duty to "take responsibility for all under heaven," to "be the first in the world to assume its worries," and so on. Stories of courageous intellectuals such as Liang Shuming, Hu Feng, and Wu Han,[4] who had championed these virtues even under the Com-

3. Gu Jianping and Xu Huaiqian, "Dangdai zhishifenzi de jiaose zhuanhuan: Fangwen Qian Liqun fu jiaoshou" (The transformation in the roles of contemporary Chinese intellectuals: An interview with Associate Professor Qian Liqun), *Beijing daxue xueshu lilun fukan* (Beijing University supplement on scholarly theory), March 1, 1989, pp. 1, 4.

4. Wu Han was a historian and deputy mayor of Beijing whose play *Hai Rui Dismissed from Office* (1961) indirectly but strongly criticized Mao Zedong for the disastrous Great Leap Forward policies of 1958–60. See Merle Goldman, *China's Intellectuals: Advise and Dissent* (Cambridge: Harvard University Press, 1981), pp. 34–36. On Liang Shuming, see chapter 3, note 12. On Hu Feng, see chapter 3, note 3.

munists, helped to maintain the vitality of the ideal. But whether speaking of the origins of *youhuan yishi* or of its contemporary practice, most people regarded the attitude as distinctively Chinese. In the spring of 1988 Liu Zaifu observed, "In America, if a writer or an intellectual went around all day shouting about 'the duty of the writer' or 'the mission of the intellectual,' he might seem a bit ridiculous; but in China, to be a writer or intellectual and *not* speak of responsibility and mission seems equally ridiculous."[5] I sometimes commented to my Chinese friends, in an effort to cheer them, that I admired their concern for the large issues, and wished that we in America showed the same sort of commitment. On one occasion a senior historian, a man who understood recent American history well, rebutted me in an illuminating way.

"You say our big concerns are admirable; I say they're pitiable. Where do they come from? From traditional Chinese virtues? Only in part. Do you remember the 1960s in your country, when students and intellectuals were questioning 'the system'? Those were 'big picture' worries, were they not? And why were people worrying? Because of *crisis*. They asked the big questions about 'the system' because of a fear that something was fundamentally wrong. But China, our China, has been in crisis almost constantly now for about 150 years, ever since the Opium War. We've had no choice, really, but to keep asking the 'big picture' questions—over and over again. Is that admirable or pitiable? I just hope a time will come in China when we don't need this 'admirable worrying' any more. It seems ironic, I know, but the 'admirable' Chinese intellectuals identify with China more strongly as China gets more and more *badly off*. If China were suddenly to do better, their commitment would go down. And that would be fine."

Another historian, while agreeing with her colleague's argument that a "crisis mentality" had much to do with *youhuan yishi*, was unwilling to overlook its distinctively Chinese component. "Isn't it true," she asked, "that the American antiwar

5. "Wenxue yu yishu de qingsi: Li Zehou he Liu Zaifu de wenxue duihua" (Thoughts on literature and art: A dialogue on literature between Li Zehou and Liu Zaifu), *People's Daily (Overseas Edition)*, April 14, 1988, p. 4.

movement in the 1960s was stimulated by the military draft? If the American questioning of 'the system' came about because people were worried about their own fates, then it's still different from *youhuan yishi,* whose aim is to set things right as a matter of principle, even at the cost of one's personal fate." This comment elicited a counterriposte from a younger historian. "I have a friend who is an entomologist," he said. "He worries a lot about China. I am a modern China historian, but I don't worry about bugs. Why does he worry about my field and I not worry about his? Because he *has to* worry about China. The sorry reality of China affects his life every day; if bugs bothered me that much, I would worry about bugs, too. So I'm not so sure *youhuan yishi* is purely idealistic."

Even considering its more mundane causes, there is much to admire in *youhuan yishi.* I felt this admiration most strongly when going to visit friends in their homes. On these visits I would generally walk down a chilly, unlit street, pick my way through the rubble of the Beijing street-repair projects that seem never to end, enter a barren cement-framed doorway, carefully ascend a dark—sometimes pitch-dark—stairwell cluttered with bicycles, garbage receptacles, and an occasional scurrying rat. Knocking on the door, and listening as a series of locks was undone, I would then enter a cramped apartment modestly decorated with a few prized possessions—perhaps a painting, a television set, an antiquarian piano, and always some books. In these surroundings, my friends would worry about China, the obligations of *youhuan yishi* their only surplus.

More than once on these visits, I was made to think of the Buddhist metaphor of the lotus, its blossom floating on the river surface as its roots extend into the muck at the bottom. Chinese intellectuals themselves sometimes remarked upon the incongruity between their high-minded concerns and their dreary surroundings, often finding humor in the irony. Liu Zaifu, even while pleading the case for *youhuan yishi,* referred to it as the "prevailing malady" of Chinese intellectuals.[6] A young sociologist, in declining his relatives' offer to emigrate to the West,

6. Ibid.

facetiously characterized his motives for staying: "Leave China? Like everybody else? Not me. I will stay till the bitter end, until only the smartest person—me—and the stupidest people—my government—are left here."

*Youhuan yishi* was itself one of the issues that Chinese intellectuals worried about. They wondered whether this kind of constant, depressing concern was useful. Did it constrict their vision and prevent them from functioning in more enlightened and productive ways? They were especially concerned that events in the last century and a half had seemed to transform *youhuan yishi* from its broadly humanistic grounding in Confucian tradition into more narrow, set views that could stifle independent thought and aid dictators. The transformation seemed to have two stages. First, the shocks of nineteenth-century Western imperialism and twentieth-century Japanese aggression had seemed to reduce *youhuan yishi* to a relatively simple imperative to "resist the invaders" and "save China." Then, in the 1950s, it was reshaped again, when the new Communist government introduced a heavy emphasis on loyalty to itself as the representative of "the people."

In its demands for loyalty, the new government sought to conflate all of the several aspects of *youhuan yishi*. Duty to country or society became coterminous with duty to the party; opposition to China's enemies was equated with support of the party; patriotism came to mean loyalty to China's current political system. By the late 1980s the rapid decline in the prestige of the party had led, especially among young intellectuals, to a rebellion against responsibility in every form. "We don't want *anyone* laying duties on us any more," said a young writer. "We've been told what to do, what to think, ever since we were born. And there has always been a big *moral* overlay to it. 'If you don't obey, you're immoral.' This has always been the government's attitude. Now our intellectual leaders like Liu Zaifu and Liu Binyan are also telling us about our social responsibilities, and also add their big moral overlay. We don't want it! We don't want any talk of responsibility." Said another, "The older generations were so preoccupied with 'saving China' in the 1930s and 1940s that they froze their own critical judgment and were easily manipulated in the 1950s. They can't see how they were trapped by their own 'responsibility' ideas. And they want us to *follow* them?"

To the older generations these attitudes were irritating but not easily dismissed. Many sympathized with the young in their strong desire to be free from party control, but they were pained by the rejection of basic ideas of social responsibility. "Some youth," as Liu Zaifu saw it, "have developed an 'anti–social consciousness'—the attitude that, since society is hopeless, I will care only for myself. This is the very opposite of *youhuan yishi*. It's too bad. The young don't realize that prior generations of Chinese intellectuals also faced some very hard times earlier in this century. One of the most valuable things to come out of May Fourth times was the idea of *resisting despair*. Lu Xun's story called 'The Passerby'[7] shows it well: a man traveling along a road stops to rest at a roadside stand. He doesn't exactly know what his destination is or how he will get to it, but after a short rest he *keeps going*. He won't give up just because things seem hopeless. In fact, you might say he keeps going *just because* things seem hopeless. This determination to 'resist despair' could be found in Lu Xun's generation; I wish I could find it among our young people today." A younger writer who was listening nodded his head and said, "The Communist party has given responsibility a bad name."

## The Responsibility of Expression: Two Traps

The logic of *youhuan yishi* demands that one express one's worries, and it is fairly easy to do so in private—indeed, sometimes so volubly as to amaze an outsider. But public expression carries serious risks.

One of these might be called "the personal risk trap." It is built upon two conditions: (1) certain criticisms of the party

7. Lu Xun, "Guo ke" (The passerby) (1925), *Selected Words of Lu Hsun* (Beijing: Foreign Languages Press, 1956), 1:332–38.

and state are widespread and strongly felt, and (2) the party's practice of making the person who steps forward with criticisms a scapegoat is very familiar. This technique for stifling dissent is known, among other names, as "killing a chicken to frighten the monkeys." The person who speaks out also elicits responses from those who agree with him or her, but under the conditions of the "personal risk trap," these responses are a combination of two seemingly contradictory elements: admiration and distancing. Others are excited when someone speaks out, but veil their excitement in order to avoid the official shadow that will fall over the speaker. They will want to applaud, but will take care not to be the first to applaud. They will join in if somehow general applause breaks out, taking advantage of the anonymity of the crowd and the protection afforded by the vulnerability of the one who stood forth to criticize. Thus the larger a dissenting crowd becomes, the more easily it can grow even larger.

When the "personal risk trap" is operating properly, which is most of the time, it stifles dissent and enforces an artificial stability.[8] In those unusual times when its operation comes undone, the effects can be highly volatile. Two examples of this are the sudden rapid swells in popularity of Liu Binyan in 1980 and Fang Lizhi in 1986. In these cases, the original "crowds" were readers of fiction and reportage (for Liu) and student audiences (for Fang), but both groups of supporters propelled their leaders to national prominence. The undoing of the "risk trap" was also clear in the astonishing growth in crowd size at Tiananmen between mid-April 1989, when a few thousand marched on the square, and mid-May, when one million people packed the same space and residents in the small back alleys throughout Beijing expressed support. The regime itself is aware of this potential volatility; that is one of the reasons why it asserts, at the earliest possible stage, that dissenters form only "a tiny minority" of Chinese society.[9]

8. Since the trap does work most of the time, dissident expressions seem "abnormal," and consequently the words "normal" and "natural" sometimes become antonyms. Self-censorship and playing the political language game become the "normal" state of life; it is abnormal to allow more "natural" feelings to become publicly visible.

9. Although both the Chinese people and the Chinese regime are well aware of the

Why do individuals step forth to defy the "personal risk trap"? Isn't it foolish to do so? In my experience, none of those who make such a move, whether at the national level or in local work units, are naive about the consequences. They try to calculate the effects of their actions in advance.[10] They act on a variety of motives, from idealism and raw courage to the hope that speaking out will bring fame, admiration, and perhaps even international notice and a chance to leave China. In calculations of whether to take a risk, the support of a powerful person often weighs more than the number of relatively powerless people who will applaud from a distance. The powerful supporter can be a sympathetic official (perhaps expressing himself privately, but promising key support within official circles, if necessary), a relative (the children of high officials are among the most successful at flaunting the "risk trap"), or others within a social web built by the trading of favors. One's own trading position is of great importance, as is a sense of timing. It is critical to study the shifting political winds for opportune moments. In cases of some prominence, foreigners can be a factor, because foreign notice can offer at least some protection to the speaker. But none of these calculations can ever be precise, and they can turn wildly inaccurate when unpredictable factors intervene. Dissenters must always command the courage to take serious risks.

The few whose motives in speaking out are most idealistic present a poignant irony. By taking on personal risk for the common good, they exhibit a public-mindedness that has been increasingly hard to find anywhere else in their tired, battered society. The "risk trap" discourages them; it is like a heavy tax

mechanics by which lonely voices speak for repressed majorities, foreigners can still be misled by surface appearances. For example, Leo A. Orleans describes the student demonstrations of late 1986 by saying, "This short-lived turmoil seemed almost an aberration; it was handled gently by the authorities and, by now [1988], most of the overt dissent seems to be limited to a relatively small group of vocal and highly publicized intellectuals." *Chinese Students in America: Policies, Issues, and Numbers* (Washington, D.C.,: National Academy Press, 1988), p. 47.

10. The few exceptions I saw to this generalization came in the days immediately following the June 4 massacre. Several people—workers as well as students—were overcome with rage and clearly not calculating the consequences of the invective they were hurling at their government.

that the regime levies on these few remaining stores of public idealism. The irony is that the regime continues to exhort the Chinese people, as it always has, to be altruistic and self-sacrificing.

A dissident who speaks out on an issue can hope that others will follow, but the relation between leader and followers in such matters is paradoxical. Although speaking out is the necessary first step in liberating repressed public opinion, it can have the opposite effect, at least briefly: it can *reduce* the inclination of others to stick their necks out. Once a brave (or foolhardy) person has stepped forth to say what everyone else wants said, the minimal purpose of the intimidated majority has been served. To repeat the message adds little benefit while incurring an almost equal risk for the second voice. After the first declaration, those in the majority can label the dangerous idea as "so-and-so's," subtly disavowing their responsibility for it even as they enjoy repeating it.

An invisible line separates the speaker and his or her relatively silent admirers. Superficially this line supports the regime's "tiny minority" claim and is yet another reason why that phrase is useful in the official language game. The line demarcates not different opinions but different roles: those of actor and observer, or even, in extreme cases, something like bullfighter and fan. Beijing intellectuals had differing opinions on how well advised Fang Lizhi's blunt outspokenness was; but even those who criticized his tactics would say, "Anyway, I'm glad there's a Fang Lizhi," or "China needs a Fang Lizhi." The little word "a" in these oft-repeated phrases is significant. In Chinese it is a bit more prominent, and it well bespeaks the tendency of the majority to back off and let one hero represent its views.

The many who watch and silently applaud sometimes fail to appreciate the emotions experienced by the few who speak out. When someone courageously stands up on behalf of everyone else, those who listen naturally attribute great confidence to that person, and themselves feel a temporary warmth inside. For the person at risk, however, speaking out breeds neither warmth nor confidence; indeed, it *consumes* those two resources and in their place leaves feelings of gnawing emptiness and vulnerability. Those who admire the hero frequently offer their support in private, which does help to fortify him or her. But the admirers, wishing to hear more truths revealed in public, often pressure the speaker to act again, by posing questions that have obvious but taboo answers or by issuing invitations to give public lectures on sensitive topics. The admirers eagerly consume whatever new statements they can elicit, but also consume the emotional resources that allow the speaker to stand forth.

Because the gap between the emotional experiences of the hero and those of his or her admirers is not well understood by the admirers themselves, they can find apparent lapses in their hero's courage puzzling and sometimes respond by criticizing the hero for not pressing the momentum of protest. The followers want the heroes to be fearless—indeed, to be martyrs to principle if necessary. This ideal is animated by examples of heroism in Chinese history, which are sometimes used as standards to measure contemporary figures. In recent years many have invoked the example of Tan Sitong, the late-Qing reformer who was executed in 1898 by order of the conservative empress dowager Cixi after failing in a plot to overthrow her rule. While his fellow reformers Kang Youwei and Liang Qichao both fled to Japan—Kang with the help of the British in Shanghai and Liang after taking refuge in the Japanese legation in Beijing—Tan Sitong is said to have offered himself as a martyr, declaring that because every revolution requires bloodshed, it might as well be his own. When Fang Lizhi took refuge in the American embassy after the June 4 massacre, some Chinese intellectuals compared his actions unfavorably with Tan Sitong's. They criticized Fang for passing up an opportunity to confront the regime, for seeking refuge while the students and workers he had inspired suffered death and imprisonment, and for "bringing his case to a foreign court" by going to the Americans. The point of nearly all the criticisms was that Fang should have chosen prison not only for the sake of his personal image but because the sacrifice would have helped China by further discrediting the regime.[11]

The special dynamic between hero and spectator extends beyond China's borders. Many overseas Chinese, as well as non-Chinese with sentimental attachments in China (I include myself here), exemplify the spectator role as much as do people inside China. Through the press, especially the Hong Kong press, we sometimes watch China as if it were a morality play with an unpredictable script, hooting at the villains and coolly evaluating the performance of those heroes who courageously decide to play a part on stage. The moral ambiguities implicit in this spectator role frequently go unperceived. Seldom do we reflect on the arrogance of the person who, while watching from a position of safety and comfort, evaluates the "performance" of the person who knowingly puts safety and comfort at risk.[12]

During the 1980s, as the dangers of running afoul of the "personal risk trap" declined markedly from what they had been in the 1970s and earlier, there was a small but growing tendency to defy it. A remarkable case came in spring 1989, when leading intellectuals signed three petitions supporting Fang Lizhi's call for a release of political prisoners and other democratic reforms. This was the first time in Chinese Communist history that intellectuals had, as a group, publicly opposed the top leadership on a sensitive issue. The concept of a petition itself undermined the "personal risk trap" by representing a number of people who were willing to stand together in assuming risk— in form equally, although it was clear that those fingered as "organizers" would be most vulnerable. The first petition bore

11. The regime, for its part, appropriated the anti-Fang sentiment among intellectuals and presented it to Americans—successfully, in some cases—as popular support for itself.

12. The problem is symbolized in my mind by the image of a Chinese student whom I met at the University of Virginia in early 1990. He approached me to say that Fang Lizhi was his hero and could be a model for all Chinese. "But," he asked, "why did Fang go into the U.S. embassy? I wish he had been more like Tan Sitong. When he went into the embassy, he was not the Fang Lizhi I was rooting for." The image sticks in my mind partly because of the young man's dress: he wore a new Adidas jogging outfit and had a Walkman speaker in one ear.

thirty-three names, most of them belonging to senior and distinguished humanists; the second carried the names of forty-two equally senior and distinguished natural scientists. Shortly after these two petitions appeared, the government spokesman Yuan Mu delivered an austere warning about "illegal pressure" on the government. Angered by the menacing announcement, a third group, primarily young social scientists, produced another petition within twenty-four hours. They stopped gathering names when they had forty-three—one more than the number of signatures on the second petition. The point was to show that they could defy the "risk trap." "We were saying," said one of the young signers, "that if the government takes out its nets to catch people, more of us are just going to jump into that net." The student marches in spring 1989 obeyed the same logic: the harsher the government warning, the larger the next day's march.

The principle behind these forms of protest—"spread the blame wider so that each person's portion will be smaller"—defied not only the "risk trap" but another of the system's standard control techniques: pardoning those charged with crimes if they "earn merit" by informing on others. The process of confessing and then shifting blame elsewhere is supposed to "educate" a person; in concentrating all the blame for an act of protest on an iniquitous few, this process also creates a set of negative examples to "educate" the whole community. One young writer of literary reportage had built his optimism for China's future on the hope that a habit of mutual support would gradually supplant the mutual incrimination encouraged by the state. "During the [1957–58] Antirightist Campaign," he said, "intellectuals would lighten their own punishments by selling out their colleagues and friends. [The poet] Shao Yanxiang, hoping to save his own neck, criticized Liu Binyan. But it didn't work; very quickly Shao himself was punished. Shao and Liu were both sent away for twenty years. But in the late 1970s, when they were exonerated, Shao immediately apologized to Liu Binyan. Then in 1987, when Liu was expelled from the party in the 'oppose bourgeois liberalization' campaign, Shao did an even more wonderful thing. He published an essay called 'I Died in 1958,' meaning that his integrity died when he sold out Liu Binyan. It was an honest, beautiful eassy, written in the teeth of a crackdown. He called it 'I Died in 1958,' but his other meaning was 'I awoke in 1987.' "

This young writer had a larger theory of how the rejection of the "personal risk trap," and the growth of a community of mutually supportive intellectuals, could contribute to a better future for China. "Deng Xiaoping does not have Mao Zedong's prestige," he said, "and whoever follows Deng will have less than he. Power will inevitably become more dispersed, making it harder to persecute intellectuals and possible for us to have a greater effect. If we can support one another—I don't mean agree with one another, but just support one another's right to speak and work honestly—then we can do some good. It will be slow. We have to be patient. We face the tremendous task of educating our common people, whose own lives are preoccupied with basic questions of food, clothing, and shelter. But if China is to become a healthy, democratic society, *we Chinese* must be the ones to accept these burdens and challenges." He paused as if he had trouble continuing. Then he said, "This piece of land called China is *our* piece of land. Ours. If we don't fix it up, who's going to? Moreover we—I mean each of us individually—will always have to face the question of personal sacrifice. There is no way that China, in my lifetime, will have a comfortable living standard like that in Western countries. I know that. I have simply decided to accept the fact. I have no plans to leave China. But even inside China, I face the sacrifice question. I know perfectly well that if I were to parade some flattering language in front of my leaders, and stop telling the truth in my investigative reporting, I would quickly get some small raises and privileges and could live a little bit better. But why? My life is still basically passable in its present state, and the worth of doing something significant is greater than the small increase in living standards."

"Besides," he went on, "once you compromise with the state system, you are drawn into it more and more. You are pulled from within by your vested interests and molded from without by the expectations of others. Gradually you are left with only two choices: either abandon your own integrity and just be a spokesman for the state—which means you agree to die, except for your body—or keep your values hidden while you try to climb to a position where you can do some good. Personally I don't like either alternative. To climb within the system means you have to be constantly vigilant and protect your values from corruption. That's a big strain. Besides, in our autocratic system, you have to get *very* high before you can affect the basic policies. During the Cultural Revolution, even [Premier] Zhou Enlai was reduced to the role of softening the idiocies of Mao. Idealistic officials at all levels seldom have opportunities beyond this one of softening the effect of mistakes. I know some who have spent their lives waiting for a chance to do more, and they're still 'storing up capital' even today. Sometimes they even 'sacrifice' other people in order to preserve their positions. But somehow the more capital they store up, the less they speak out. This is because one of the punishments for speaking up is to have your capital destroyed. It's ridiculous. Having a lot of 'right to speak' becomes the reason for not speaking."

This is the second "trap" for potential dissenters—the dilemma between speaking out and building credibility for use in the future. Although perhaps recognizable in any bureaucracy, this credibility dilemma is especially acute in a system like China's. Those who must face the dilemma personally are people in or near official positions who dissent from state policy, such as intellectuals who wear an official hat. Beyond this circle, many others observe the performances of those confronting the dilemma and offer their assessments. Some were more forgiving of the conflicted official than was the young reporter quoted above. "There is a big difference between values and tactics," said an older reporter. "I would never be an official myself, but I can understand what [the minister of culture and creative writer] Wang Meng is doing. I would much rather have Wang Meng in that position than certain other people. I even think, actually, that Hu Sheng [president of the Academy of Social Sciences and a hard-liner] is probably doing his best. I think we have the best chance of moving forward if we have both: people criticizing from the outside and people working quietly on the inside. Sometimes the people on the inside complain that the ones on the outside, if they become too noisy, can be counterproductive. The insiders are maneuvering within very complex balances, and a strident outside voice sometimes can wreck the balances by giving the hard-liners an excuse to crack down. So I can understand the insiders' view, at least in principle. What bothers me about it is that everything is so invisible. The key questions turn on people's private thoughts, and you can never really know what those are. All the officials wear masks and are constantly suspicious of what lies behind the masks of others. This helps to explain why there is so much intrigue in Chinese politics. It also means that you can never finally judge an official until he is dead. Who can be sure about Zhao Ziyang as long as he is still living? Hidden views could always emerge. He might also die with a lot of his views still bottled up, to be unknown forever. But at least, when he dies, he can be placed in history. Not before."

Others forgave the compromises of "good-hearted" officials out of the recognition that the difficult choices they faced every day were not of their own making. A professor at Beijing University defended her university president, Ding Shisun, on his handling of student demonstrators. "He's caught in the middle. The students demonstrate over big questions of society and the world, not over campus administration. But whenever they demonstrate, the political leadership points a finger and says, 'Look, your students are acting up; you must be running things badly.' If President Ding speaks for the students, the top only blames him more; if he resigns in protest, he knows the top will retaliate by appointing a heavier-handed successor. He's stuck."[13]

13. The mood and events of 1988–89 did eventually force President Ding to make a choice, and he paid for it with his job. In winter 1989, well before the student demonstrations, he published an article entitled "Beijing University Is Facing a Challenge," in *Daxuesheng* (The university student) (Beijing), no. 1 (1988), in which he said (1) that student demonstrations were not caused by campus problems and (2) that, because he understood what those larger problems were, he was "not afraid" of student

The director of a scientific research institute offered a more innocuous example of calculating how and when to oppose the leadership. "When the Japanese emperor died recently, I wanted to offer my condolences. I didn't intend, or wish to arouse, any political implications—just offer my personal condolences. But the Ministry of Foreign Affairs, which had already sent the state's official condolences, prohibited me from adding my own. If I had disobeyed, it would have been a 'grave violation.' It crossed my mind to disobey anyway. I have the strength. I have challenged my leadership in the past and am willing to take risks again. But then I thought, On *this* issue? Or on something more important? Like Chinese science or Chinese democracy? So I obeyed." A young journalist to whom I relayed this story was sympathetic." I always mix a few 'appropriate' false statements into my reporting," she said. "I do it in a way that I believe my readers will understand. I do it because I believe that it is better to say seven true things and three false things than to say ten true things, zero false things, and be rejected." Her senior colleague Dai Qing, whose greater personal prestige and connections allowed her to be more frank and yet avoid rejection, could afford to take a position that others envied. "I do not judge those who are on 'the inside,' doing their best," said Dai Qing. "Indeed, I support them. But that is not my own preferred role. I prefer the role, which I believe is the intellectual's proper role, of simply telling the truth. I want to tell the truth without always having to ask, 'What will happen in consequence?' I believe that the long-term consequences of telling the truth can only be good and that the short-term consequences are too hard for us intellectuals to predict. I *do not* believe it should be our role to look at the political factions at the top and try to calculate how this or that statement is going to help or hurt the relatively more enlightened group. That kind of calculation is their business. Our business is to discover the truth and to tell it." But the question of the relation between

demonstrations. After the "turmoil" in the spring, the top leadership ordered President Ding fired.

knowledge and its use, which seemed so clear for Dai Qing, was problematic for others.

## The Problem of "Knowledge for Use"

The Chinese notion that intellectuals should put their knowledge to practical use in the world is implicit in their obligation to "care for society," which, as we have seen, arises from three historical sources: the Confucian tradition in which the literatus is expected to serve "all under heaven," and to do so by offering wisdom for use by political authority; the sense of national crisis that has assailed China, on and off, for more than a century; and the Communist party's demand that intellectuals limit themselves to technical functions and become the "docile tools of the party." In recent years intellectuals have vigorously debated how to put knowledge to use—and, indeed, whether to do this at all.

The burden of these accumulated calls to responsibility has produced feelings of futility in the face of problems that extend beyond China's political system to the nature of Chinese culture and even "national character." Although such daunting questions impart a sense of urgency and even, to some, a feeling approaching panic, they also reduce the sense that anyone, especially intellectuals in their merely advisory roles, can do much to help. One young writer who was trying to distance herself from the intellectuals' "worrying mood" observed, "The intensity of the intellectuals' worries contributes to the size of their questions, and the size of the questions only adds to the worries. The worries are so big that they cover the whole of 'Chinese tradition.' But what do you do after you have worried about all of tradition? Just worry some more? Worrying about tradition has itself become a tradition. The intellectuals want to 'shake the country awake.' But most of their thinking and talking is quite disconnected from the actual processes of society. Over the ten years of reform [in the 1980s], certain progress has come; but it has come—or not come—quite independently of the frenzied concern of intellectuals."

I put the question of the practical effect of intellectuals' worrying to Wang Meng, the author of "The Butterfly," who in early 1989 was still minister of culture. His answer exhibited the dazzling imagination and sprightly humor for which he is widely admired, as well as the circumspect regard for official policy that brings him more mixed reviews. "What good does it do," he asked, "to worry constantly about great, unsolvable questions? It reminds me of monks worrying about whether there is an afterlife. They can do a first-class job of worrying, and do it all day, but at day's end are they any nearer to a solution? Meanwhile they also have to handle the question of three meals per day. I think in the long run they'd be better off putting their worry into the 'three meals' question. And that, by the way, would be true whether there is an afterlife or not. My view is that we should all do our best with the immediate tasks that lie before us. If I make teacups [Wang picks up his teacup and regards it from several angles], then I should work as hard as I can to figure out how to make the best possible teacup. If we all did that, China would automatically be better."

In later interviews I asked others to comment on this informally expressed view from the minister of culture. Some took sharp exception to its implied support of the party's position that intellectuals should limit themselves to technical tasks. "The party wants us to be production specialists in the 'commodity' of knowledge," complained a young writer. "They want us to help 'build society' but not question the blueprints. Stalin referred to intellectuals as 'screws' in the state edifice, and our party elders still like that idea and still use that ugly term. Wang Meng means something different. He's not nearly that bad. But he purposely expresses himself in an ambiguous way that will keep the old men happy. It's extremely clever, but I don't like it."

Many others, after distancing themselves from the official flavor of Wang Meng's idea, acknowledged substantial agreement with it. A middle-aged computer scientist favored the emphasis on personal responsibility. "The trouble with all the worrying," he said, "is that people neglect their daily work as a result. And they don't notice the harm in neglecting their work, because they are so confident of the moral rightness of worrying about 'all under heaven.' We should all relax for a moment and realize that it is easier to criticize others than to do something yourself. *Start with yourself,* I say. Do your own job well. If you're worried about education, go down and volunteer at your local school. I like the analogy of soldiers fighting in a war. If they start debating the question 'Will we win the war?' you know for sure they're going to lose. The army that wins is the one that fights all out, not the one that stops to ponder big questions."

A senior professor of art history agreed with the emphasis on paying attention to one's own work, but insisted that it was essential also to consider the "big questions." "You don't want an army that fights 'all out' if it doesn't know what its goal is," he said. "Personally I agree with Wang Meng that each of us should do our 'little bit,' whatever that may be. I would only add that the 'little bit' *has* to be aimed at contributing to democracy and its related ideals. I, for example, am a teacher. My teaching is a mere 'little bit,' but I make very sure that it is correctly directed. And my sense of 'correct direction' comes exactly from my 'big worries.' " A young writer was even more positive about the responsibility of intellectuals to guide society. "It *should* be the role of intellectuals to reflect on big questions," he said. "Solve all the problems? No. But just raising the questions serves an important purpose. Recently the general mood of intellectuals has been very depressed. But personally I do not feel depressed. I actually think, sometimes, that the general sour, questioning mood is a good atmosphere for thinking. It is certainly better than the mindless 'hurrahs' of a political campaign!" A senior editor who had experienced many setbacks in life echoed this notion that disillusionment, whatever pain it brings, also clears the head. "I agree with Wang Meng about doing something practical," he said. "I work hard every day on my magazine. You could still say that I have a sense of mission about helping China, but my practical expectations are very modest. My only demand of myself is to be *clear in my own mind.* Even if I die editing my magazine, I'm determined to die clearheaded. During the Cultural Revolution I saw too many people die muddleheaded."

One group of intellectuals in Beijing espoused a critique of "knowledge for use" that was so radical as to undermine all the views we have just described, including those of both Wang Meng and his critics. This group was self-consciously modern minded and mostly young—although one of its most articulate spokesmen was the middle-aged maverick Li Tuo. To them the issue was not whether knowledge should be applied to big questions or to practical problems but whether it should be conceived of as having uses at all. They rejected not only the Communist party's notion of intellectuals as mere technicians but also the deeply rooted Confucian assumptions about a scholar's fulfillment through the offering of advice to the state. "The Confucian ideals of 'speaking for the people' and 'assuming responsibility for the world' are very attractive," Li Tuo explained. "They reflect high character and offer the possibility of individual perfection. But I question them. We all need to question what their actual effects are."

"In essence," said a younger scholar in this group, "the Confucian idea of 'use' has always meant 'political use.' This might have been all right in ancient China, but today it means that the Communist party has an immediate claim on a scholar's loyalty. Our knowledge is to be offered upward, for 'use' by the political authority. This attitude supports the party's efforts to instill the 'mother-son' conception of our relation to them. They have nurtured and supported us—so they say—and therefore we must owe everything to them; our function is to serve them, whatever else happens. We feel that we *must*—somehow—get out of this mold. It's not easy. Our conscious rejection of 'knowledge for use' is aimed in part to help us in that escape.

"But it is more than that. We also want to escape the panmoralism that is implicit in the Confucian conception of knowledge. The Confucian ideal is not just that knowledge be for use but that its uses, ultimately, be for great, noble, and exalted ends. Pardon me if it sounds peculiar to speak against the 'great' and the 'noble,' but our experience in China has taught us two things about shining social ideals. First, they can scorch the individual right out of existence. What can a single person do in front of a 'noble ideal' that demands personal sacrifice for the sake of a huge and glorious motherland? Second, serving a noble ideal causes people to stop thinking for themselves and even to be proud of it. Why raise questions if it is obvious that you and your exalted movement are doing so much good? In China we have had enough of this. How could it happen that so many people were persecuted and killed during the land reform [of the early 1950s]? Or hounded to suicide during the Antirightist Campaign [of 1957]? Was this because we were afraid to speak out? No. Most people at that time did not even think of speaking out. They were convinced that the cause was noble—so wonderfully, almost transcendentally high-minded that it didn't matter what was done in its name. It didn't matter how many human beings were destroyed on the road to the shining ideal. It is not only China, I believe, that has had this problem. In the West didn't you have 'religious wars'? Wasn't imperialism pursued with the idea of 'civilizing the world'? But in the West at least you have legal systems that can save little people from the good intentions of the powerful. In China we are still as exposed as ever. Why is our leadership willing to lie? Willing to kill? Only to protect its vested interests? Not so, I believe. For that highest, oldest, most detestable group of 'revolutionary' leaders, it's still a matter of 'doing what's necessary' for their 'noble ideal.' "

Li Tuo argued that the idea of "knowledge for use" was not only dangerous in the minds of the state's rulers but also of dubious value for intellectuals who advocate reform. "I see a circularity," he said, "in the pattern of Chinese intellectuals seeking reform over the past century. Each generation has thought that, by 'putting their knowledge to use,' they could 'save China' within their lifetime. Yan Fu and Liang Qichao [in the 1890s] thought it;[14] the May Fourth generation [in the 1920s] thought it; now we have Liu Binyan and Fang Lizhi similarly hoping to

---

14. On Yan Fu, see Benjamin Schwartz, *In Search of Wealth and Power: Yen Fu and the West* (Cambridge: Harvard University Press, 1964). For references on Liang Quichao, see chapter 4, note 14.

save China. But so far, each of these efforts has ended in sham-bles, and with the need to start once again. To me, the present reform effort in China seems like Liang Qichao all over again. The issues are the same—how to go out and 'make' China strong, wealthy, and democratic. Intellectuals keep designing strate-gies, but China keeps ending up where it started. However modern we think we are, we fall into the pattern of 'knowledge for practical use.' We need to forget that idea and pursue knowledge for its own sake. If we do, we will be happier and more fulfilled as individuals and will also allow China to grow through and beyond the 'practical circularity' that has been plaguing it.

"Look how democracy came about in Europe," he continued. "What was the role of intellectuals? Hobbes, Locke, and Rous-seau, as I understand it, did not sit down to 'save Europe', trying as a Confucian would to put their knowledge to use. They were basically trying to *analyze* the world, not save it. Rousseau, as I understand it, was actually a kind of bookworm. Now, did these thinkers have an effect on European democracy? Of course. But is this because they *set out* to have effects? No. They set out to discover truth. But it's hard for Chinese intellectuals to behave in this way. It requires conceiving of knowledge in a radically different way.

"Moreover, the last hundred years, during which this West-ern concept of the intellectual has come to China, have been a terrible time to expect Chinese intellectuals to accept it. The various shocks from the Western impact and the Japanese inva-sion caused the traditional ideal of 'serve all under heaven' to become 'serve the Chinese nation'; then 'serve China' became 'save China,' and 'save China' amounted to 'rebuff the foreign-ers.' All very *practical*. Even natural science—which should be a fairly pure case of knowledge for knowledge's sake—was espoused during May Fourth times under the banner *kexue jiuguo*, 'science to save the nation.' [The Hong Kong philosopher] Tang Junyi has said that China has no history of science, but only a history of technology. He was speaking of Confucian times, but it's just as true today."

Another who agreed with Li Tuo argued, "If you carefully

analyze the prominent ideas in twentieth-century China, you can see that nearly all of them are rooted in the notion of 'knowledge for use.' Lu Xun's famous story about Ah Q raises the question of flaws in Chinese national character, and does it with great power and insight. But he grounds his inquiry, ultimately, in the mood of the heartfelt sigh. 'What are we *to do?'* he is asking. He raises, basically, a technology question, not a science question. The study of Chinese national character should be approached as a matter of true or false, not as an exercise in hand-wringing. Or look at Mao Zedong, and all of his 'developing' of the great 'theory' of Marxism-Leninism. The theory was an afterthought, I say. Mao Zedong was attracted to Marxism for its practical use, for its promise to make China strong and advanced. Look at our contemporary intellectual dissidents. Who among them would not give up writing or research if there were a chance to be an official and have a practical effect? The makers of [the 1988 television series] "River Elegy" aimed to suggest that Western values be transplanted wholesale into China. But they contradicted this conscious goal in the way they couched their presentation. Showing emotional national symbols such as dragons, mountains, and the Great Wall, and applying a sonorous voice-over that made the whole thing seem momentous and ever so noble, they simply ruled out, as morally unthinkable, any role for knowledge other than practical use."

As I listened to these astute and fiercely independent-minded people, who became more animated as their arguments unfolded, I could not help reflecting that they, too, seemed motivated "at bottom" (one of their favorite phrases) to help China. How much of their advocacy of "truth for its own sake," after all, stemmed from the conviction that this maxim could lead China out of the box it was in? Their theory challenged some fundamental assumptions in their own culture, but in the end the theory itself seemed to spring from that culture and to exemplify some of the very values it aimed at overturning. They seemed vaguely to recognize this problem. The effort to get completely free from "the invisible hand," as Li Tuo described the implicit working of Chinese tradition, demanded not only social analysis but self-dissection of a most difficult kind. The first step seemed to be to dismantle the received concept of responsibility. But what was the alternative? What new responsibility was there? Without falling into "invisible" habits? It was a perilous question.

## New Definitions of Responsibility

In fall 1988, I attended a conference on literature at the Chinese Academy of Social Sciences. It did not take long for the meeting to transform itself into a debate over contemporary China and the duty of the intellectual. A literature professor in the "dismantle responsibility" group said, "After the Japanese invaded in 1937, we had a slogan that proudly claimed 'there is no quiet desk in north China'—all the scholars were busy 'resisting Japan.' But I say we *should* stay at our 'quiet desks.' I have a topic to propose to this group: the grammar of ancient Chinese. Precisely because it is *use*less, it can remind us that our role is to produce knowledge, not other things. We have to get away from the idea [expressed in a traditional proverb] that 'every individual bears responsibility for the fortunes of the state.' That hasn't been true elsewhere. Archimedes stayed at his work when Greece was invaded. In Nazi Germany, Heidegger didn't stop work on his metaphysics. Why do all Chinese scholars abandon their work because of crisis?"

This view—which I believe the speaker deliberately simplified in order to startle the audience—represents one attempt to locate a modern Chinese concept of responsibility beyond the reach of practical use. Especially among younger scholars, an attitude reminiscent of Daoism—that transcendence can result from passive nonengagement—seemed a good alternative to the regime's insistence that responsibility entail loyalty to the state. The position also bore the attraction of seeming both Western and modern—attributes that had automatic appeal as counterpoints to the situation in China. Finally, the stance offered liberation of the individual and lent respectability to the pursuit of one's own career.

Yet many in the middle and older generations still argued

that notions of responsibility should—if freely undertaken by the individual—include responsibility to society. Liu Zaifu, for instance, argued, "Young people are quite right to be deeply skeptical of the externally defined 'group consciousness' that destroys the exercise of individual conscience. Whether in Confucian times or in Communist times, that kind of imposed morality has always produced hypocrisy. In fact, the appearance of hypocrisy is a sure sign that responsibility has lost its roots in conscience. The ancient Chinese admired 'filial piety,' for example. But when filial piety became an official virtue of the empire, and one of the qualifications for holding office, it lived in form but died in spirit. It led to the paradox of 'the filial living apart from their fathers.'[15] The young see this hypocrisy in our official values today and are quite right to reject it. But why should they also reject the guidance of their own, independent social consciences? I would put it is this way: intellectuals and society should have mutual respect. Society must show respect for the independence of intellectuals. And intellectuals should respect society enough to offer it their honest and concerned criticisms. This assuredly is responsibility; but it is a responsibility that can be free from hypocrisy, and free from politics."

A young scholar who opposed the strictures of social responsibility was present when Liu made these comments. Liu's warmth and eloquence seemed to move the young man, although he remained reluctant to embrace Liu's position. "The way you put it," he said, "I can accept the idea. It's the same idea I have in my own heart—you know? But why talk about it? As soon as you pronounce the word—as soon as you make it public—it gets corrupted. Our consciences need some space to grow. We don't need moralizing words—words only open the way for a return of the handcuffs."

15. This material, provided in an interview, is substantially repeated in Liu Zaifu's published dialogue with Li Zehou (see above, note 5). The phrase "the filial living apart from their fathers" is from *"shen ju"* (Examining promotions), vol. 15 of the *waipian* (outer chapters) of Ge Hong (A.D. 284–364), *Bao Puzi* (Taizhong: Chuangyi Publishers, 1981), p. 171. Ge Hong was referring to the collapse of official morality at the end of the Later Han dynasty (A.D. 168–221).

The young man's admission of an underlying sense of responsibility was, I discovered, fairly common among those who presented explicit arguments against the idea. The professor who had advocated "staying at the desk" to study subjects such as ancient grammar, even if one's country was in crisis, in spring 1989 was at Tiananmen Square—signing petitions, debating issues, and even carrying water to the protesting students. Had concern for China suddenly displaced his advocacy of pure research? I doubt it. His concern for China had underlain his advocacy of "staying at the desk" all along. The phrase was not a plea to abandon social and political responsibility but a dramatic way of stating that scholars should guard their independence.

Recalling the markedly different atmosphere of fall 1988, when scholars complained of *mei jin* ("no zest") in life,[16] I now realized that there had been evidence then, too, of an underlying interest in political engagement. The problem of *mei jin* had arisen because a seemingly moribund government, while leading China nowhere, was also, for the time being, leaving the intellectuals alone. For any scholar truly interested only in working at the desk, those would have been good times. But on the contrary, the lack of provocation from the government left intellectuals with no focal point for protest, and the result was a frustrating sense of listlessness. The advocates of pure research were among those complaining of *mei jin*. Desk work was not a satisfying replacement for their concern for China.

I began to wonder what, at least hypothetically, the concerns of a Chinese intellectual might be if the all-consuming battle with the state could finally be won or in some other way completely avoided, so that their own unconstrained interests could emerge. Many, especially among the young, speak of an ideal situation in which there would be more room for the concerns of "the individual" or "the self." By this they do not necessarily mean narcissism or selfishness, as the official language of the party frequently charges. "The concerns of the self," said

16. See above, pp. 122, 232.

a young writer, "do not have to be concerns *for* a self, or even about a self. The key point is that, whatever they may be, they should come *from* the self." Her point seems to be borne out in the work of Chinese intellectuals who have managed to put the greatest distance between themselves and the state, and to draw closest to expression of "the self."

At an exhibition of contemporary Chinese painting and sculpture at Beijing's Central Art Museum in spring 1989, most of the flamboyantly modernist works were as personal, and as far removed from the party's prescribed Socialist Realist style, as they could be. Yet many of the pieces also invited interpretation as commentary on Maoism, on traditional Chinese culture, or on other social and political issues. "The point," explained one of the bohemian-looking young artists, "is not to reject social concerns. Why can't I have my own opinions about society? The point is to reject the social convention that says we are all supposed to 'fit' our perceptions into words and forms that are considered standard—by the Communist party, by the opponents of the Communist party, or by somebody else. Chinese culture demands that we fit, and we don't want to. But that doesn't mean we have no opinions about the world. Why should it? The questions are totally unrelated."

A young writer who agreed with this view pushed it further by arguing that intense concern with the self actually leads to the most universal of concerns about the world. "Why do we feel that Dostoyevsky has transcended to a level where truths are universal?" she asked. "It's because he looks so deeply into the individual, and leads us to see truths that are so elemental, that we know intuitively that they must hold for all human beings. This is what attracts us young writers—me, at least—to a focus on the individual. You can view it as my private rebellion against Socialist Realism, which insists that writers start with 'general truths' about society and show how these mold individuals—who then become mere demonstration items for the general theories. In a sense I'm dealing with the 'general' and 'individual' levels just as the party theorists do, but in exactly the opposite direction. My way is better."

The stress on individualism in views such as these seems to represent a fundamental break with both Confucian tradition and the Communist party. The notion of a kind of social responsibility that grows out of individual freedom does have precedents among May Fourth thinkers, who in turn had developed such ideas under strong influences from the West. But the May Fourth interlude was brief, and it remains to be seen how long-lived this kind of individualism will be among the young Chinese of today. Its popularity among university students is fairly superficial—it is exciting theory more than assimilated practice. And older generations, who remain preoccupied with more conventional notions of responsibility, show little interest in the idea.

Dai Qing, whose practical bent kept her at some distance from the involuted debate over responsibility, expressed a compromise view—widely accepted among the middle and older generations—that the role of intellectuals should be to tell the truth and that truth telling was itself a kind of social responsibility. "I agree with the critics of responsibility," said Dai Qing, "when they say intellectuals should pursue knowledge without having to think about all its social effects. For example, as a writer I resist the idea [long promoted in Chinese Communist literary theory] of being 'responsible toward readers.' I don't know my readers personally. I can't see them. My sense of responsibility is toward the truth. Discovering and writing the truth is what excites me about my work on the Trotskyites in the 1930s and 1940s. But on the other hand, I have a faith that uncovering the truth will, in the long run, one way or another, be beneficial—or 'useful,' as the critics of responsibility say. I see nothing wrong with knowledge being useful in this sense, so here I disagree with them."

After listening to many views in the debate over responsibility, I concluded that there was still widespread acceptance of the idea in one form or another. Some continued to speak unapologetically of a "sense of responsibility" or even a "sense of mission" as the high calling of the intellectual. Others, who rejected such language as pompous, continued in practice to assume, in basically Confucian form, that it was a primary duty of theirs to offer criticisms and ideas for the improvement of society. And, as we have seen, even those who were in revolt against received notions of responsibility were fundamentally motivated by their own political and social values.[17] The structure of opinion on this issue—where broad agreement on a value was surrounded by disagreement on how to implement it—had a parallel in the related issue of how to push toward democracy.

## Advancing Democracy

To Chinese intellectuals in the late 1980s, the ready answer to the question "What should be done?" was "Build democracy." It was easy to reach a consensus on this because the term was used vaguely, and because it could be held as a long-term ideal even by those who saw difficulties with immediate implementation. There was little discussion of the eventual shape of a "Chinese democracy,"[18] but much talk, and sometimes sharp disagreement, about what China should do *next*. What steps will begin the evolution of Chinese democracy?

Many in the older and middle generations argued that the Communist party, however despicable, still offered the best avenue for hope. Although the example of Mikhail Gorbachev did much to inspire this view, its real force derived from people's sense that there was no alternative. "The Communist party," said an elderly historian of music, "has monopolized so much power for so long that it has made itself indispensable. Who could replace them? Who—given our present situation—could

17. I found only two kinds of intellectuals who might indeed be viewed as entirely free from the syndrome of "taking responsibility for China." These were, ironically, not those who advocated such freedom, but (1) those whose compromises with the regime, whether willing or forced, had reached the point where they became simply the tools of others, and no longer asked why; and (2) the most callous among the cynical young. Although the cynicism of most young Chinese remained tied to a hope that China will do better, some had abandoned this hope and rejected all responsibility in favor of satisfying their own immediate needs and desires.

18. For reasons discussed above, p. 199.

we possibly expect to overthrow them? How do you get a dragon out of your garden?" A senior editor who admired the student democracy movement of 1989 nevertheless worried about what would have happened if it had prevailed. "The Communist party may be unfit to rule, but would the complaining youngsters be any better? I think they would be even worse. And I'm not just speculating. They *were* even worse during the Cultural Revolution, when we saw 'young rebels' kick out party secretaries and take power themselves. The young people today always misunderstand me when I say this, but I always say that we must reform from within the party."

There was disagreement on how the party might be democratized. Many admired the political scientist Yan Jiaqi's essays on democratic theory for their refutation of the idea of "personal rule." Yan argued that since human beings are imperfect, any leader must be imperfect, and democratic decisions are possible only through a process that no single person controls. If the fruits of this democratic process are flawed, the corrective mechanisms must also be impersonal, and a legal system must shield the democratic process from intervention by powerful individuals.[19] Some considered Yan's carefully reasoned disquisitions too theoretical because they did not answer the question "What do we do *now?*" But raising the issue of immediate action too concretely brought one dangerously close to questioning the legitimacy of Communist party rule—a question so sensitive that most people, even in private, addressed it only tangentially. The subtle and not so subtle pressures to observe the taboo on this question had caused what one young writer called mental "detouring" (*rao*). "The question of Communist power is a big unmentionable," he said. "Even people who say the party is rotten can't bring themselves to utter the words 'Down with the party.' The question of party power sits there in the middle, related to all kinds of other questions, but whenever

19. Yan Jiaqi, "Zhongguo ruhe fuqiangqilai" (How China can become strong and wealthy), *Dagongbao* (Hong Kong), March 23, 1988, p. 9, translated in David Bachman and Dali Yang, eds., *China's Struggle for Democracy* (Armonk, N.Y.: M. E. Sharpe, 1991), pp. 83–90.

we get near to it we *rao*. Analyze China's economic difficulties? Pretty soon you have to *rao*. The problem with education? You have to *rao*. Literature and art? *Rao*. We do it so much that the pattern feels natural."

But the routes of these detours were fruitful in themselves. People proposed "peripheral" changes as ways of bringing about systemic reform in the long run. The first step, a computer scientist believed, should be "to admit, in public, what everyone in private knows and talks about: that there are clearly two factions in our leadership—the reform-minded 'open' faction and the more Leninist-Stalinist 'conservative' one." Such an admission, he argued, could be the first step toward honest competition within the framework of the party.

Others made the argument that freedom of the press was a key to reform.[20] Under China's authoritarian system, bad news was considered to reflect poorly upon rulers; therefore it was forbidden to report bad news forthrightly. Even colossal disasters such as the 1976 Tangshan earthquake that killed hundreds of thousands were reported under headlines such as "Courageous Rescue Workers Save Thirty Miners." Journalists who dared to report bad news were blamed as if they were the cause. (In 1979 Liu Binyan protested this attitude, saying that journalists merely hold up "mirrors" to society;[21] and the poet Ai Qing wrote, "If you are ugly / Don't blame the mirror."[22] How, argued the free-press advocates, can we solve our problems if we cannot even set them forth honestly? This seemingly simple question harbored a far-reaching agenda: a free press would not only expose problems but end the top leadership's monopoly on public analysis of them; it would, moreover, check abuses attributable to the government—such as official corruption and the bullying of people in work units. Eventually, according to

20. For a sample of this view, see Liu Binyan, "As a Sign of Political Maturity, China Needs an Independent Newspaper," *Los Angeles Times*, April 6, 1988, op-ed page.

21. Liu Binyan, "Listen Carefully to the Voice of the People," in *People or Monsters? and Other Stories and Reportage from China after Mao* (Bloomington: Indiana University Press, 1983), p. 5.

22. Ai Qing, "Flowers and Thorns," *People's Daily*, July 10, 1980.

this argument, a healthy, open "public opinion" would emerge and naturally cluster around various issues; these clusters would lead to "pressure groups" and eventually the competing parties of a democratic system.

Another reform some proposed as pivotal was to end the power of work units over people. "If there is one change I could make," argued a journalist, "it would be to give people the simple right to resign from a work unit and find work elsewhere, and to give other work units the right to hire them. That one change would lead to much more. It would mean, overnight, that party secretaries would have to treat their good workers better or risk losing them. Even slightly better treatment of workers would greatly help their morale. Their better work would improve the economy. Of course, our leaders say that ending this power of party secretaries amounts to opposing the leadership of the Communist party, which is one of the Four Basic Principles. So my one simple change is, I know, not so simple." Others got at this point through euphemisms, calling for "ownership reform"—meaning an end to state ownership of work units and the possibility of ownership by universities and other institutions, by local governments, and by individuals through shareholding.[23] Its advocates argued that this reform was essential to ending the decades-old alienation workers feel toward workplaces that, as one senior journalist put it, "belong to everybody, and therefore belong to nobody—except 'them,' the officials, which only adds the spice of resentment to people's general indifference."

Some saw ownership reform as a key not only to economic advance but to democratic progress as well. "We can't have democracy," said a young philosophy professor, "until people are willing to say what they think. And people will not say what they think until they know what their livelihood will be insulated from the consequences of what they say. Our present work-unit system is deliberately designed to control people by manipulating their livelihood contingencies. Therefore the work-

23. See Nicholas D. Kristof, "Chinese Economists Urge End to State Ownership," *International Herald Tribune* (Hong Kong), January 11, 1989, p. 1.

unit system has to be changed, and the only way to change it is by ownership reform."

"If all that seems too abstract," he continued, "let me tell you a story that puts my point better than I ever could. A few days ago a friend came from Hong Kong and brought me a Hong Kong newspaper. It carried a report from Shekou, in Guangdong province. Shekou is one of China's 'special economic zones,' where foreign and Hong Kong companies can operate. Under such conditions, political thought can become, as our government puts it, a bit 'disorderly.' Seeing this, our central leaders sent down an 'ideological work team' to lecture to the young people and get them into line. The team was accustomed to having people listen as quietly as rabbits and then either agree or at least pretend to agree. But what happened in Shekou? The young workers started to talk back! They said the work team's 'line' was outdated, outmoded, false, hypocritical, and so on. The work team couldn't believe it! One of the old ideologues got mad. He stood up and singled out one of the young workers for interrogation. 'Who are you?' he demanded. 'Do you dare to tell me your full name?' He must have been sure that this would shut the youngster up and also warn the others. But no. What a surprise! The youngster stood up, stated his full name and place of work and then added, 'My boss is from Hong Kong, and he doesn't care what I say as long as I work well. I'm not afraid of you.' "

"That youngster," the philosopher continued, "still should have been afraid, and probably knew it. But the story still shows what a big difference the 'ownership' question makes."

Some, for all their commitment to democracy, could produce no suggestions on how to nurture it. Many of these could embrace only a general faith in education. "I see no way out," said a senior professor of art, "—except education. If we can get our government to invest in education, at least we can hope that the next generation will do better." A professor of international relations agreed, but insisted that the nature of education, not just funding levels, would have to be revised. She was one of the few people from whom I heard a kind word for

Commissioner of Education Li Tieying, who was a favorite lightning rod for the intellectuals' complaints about the regime's neglect of education.

"I do have a bit of hope for Li Tieying," she said in early 1989. "Recently he commented that we should do away with educational guidelines and just let teachers teach. I think this is an important first step toward getting rid of the 'political education' that begins in primary school and extends through college. 'Political education' courses give high grades for mediocre work, students make fun of it, and teachers find it an unpleasant burden. Moreover, to judge from the results, it is counterproductive. Just look at the children of the high cadres. They're the ones with the best political education, right? And yet they are also the best at arrogance, at high living, and at only caring for themselves. If you find students who still want to help China, who have *youhuan yishi*, who are frugal and work hard, you'll discover that they're usually the ones with the 'worst' political education, the ones from the families of the 'stinking intellectuals' whose 'class nature' has always been the target of political education. Objectively speaking, political education has failed by both positive and negative criteria: those who have it often behave poorly, and those who don't, often behave well. To abolish it would be a step forward."

## The Debate Over New Authoritarianism

One of the potential routes to democracy that Chinese intellectuals debated, especially in the fall of 1988, was called New Authoritarianism. Its advocates argued that China's difficult transition to a democratic system could best be managed by an enlightened dictator. Dai Qing was an important early proponent of this approach.[24] In her case the idea had grown out of

24. The first to broach the idea of New Authoritarianism were Zhang Bingjiu, a doctoral candidate at Beijing University, and Wu Jiaxiang, a member of the Communist party's Central Policy Research Section and a close associate of Zhao Ziyang. Other early proponents included Su Xiaokang, the distinguished writer of reportage and coau-

a meeting in September 1988 to commemorate the constitutional monarchists of the late nineteenth century, and had sprung from their proposal that China be led by a largely symbolic authority figure presiding over a constitutional government.[25]

New Authoritarianism has two basic tenets. The first is that a benevolent authoritarian can order a series of economic and political reforms into place and then abolish his own authority, leaving a democratic system behind; the argument for this approach is that it is best suited to China's authoritarian traditions, backward economy, and unenlightened populace and that democratic means would prove slower, less efficient, and likely to end in chaos. The second tenet is that economic reform should precede political reform, since economic development produces the middle class that is the political foundation for democratic reforms.

Advocates of New Authoritarianism cited the Four Little Dragons of South Korea, Taiwan, Hong Kong, and Singapore as examples of the theory's success. Each of these places seemed to demonstrate that impressive economic growth could occur within an authoritarian political structure; and Taiwan's progress in developing democratic institutions struck many Chinese as attributable to the willing abdication of the last dictator, Chiang Ching-kuo. Some advocates of New Authoritarianism also invoked Mikhail Gorbachev as an example of an all-powerful leader using his authority to reform a dictatorial system. The Gorbachev example was especially impressive because it demonstrated that even a Marxist-Leninist system, like China's own, might successfully be dismantled by a determined leader. But Gorbachev's reform priorities—*glasnost* (political reform) first and *perestroika* (economic reform) second—did not fit the

thor of "River Elegy," and Wu Guoguang, a high-level editorial commentator at *People's Daily* and deputy to Bao Tong, a close associate of Zhao Ziyang's. For more on New Authoritarianism see Liu Jun and Li Lin, *Xinquanweizhuyi: Dui gaige lilun gangling de lunzheng* (New Authoritarianism: Controversies on the theoretical program of reform) (Beijing: College of Economics Publishing House, 1989); see also *Beijing daxue xueshu lilun fukan* (Beijing University supplement on scholarship and theory), March 5, 1989, special issue on New Authoritarianism.

25. See above, pp. 193–94 for a full statement of this view.

New Authoritarians' theory and were sometimes used in contrary arguments. Even so, groups within China's top leadership saw the opportunities the theory afforded them. Zhao Ziyang's reformist faction embraced the theory in late 1988 as a way to bolster its sagging political position; other, less reform-minded leaders may have seen the argument as at least a temporary rationale for the continuation of a dictatorial system. The quasi-official sponsorship that developed weakened the idea among intellectuals, notably Dai Qing herself.

Those intellectuals who supported New Authoritarianism had to counter the charge that they were using fire to fight fire. They insisted that acceding to a dictator was a means only, that their final goal was the same as that of democratic reformers, and that they were offering a practical alternative to "romantic democratization." "Look at the work-unit system," argued a young reporter. "How do you make it more economically efficient? Work units are thoroughly entangled in spoils systems and vested interests that have grown up around private connections and political maneuvering. How do you get from there to 'market efficiency'? The interests are too deeply entrenched. Any move to reform the state-run work units immediately brings tremendous resistance. You need a strong authority to break through those interests and insist on reform. What would happen if you tried to do it 'democratically'—if you just said that, from now on, managers would be free to make decisions based on efficiency? There would be two big problems.

"First, who would make those 'market' decisions? Most of the people now in charge would have no idea how to do it. They reached their current positions because they are clever about politics and good at brokering connections. That's what they're good at, not economics. Second, even if managers were willing to fire incompetent workers, what would society then do with all the fired workers? Do you realize how many there are? They would become a tremendous force of opposition to this kind of reform. To make it work you need society-wide policies, strongly enforced." At this a senior professor of history nodded agreement and told the story of a courageous factory manager in the northeast who decided to hire and fire in her unit on the basis of productivity. "Some workers dragged her out and shot her," he said, showing no sign that he doubted the story. "This may be an extreme example, but it illustrates the problem."

"It's peculiar," said a young lecturer in philosophy, discussing the means and ends of reform. "It's like looking through a glass wall. We can see where we want to go, but know we can't go straight there without triggering disaster. If we try to go straight to democracy and a market economy, there will be chaos, and from chaos will certainly grow authoritarianism—not the new kind, but the *old*, feudal authoritarianism. Feudal authoritarianism is what sprouted from the chaos of the Cultural Revolution, and it happened in countless large and small localities all across China. It is what grows naturally in China, and it will sprout again if chaos reigns again."

Critics of this school countered that the "new" authoritarianism would prove fertile ground for the more familiar form. What, they wondered, ensures that the benevolent ruler will remain so? What recourse is there if he turns despotic? By what process will he be chosen in the first place? Have we not seen strongmen promise democracy before? What is to guarantee that it will be different this time?

Other critics questioned the connection between authoritarian rule and efficient economic development. While granting that the Four Little Dragons apparently provided evidence of the linkage, they cited other authoritarian states as counterexamples, including Burma, Uganda, Haiti, Albania, and North Korea. Those critics concluded that the alleged connection between authoritarian rule and economic growth was more complex than the New Authoritarians were allowing. Fang Lizhi made the point with characteristic irony: "Does the low efficiency that we observe in China today result from the fact that we have had insufficient authoritarianism in recent times?"

A young literary scholar pointed out that the very name of the theory, *xin quanweizhuyi* (literally "new authority-ism," which lacks the autocratic connotation of the English word "authoritarian") was subtly, and perhaps purposely, misleading. "The question is not whether we want political authority or not," he objected. "Democracy also provides authority. The question is *what kind* of authority we want. We should cast our debate in terms of 'democratic authority' versus 'dictatorial authority.' That would make people realize better what is at stake." Another young man complained, "The supporters of New Authoritarianism often use a dangerous metaphor. They say the New Authoritarian will be *guodu* ['transitory'—literally 'cross-ferry']. But let's look at this ferryboat. People take it for granted that a ferry will reach the opposite shore. At least they normally have no fear that the pilot might head off on his own or take them all hostage. But this is precisely the fear that we have—and ought to have—about New Authoritarianism. The *guodu* metaphor is misleading. It makes a perilous gamble seem harmless." China's history provided ample support for this point. "In the 1940s," said a middle-aged literary scholar, "Chinese intellectuals subordinated themselves to a 'new' authoritarian party, the Communist party, which promised it would bring 'socialist democracy' in the long run. And look what happened. I think German intellectuals learned the same lesson when they thought a strong new authority might clean up Weimar."

Many feared that backsliding was a greater danger in China than elsewhere because of the Chinese cultural habit of looking to an absolute authority—a strong and just "savior king"—to set things right. "Peasant rebellions through Chinese history," observed a senior scientist, "have pinned their hopes on enthroning a wise new emperor, someone whose sage understanding is beyond the reach of ordinary people, but who uses his wisdom and power in their behalf. New Authoritarianism makes the same mistake of reinvesting faith in government by men. We need government by law." Fang Lizhi apparently had similar thoughts in mind when, after his release from the American embassy in June 1990, he gave his reasons for declining a leadership role in any overseas Chinese democracy organization. "If Chinese are waiting for the appearance of a superhero," said Fang, "I am not that man. Moreover, I think that this expectation is in itself an unhealthy one. . . . Chinese too easily tend to put all their hopes on the next leader, only to become disillusioned."[26]

Opponents of New Authoritarianism also vigorously challenged the claim that an absolute leader was necessary to prevent chaos. "Where has all the chaos in our country come from in recent times?" asked a middle-aged poet. "From democracy? From the people? No. Why can't we see the plain facts that lie before us? The main causes of chaos in the People's Republic of China have been the anti-intellectual campaigns, the Great Leap Forward, the Cultural Revolution, and the constant jockeying for power among our top leaders. Just look at all the chaos-creating slogans and commands that have coursed through our society over the years: 'Never Forget the Class Struggle,' 'Down with Imperialist Running Dogs,' 'Bomb the Revisionist Headquarters,' 'To Rebel Is Justified,' 'Smash China's Khrushchev,' 'Political Power Grows from the Barrel of a Gun,' 'Learn from Lu Xun's Spirit of Thoroughly Thrashing Drowning Dogs,' 'Criticize Lin Biao and Confucius,' 'Oppose the Move by Unrepentant Capitalist-Roaders to Reverse Correct Verdicts,' 'Oppose the Vendors of Spiritual Pollution,' 'Oppose Bourgeois Liberalization,' and many, many more.[27] Who started all this? Democrats? Peasants? Of course not. Authoritarians did. Chaos in China comes from the top, not the bottom. And now someone tells us we need an authoritarian to *prevent* chaos?"

Others who espoused this view acknowledged that a certain chaos could indeed come from below, but held that, in a democratic system, some small chaos could be contained within a larger stability." "Ever since Mao," argued a young writer, "the government has always called for 'stability first and foremost.' It knows that popular sentiment against chaos is strong because people remember the Cultural Revolution. The government

26. Orville Schell, "The Liberation of Comrade Fang," *Los Angeles Times Magazine,* October 7, 1990, p. 38.

27. This statement was made in spring in 1989, before the bloody crackdown at Tiananmen. By now, I feel certain, the poet would want to add to his list a slogan that appeared in the 1990 effort to "educate" the Chinese people about the "true nature" of massacring peaceful demonstrators: "Imitate the Spirit of the Heroes Who Suppressed the Counterrevolutionary Rebellion."

exploits these memories by calling for stability as a way to get people to bottle up their discontents and be docile. But is that real stability? Or is society more stable when people have the satisfaction of saying what they think? In the late 1970s, when the slogan *anding tuanjie* [stability and unity] appeared, everybody supported it. It sounded fine. It took me a few years to realize that actually the slogan was self-contradictory at a deep level. The demand for unity requires that everyone with differing opinions pretend that they don't have them. But this naturally breeds instability. If a society wants stability, it must let those various opinions come out. But then, of course, it won't have unity—at least not on the surface. To me the genius of a democratic system is that it distinguishes two kinds of unity: unity of opinion, which cannot be achieved among groups of thinking people, and unity in agreeing to play by the same rules. In such a system, surface chaos can go together with underlying stability."

Sensitive to a possible objection to his argument, the young man continued, "The New Authoritarians like to talk about 'national conditions.' They argue that China lacks the social and cultural conditions necessary for observance of a set of democratic rules. But how do they know? Has anyone really tried it? Why can democracy work in places like India and Turkey, but not in China? Are we to believe that Chinese peasants, after all the politics that has been forcibly brought to them over forty years, are less ready to handle politics than Indian peasants? Besides, if we keep saying that we will put off democracy because national conditions might be inappropriate, we only strengthen those very national conditions. We create a self-fulfilling prophecy. The way you learn something is to try it. Which Communist leader in the 1940s said, 'Stop! Wait! Are China's national conditions ready for Marxism-Leninism?' If they took a risk in trying Marxism then, there certainly is no greater risk in trying democracy today."

In one sense the debate over New Authoritarianism was highly satisfying to Chinese intellectuals. It offered the chance to focus clearly on some of their most cherished values and to have it out with the opposition. But at a deeper level the debate was less satisfying. Although, by early 1989, it had largely succeeded in discrediting New Authoritarianism as a solution for China, it failed to yield its own practical answers to the big, pressing, and terrible questions that continued to fuel *youhuan yishi*: What can be done? What can *we* do?

# AFTERWORD

# "Here in the Woods..."

This book was conceived as a report on China to Westerners, not as an analysis of China for Chinese readers. Chinese intellectuals who read it may, I think, feel somewhat gratified to see their domestically unpublishable worrying spelled out in black and white between the fancy covers of a Western book. But they will gain little exposure to new ideas, and this may disappoint them. Many who agreed to be interviewed for this project said that they would eagerly await my "conclusions"—in the belief, I am afraid, that a foreigner's distinctive angle on things would be especially illuminating or, as they often put it, "more objective" than their own.

To these friends I feel a duty here to *biaotai* (Chinese political slang for "reveal an opinion") and offer just two brief conclusions. First, as a citizen of the modern West, I find the Chinese intellectual's stubborn habit of worrying about his or her whole society impressive and even fortifying. Although the habit prevents Chinese scholars from making the greatest possible progress in their special fields, Western scholars face the opposite problem: their special fields have become ever more narrow, and competition within them has left intellectuals with less time and inclination to stand back and appreciate, much less take responsibility for, the overall directions of society. The potentially disastrous consequences of problems like environmental degradation, and the seeming intractability of social problems such as drug abuse and a faltering education system, deserve more conscientious *youhuan yishi* than Amerians give them.

Second, I agree with those Chinese intellectuals who argue, "Patriotism should not be our highest priority." If *youhuan yishi* is taken to imply that China should be viewed as a special place, where unusual rules apply and human life is different, then I am opposed to that dimension of *youhuan yishi.* In my view such assumptions, while often convenient ways to protect Chinese pride, have done great harm to China. Chinese intellectuals enjoy criticizing excessive pride among their rulers, but the blinding effects of pride are not limited to imperious leaders. The intellectuals themselves have made "Chineseness" such a powerful category, one that carries such strong moral connotations, that it obstructs normal lines of observation and reflection.

Let me illustrate the point with a story about a Chinese graduate student in American studies whom I met at a conference in Tianjin. His is a good test case because, on the surface, he was about as far from conservative Chinese chauvinism as one could be: young, extroverted, educated in international studies—and open in his expression of naive enthusiasm for everything American, together with sheer contempt for the Chinese government. He was doing a research project on Mark Twain, and began asking me—"the professor of literature from America"—about some stories by Twain that I had never heard of. I pointed out to him that I study Chinese, not American, literature and that he, as a specialist on Mark Twain, clearly knew more about that author than I did. I added that I thought this fact was "a healthy thing." The young man appeared thunderstruck. "Couldn't be," he murmured. "You're an American professor." I foolishly sought to wrench his world back into balance by observing that perhaps, on the other hand, I might know some things about modern Chinese literature that were unknown to him. But this only made matters worse. "What? I'm *Chinese,*" he objected. When I named some Chinese authors from the 1910s whom I suspected he would not know, and asked him his views on them, he seemed not to recognize the names. To my dismay, he simply backed away from the group we were standing with, gently shaking his head, apparently in deep and pained struggle with the notion that a Chinese and an American could intrude so brazenly onto the turf of the other.

Even among some of my best Chinese friends—mature intellectuals and people who long ago had understood that I mean China well—I usually found it necessary to maintain a careful balance in any statements I made during discussions involving sensitive issues of Chinese pride. My friends could be pouring forth their harshest criticisms of Chinese politics, society, and culture—including, yes, the very problem of Chinese pride; but if I joined the discussion, it was always better if I balanced any criticism of China with either praise for something Chinese or criticism of something American. This was not hard for me to do, and I was happy to do it for my friends because it reinforced their sense of self-respect. But I do worry about the larger implications of such necessities. What limitations of vision result when so many issues must be conceived in part as matters of Chinese pride? As China faces complex and inexorable pressures to join the modern world, does it help to maintain such a profound distinction between "Chinese" and "foreign"? Must we acknowledge Chinese "specialness"—which is a code for "superiority" and, in turn, often a heartfelt attempt to banish the notion of "inferiority"? Would China not get a squarer look at the world, and at itself, and adjust itself to the world more efficiently, if sweeping, morally charged terms such as these could simply be set aside?

With very few of my friends in China did I ever raise these questions directly. I was always stopped by the fear that, as a foreigner, no matter how good a friend, I might only stimulate defensiveness and exacerbate the very problem I was seeking to diminish. But here, with the advantage of distance, I offer my sincere opinion and hope for the best.

After leaving China in June 1989, I spent two months in Hong Kong before returning to the United States, first to Los Angeles for a month and then to Princeton, New Jersey. Along the way, I found it both intriguing and frustrating to observe an ever-growing distance between what I remembered of life in Beijing and the interpretations I heard of the dramatic events that had just taken place there. The farther I moved away from China in time, place, and culture, the more it seemed to me that perceptions of the crisis were colored, and sometimes distorted, by local concerns. As I read and listened to sincere, intense debate, I often felt the need to remind myself, "No, that's not the way it was. Don't forget how it actually was."

HONG KONG. The first stage in my "distancing" from events in China came in Hong Kong, where the populace faces a return to Chinese rule in 1997. Hong Kong's initial reaction to the massacre was reflexive: vivid television images elicited outrage and panic. There were huge demonstrations, with protest banners everywhere. One banner in a working-class section of Kowloon read, "There are two abominations in today's world—AIDS and Li Peng."[1] This kind of immediate, unconditioned response was quite similar in spirit to the immediate reaction in Beijing—except that in Beijing, of course, public demonstrations were impossible. What interested me in Hong Kong was the second, more reflective stage in the response to the massacre. After the initial shock had passed, the expressions of outrage and open defiance receded. Many people rededicated themselves to emigrating—or at least securing a foreign passport that would allow them to emigrate—before 1997. Others, especially among the wealthier classes, reasoned that the col-

---

1. Although Chinese and Hong Kong public opinion has held several of China's hard-line rulers responsible for the massacre, Li Peng has, fairly or not, borne the greatest blame. The targeting of Li intensified after he accepted the duty of reading the repressive speech "explaining the emergency that requires martial law" on Chinese television. His bumbling, fatuous performance in this role made him appear as something between a tyrant and a clown. On the Chinese grapevine of "alleyway news," Li Peng jokes easily came to outnumber those aimed at any other leader. In late June 1989, a Hong Kong newspaper carried a story about twenty people in the city who happened, unfortunately, also to be named Li Peng. In the days after the massacre, they received taunts in public and threatening phone calls. One had formally applied for a change of name. See "Li Peng Makes a New Name for Himself," *Hongkong Standard*, June 30, 1989, p. 1.

ony would do best to cooperate with Beijing's repressive rule—
to lie low in the hope that Beijing would focus its repression
elsewhere and treat Hong Kong, it's "money tree," with special
consideration. The people who took this view had material and
emotional investments in Hong Kong and understandably feared
that they could lose much by "angering the dragon." Nevertheless, I found their position puzzling. I wondered whether these
people could be so out of touch with the ways of the leadership
in the People's Republic as to suppose that "lying low" would
work. Did they really imagine that their wealth—fantastic by
mainland standards—would cause China's rulers to keep their
hands off, rather than produce exactly the opposite effect?

I checked my response with a friend from Beijing, a quiet
and normally apolitical scholar who was visiting at the University of Hong Kong. "I've heard Hong Kong people say those
things, too," he said. "They're naive. Hong Kong's only hope
is that the Beijing government will change—I mean change
*fundamentally*—before 1997. Anything else is a sheer dream.
But they can't understand. I guess there's no cure for this except
to live in China." His response, and the desperation it bespoke,
highlighted another difference between the people of Hong Kong
and Beijing vis-à-vis the Communist state. Hong Kong citizens
who seek an accommodation with the Beijing government do
so in order to preserve all that they have built up; Beijing people, who have no comparable wealth or status to protect, feel
that they have little or nothing to lose. When they are allowed
any room to rebel, they take advantage of it with more abandon.

Other ironies in the mutual misperceptions of Hong Kong
and Beijing began to occur to me. Viewed from Beijing, for
example, Hong Kong seems extremely attractive not only for
its wealth but for its freedoms. Beijing intellectuals cherish every
chance to read publications from Hong Kong, especially the six
or seven monthlies that are filled with news, rumor, and analyses that cannot be published inside China. In Beijing, these
magazines contribute to Hong Kong's image as a bastion of defiance against repression. Beijing intellectuals tend to assume that

people in Hong Kong, because of their environment, must be stronger in their commitment to freedom than many on the mainland and thus natural leaders in opposing tyranny. But this image is largely an illusion. The latitude of the Hong Kong press is the result less of its intrinsic strength than of the absence of repression. Courageous editors in China, such as Shanghai's Qin Benli,[2] must be far stronger than Hong Kong editors in order to carve out space for free speech. And although Hong Kong editors are savvy about conditions in China, their readers, on the whole, are no match for Beijing intellectuals in understanding the stark, hard-bitten realities of life under repression. And so even as some in Hong Kong badly underestimate the "dragon" that resides in Beijing, many in Beijing overestimate, just as badly, the "dragon slayers" they see in Hong Kong.

OVERSEAS CHINESE. The next stage in my distancing from China came as I left Hong Kong for California, where I spent August 1989 and where the large overseas Chinese community was still abuzz over the massacre and subsequent crackdown. But the overall perspective of this community was noticeably different from those of their cousins in either China or Hong Kong. The Chinese in California were concerned spectators looking at Beijing as a stage upon which a great moral drama was being played. In late August, a group of leaders of the Front for a Democratic China,[3] including Wuerkaixi, Yan Jiaqi, Wan Runnan, and others, came to Los Angeles and spoke to a packed auditorium at the University of Southern California. Sitting in the crowd, I could overhear comments on which of the celeb-

2. Editor of *World Economic Herald,* famed for its truth telling before Qin was forced out in late April 1989.

3. The Front for a Democratic China was founded in Paris in the summer of 1989 by intellectuals who had fled China after the June 4 massacre of that year. With a membership of about three thousand, it holds periodic conventions and publishes a journal called *Democratic China,* but has lost some of its momentum because of infighting and an inability to stay in touch with its constituency inside China. For an overview of Chinese dissident groups in exile as of 1991, see Geremie Barmé, "Traveling Heavy: The Intellectual Baggage of the Chinese Diaspora," *Problems of Communism,* January–April 1991, pp. 94–112.

rities had "spoken better," almost as if the audience were judging a competition. Wuerkaixi, who was ill, got the biggest ovation when he arrived late and almost collapsed on the stage. Afterwards he was surrounded by autograph seekers.

Many in this audience were professional people who by now were longtime residents of California and members of the American middle class. If they had visited China in recent years, they were likely to have been accommodated as Americans, in comfort and security that separated them from the local populace. The audience also included students from China, for whom the speakers' words more easily evoked a sense of ordinary life in China. But it struck me that even these Chinese students now stood several places removed from their compatriots at home. One of the biggest concerns for many had become how to extend their residence in America, perhaps permanently; the crackdown on the democracy movement had brought new urgency to the issue because of the danger of reprisals upon return to China.[4] The understandable concerns of these students caused them, I felt, to see their own predicament as a more significant part of China's unhappy situation than it deserved to be. Although they faced certain dangers in California, what student in Beijing would not leap to trade places with them? Around that time I received a letter from Beijing, hand-carried by a traveler, in which a friend expressed irritation that Chinese students would use the opportunity of their appeal to the American Congress to stress their own plight. Why not concentrate their message on the "basic problem here in China"?[5]

Whatever their distance from China, most overseas Chinese, including both recent arrivals and longtime residents, shared a revulsion at the crackdown. But there was one segment of the more established Chinese-American community that was not so moved. It consisted of intellectuals or professionals who had come to the United States in the 1940s or 1950s and whose

4. For some the democracy movement brought an opportunity to strengthen cases for visa extension or permanent residence that were already under way.

5. Despite sympathy with the writer of this letter, I did not hesitate when Chinese students asked me to write letters in support of their lobbying effort.

thinking had been shaped as much by American experience as by Chinese. Many, like their colleagues on the mainland, had sympathized in those years with the basic principles of the Communist revolution. Some experienced a certain guilt at the "bourgeois" status they had attained. Some who thought they had abandoned China when it needed them felt that guilt all the more. Moreover, because China had "stood up in the world," it had given them as Chinese a respectability they needed and wanted in their daily lives, especially when they encountered racial prejudice in America. A Chinese professor who had lived for many years in Princeton, New Jersey, felt that his "stature in this upper-class community" depended upon "a strong China"—by which he meant a strong Chinese government. During the Cold War years he had to hide his sympathy with the Communist government, turning it into a more intimate sympathy and thereby strengthening the professor's sense of personal commitment.

For all these reasons—and because they have been separated from China for many years and only partly grasp the severity of the crisis there—this group of overseas Chinese intellectuals remains reluctant to let go of its basic support for the Chinese government. Although no one can quite defend the massacre, a retired professor at Columbia University who had left China in the 1940s commented in fall 1989, "At least [the party leaders] could make the army obey. That's better than the Chinese government could do in the 1940s." This statement struck me as not only sincere but deeply felt; yet I couldn't help imagining how repugnant it would seem to intellectuals in Beijing, who earnestly hoped, for several days in May 1989, precisely that the army would *not* obey. The comment revealed how far the outlook of the overseas Chinese, conditioned by their experiences abroad, could diverge from attitudes inside China. It also caused me to judge the professor rather harshly: could it be that he didn't know what life in Beijing was like? He still had siblings living there. Did he know the situation, and yet consider his own need to identify with a "strong China" to be more important?

AMERICAN AUDIENCES. As someone who had witnessed the events of spring 1989, I received many invitations to speak to general American audiences. The American public's interest in China seemed at that time overwhelmingly focused on the June massacre. People were troubled by this event in complex ways, not only for its shocking cruelty but because it had challenged their images of a benign Chinese government. I was happy to see the new wave of interest in China, but felt frustrated by the preoccupation with the massacre itself, which I did not see as the main issue. If one chooses to measure the significance of the Tiananmen events by the grisly gauge of numbers killed, it would in fact rank fairly low in the series of bloody episodes marking the history of the People's Republic of China. The famine caused by the Great Leap Forward in the late 1950s killed twenty million people, or perhaps twice that number.[6] Even the spectacle of the People's Liberation Army firing on the people was not unprecedented, as many have claimed. This happened, indeed on a much larger scale, when the army suppressed Red Guards in 1967. It has happened several times in Tibet.

There were, and still are, much deeper problems in China than the massacre itself, horrible though it was. The existence of these pervasive problems could have been inferred even from Western news reports in the days before the massacre: ordinary citizens on the outskirts of Beijing were risking their lives by sitting down in front of army vehicles. University students were writing out wills—a bit theatrically, to be sure, but not in jest. Why would people do this? What drove them to the desperate point of risking everything? The answers are complex, as I have tried to illustrate in this book; but the very presence of such

6. The Communist government now acknowledges sixteen million deaths. Other estimates range between twenty and fifty million. Chen Yizi, formerly a key adviser to Zhao Ziyang, and until spring 1989 director of the Party Central Institute for the Reform of the Economic System, conducted a systematic survey in 1970–71 of the provinces hardest hit by the Great Leap Forward famine and concluded that forty-three million had died. In the early 1980s an internal report of the Chinese government estimated eighty million "deaths from unnatural causes" in China since the founding of the People's Republic.

drastic questions was, I believe, a much more telling sign about the condition of China in 1989 than was the loss of life on June 4.

As I accepted speaking invitations in the fall of 1989, I found that some of my American audiences implicitly wished that China could "get back to normal," and even seemed to want me to predict this. Instead, I had to explain that China's "normal" condition—if we take that term to describe the period just before the spring events, say, January 1989—was precisely *the problem* in the view of many Chinese people. I would then try to convey the intensity of popular complaints about corruption, oppression in the work units, and other abuses that underly the protests of spring 1989.

This approach drew a variety of responses. Students from China applauded most warmly—partly out of the old habit of cheering when someone makes statements that, although banal common knowledge, are forbidden in their country from formal public expression; and partly, I believe, out of the amusement of seeing how much a foreigner could get right. Some of the most troubling responses I elicited came from middle-class intellectuals and "liberals"—meaning people from backgrounds and with sympathies much like my own. These people dearly wanted China to be better than I was describing it to be, and sometimes insisted this was so. Their problem, as I saw it, was that their strong, well-intentioned interest in China, and in the socialist ideal, was based on a severely limited understanding of ordinary life in the People's Republic. The large gap between what they knew and what they thought they knew had been filled mostly with projections of what they *wanted* to be true.

And what did they want to be true? It often seemed they wanted China to be the counterpoint to whatever was wrong with American society. Whereas Americans are too materialistic, for example, Chinese are more balanced in this regard—look at the modest clothing they choose to wear. (In fact, even simple blue-cloth pants and white-cloth shirts are not easily available or affordable in much of China.) The ideals invoked in the official language of the Chinese state have reinforced the imaginative construction of China held by some Americans, who can be drawn to a phrase such as "serve the people" because it represents an attractive alternative to the rampant individualism that afflicts America. But these sympathetic observers have little sense for the ways in which official language is cynically manipulated in China; they therefore reach the groundless conclusion that "serve the people" sums up actual daily-life attitudes.

Occasionally I found it awkward to try to describe China to Americans who always wanted to compare China with America. After one lecture an elderly woman rose to object, "So many of the problems that you say China has—political manipulation of language, underfunding of education, and so on—are also problems right here in America!" After pointing out some differences in nature and degree of the problems in the Chinese case, I said that I quite agreed with her. "Then why do you make so much of it?" she asked. I apologized for making so much of it, but inwardly felt frustrated. How could I describe China if each statement were understood as an indirect comment on America?

Audience members often asked about U.S. policy toward China, especially the remarkable indulgence that the Bush administration showed for the Chinese regime that had ordered the massacre. I could only respond that my experiences in China did not square with administration policy. Even leaving the massacre aside, did George Bush and his advisers not grasp how detested the small group of China's top leaders were, or how unrepresentative of the thinking of the rest of the populace? Or did they know this and yet feel that American economic and strategic interests dictated a double standard for China?[7] When

7. The Bush administration denies that it uses a double standard for China, but it obviously does. To cite just one example, on May 24, 1990, President Bush announced two decisions: that he was recommending a continuation of most-favored-nation (MFN) status to the government of Deng Xiaoping, but denying it to the government of Mikhail Gorbachev (New York Times, May 25, 1990, p. A1). By law, MFN is denied to Communist governments that do not allow free emigration, unless the president declares that a waiver of this provision serves the cause of free emigration and human rights in

audiences asked me why the Bush administration would protest the massacre by announcing a suspension of high-level talks with the Chinese government, and yet two weeks after the announcement secretly send a senior mission to Beijing to smooth relations, I could only admit that I was no better qualified than others in the room to explain such behavior. But on the question of why George Bush insisted on being his own China expert, putting inordinate faith in his personal impulses, I did note the resemblance to the centuries-old pattern in the West of projecting subjective impressions onto the great unknowable "other" that is China.

I had more confidence in addressing the reverse question—China's image of George Bush. In the aftermath of the June 1989 events, Deng Xiaoping thoroughly thrashed the president in the symbolic Chinese game of face. The world had condemned the massacre, and the Chinese government had replied by blaming foreign agents for stirring up "turmoil." However implausible factually, the Deng regime's claim put the face game at a standoff, which George Bush then broke by dispatching his emissary to make amends. (In Chinese culture, the party that travels pays respect to the party that stays at home. In China's traditional foreign relations, countries sent tribute missions to Beijing, where the Son of Heaven received them.) In late 1989, when Deng threatened a cutoff of academic and cultural exchange with the United States if the Congress enacted a bill extending the visas of Chinese students in America, Bush again complied by vetoing the legislation. Immediately after the president extended most-favored-nation trading status to China in May 1990, arguing that this would preserve the benign American

the country concerned. On the surface, then, the Bush administration was committed to the curious position that in the year since May 31, 1989, the last time it had extended MFN for China, the Chinese government, which had slaughtered people in the streets during this period, had made better progress toward human rights than had the Soviet government, which had presided over the dissolution of its empire in Eastern Europe. A year later, when the president again recommended MFN for China, he cited "the support we got from China back in Desert Storm" (*New York Times*, May 16, 1991, p. A10). Yet MFN was still denied to the Soviet government, whose support in the Persian Gulf War was much stronger.

influence on the Chinese government, the Deng government answered by executing some prisoners and announcing the fact to American reporters. Chinese intellectuals, who dearly would like to see George Bush (or anyone else) defeat Deng Xiaoping in the face game, sigh that Mr. Bush sometimes seems not to understand what is going on. Anecdotes that circulate on China's oral network of "alleyway news" describe a Deng Xiaoping who gloats over his ability to manipulate naive American presidents.

THE PROBLEM OF REMEMBERING. Encountering so many views of China that were colored by other concerns, I began to feel a longing for reconnection to the place. I wanted confirmation that my memories of the mood in Beijing were accurate. I sought out people freshly arrived from China and also began to correspond with friends in Beijing—using third-party delivery and altered names as precautions.

A senior at Beijing University wrote me a letter describing at length how she and her classmates had been forcibly "reeducated" in the summer of 1989. They were made to attend all-day sessions at which they "learned from" central party documents and the speeches of top leaders. After reading aloud from these materials, they had to write essays, first on the theme "How a Patriotic Student Movement Could Have Become a Counterrevolutionary Rebellion"; then on the personal responsibility that each bore for contributing to this evil transition, and finally on their resolve to repent and follow the brightness of the party. They were told that anyone who failed the reeducation course would not graduate from the university—which also meant, as everyone knew, that they would be denied job assignments and become unemployable for an indefinite duration. Therefore this senior and nearly all her classmates dutifully read their documents and wrote their essays, longing for the evenings when, in the privacy of remote corners of campus, they could share with one another their utter contempt for the entire process. This pattern was so widely followed, she reported in her letter, that even undercover agents had become ineffective. Whenever an agent did overhear a private conversation, his or her testimony would be insistently contradicted by everyone else who had been at the scene.

A student from Hubei province who came to the United States in summer 1990 told of the traveling delegations that the regime had dispatched to his and many other schools. These groups, called Delegations of Model Heroes in the Suppression of the Rioting, were composed of soldiers who apparently had been handpicked for political reliability and good looks. The soldiers gave brief and vapid talks, which students often greeted with a purposeful stony silence. As a result, officials issued regulations requiring applause. At some point one student body hit upon the idea of responding with sarcastically exaggerated applause. The idea spread and eventually became genuinely enjoyable as students discovered the fun of inserting applause at inappropriate points. A model hero would stand up and say, "My name is Wang Weidong . . . [audience: HOORAY!] . . . born here in Xiaogan County [audience: XIAOGAN FOREVER!] . . ." In the end the officials were forced to issue more regulations regarding applause—still requiring it, but limiting it to the beginning and end of each event, with a two-minute maximum duration each time.

I noted strong evidence as well of the survival of "popular ditties" and other underground barbs directed at "Deng-Li-Yang," meaning the regime of Deng Xiaoping, Li Peng, and Yang Shangkun. The spirit of these ditties is always hard to capture in translation, but the following example is more accessible than most because it is set to the tune of "Frère Jacques" (a melody that entered China in the first part of the twentieth century and has been used with a variety of Chinese lyrics):

> Down with Li Peng, down with Li Peng,
> Yang Shangkun, Yang Shangkun,
> And the other hoodlum, and the other hoodlum,
> Deng Xiaoping, Deng Xiaoping.

Along with the ditties there have arisen codes for referring to taboo subjects. For example, the two-finger V sign, which was popular among the Tiananmen protesters, immediately became forbidden after the June 4 massacre. Yet students and workers continued to communicate the idea using the question "Do you sell roundworm purgative?" The connection was made through a widely shown television advertisement in which a customer asks, "Do you sell roundworm purgative?" and a pharmacist answers, "Yes, take two tablets!"—and holds up two fingers as if in the V sign. A later, bolder version of the joke asked, "Do you sell Li Peng purgative?"

Such examples suggest that the continuing repression in China has not crushed everyone's spirits. But letters and travelers make it clear that the suffering continues. At a meeting on Capitol Hill on May 4, 1990, Americans from government, business, and academe, together with some Chinese intellectuals, gathered to debate the pros and cons of continuing China's most-favored-nation trading status for another year. The discussion was at least fairly calm until the end of the day, when Lü Jinghua, who had been the leader of the Autonomous Federation of Beijing Workers at the Tiananmen demonstrations and who had just escaped from China, arrived at the meeting. She delivered a cri de coeur that, although simple in its message ("No trading status, or anything else, for the butchers!"), was startlingly different in tone from anything else that had been said. At an academic conference some months later, an elderly, eminent professor who had just arrived from China suddenly interrupted his commentary with an outburst so impassioned that it caused him to tremble. "Wasted! Gone! For ten years [1979–89] we worked so carefully, so hard, to build our university, to bring it back to something that could be called a university, and now it's destroyed again! We are knocked down again! . . ." He stopped only when a well-meaning Chinese colleague in the audience approached him with the advice that he "mind his health" and desist.[8]

8. The professor was scheduled to return to China shortly after the conference. In view of this fact, and because his outburst came at a public forum, the kind injunction to "mind his health" should be understood as referring to political health at least as much as physical.

Afterwards I observed an exchange over the incident between an American political scientist and a scholar from China, who like the elderly professor was a fairly recent arrival in the United States.

"He was so upset," said the American. "It was moving, but I'm afraid he lost perspective."

"Is it 'bad perspective' to express pain?" the Chinese asked, irritated.

"No, no, no," the American apologized. "It's not his fault. I just mean that being so emotional, one's judgment is affected. We have a saying in English that you 'can't see the forest for the trees.' "

The Chinese scholar then went into an extended comparison of two approaches to analyzing China—the "calm and cool" and the "close and hot," both of which she said had their place. "In some circumstances," she concluded, "I think the hot viewpoint gives one better insight than the cool one. What that professor said came closer to the reality of China than anything else I heard at this conference."

I wrote to a friend in Beijing, introducing the "forest and trees" metaphor of the political scientist. Some time later I received a hand-carried reply. "Here in the woods," my friend began, signaling his irony immediately, "we have scorpions. What would your political scientist friend, who can stand above the whole forest, say about that? If a man runs out of the woods screaming that he has been stung by a scorpion, I suppose we must still say, strictly speaking, that there may not be a scorpion. After all, you can't see it from on top of the forest. And the only evidence for it comes from a man who is far too emotional to be trusted. I will advise everyone here to put on coats and ties, and assume serious frowns, before they report any scorpion stings."

Two years after the crackdown on the Tiananmen protests, a mood of gloom and pent-up resentment persists among China's intellectuals, especially those in Beijing. (In Shanghai, Guangzhou, and other cities, the gloom has been relieved somewhat by the possibility of ignoring Beijing most of the time.)

As the euphoria and outrage over the events of spring 1989 subside, the underlying problems of corruption, stymied reform, neglect of education, and state-sponsored oppression reemerge. Yet "Six Four" ("June Fourth," as it is abbreviated in ordinary language) has definitely left its mark. There is evidence that not only intellectuals and workers but many officials as well, extending to levels very close to the top, privately disapprove of the official view of the massacre. At the most, June Fourth may eventually come to be known as a symbol of the self-destruction of the Chinese Communist party. At the least, the regime that follows Deng Xiaoping's, even if it is only moderately reformist, will certainly want to "reverse the verdict" on the massacre in order to recoup popular support.[9] But superficial gestures such as this will not be enough to alleviate China's pain or restore its morale.

9. There is a precedent for this pattern. In April 1976 another large demonstration at Tiananmen was crushed and declared to be "counterrevolutionary." But at the end of 1977, after the ruling group associated with the crackdown had been out of power about a year, the new regime moved to bolster its popularity by declaring the 1976 protests "patriotic." That new regime was led by Deng Xiaoping.

# INDEX